CAMPING
IN THE OLD STYLE

IN THE OLD STYLE

BY DAVID WESCOTT

SALT LAKE CITY

First Edition
03 02 01 00   4 3 2 1

Published by
Gibbs Smith, Publisher
P.O. Box 667
Layton, Utah 84041

Orders: (1-800) 748-5439
Visit our Website at *www.gibbs-smith.com*

Edited by Gail Yngve
Designed by Tadd Peterson
Printed and bound in the United States of America

Author's note: We have recently discovered that references cited as *Camp and Trail*, 1920,
were actually Stewart Edward White's *Camp and Trail*, 1907.

Library of Congress Cataloging-in-Publication Data
Wescott, David, d 1948–
    Camping in the old style / by David Wescott.— 1st ed.
        p. cm.
    ISBN 0-87905-956-7
    1. Camping—United States. 2. Camping—United States—Equipment
and supplies. 3. Outdoor life—United States.
    4. Woodwork—United States. I. Title.

GV191.4.W47 2000
796.54—dc21   99-045255

To my parents,
who took me early to the woods.
I can still smell the ponderosa pines of the Sierra foothills,
and I still have my original army pup tent.

To my wife and family,
who have let me go out to play — to practice and
share with others the things I've come to love — and to help
me keep traditions alive.

Weighing-In (ca. 1935)

CONTENTS

Camping has two purposes: to make us acquainted
with our own souls, and to renew our acquaintance with
each other. To camp badly is to frustrate both.
—Unknown

ACKNOWLEDGMENTS

In her younger years, my wife was a horse enthusiast, and even to this day, the sight of a horse in full gallop brings tears to her eyes. The slow-motion replay of the same event has an even more profound impact—flared nostrils, muscles flexed and relaxed in a fluid motion, everything extended in full stride. I must admit that even though horses make me sneeze, the sight of such perfection—an animal bred for speed, doing its thing—raises goose bumps on my flesh and a lump in my throat.

I am by no means what one might call a sports enthusiast, a highbrow, or any other special-interest fanatic. But when it comes to the well-played game, a fine work of art, a well-told story, or any talent, skill, or craft that is put on display by true masters of a discipline, I am not unlike anyone else in that the quality of their performance based on the solid underpinnings of their art touches me.

And so it is with camping and woodcraft. Through a thirty-year career of living in the outdoors, as well as twenty years of youth spent practicing for that career, I have sought out only the best and brightest in the field to be mentors.

MASTERS OF THE WELL-PLAYED GAME

A long list of people have helped shape my thinking on this great subject of camping, but at this writing only a few of the most influential come to mind.

Rulon Skinner, who taught the first camping-skills class I ever attended and gave me a "B" instead of an "A" on my final exam because I put down air instead of oxygen as one of the elements of the fire triad, teaching me that only precision and accuracy would be tolerated; Darry Wood, a true master craftsman and woodcrafter, who challenged me to comprehend that the beauty of woodcraft is that form and function are equal partners and when brought into balance through such mundane camp furnishings as guy lines, axe handles, and knife edges, camp life becomes that much more pleasurable; Errett Callahan and Steve Watts, two great friends from the South who have shown me that thinking about the past and honoring that heritage is a task we all should pursue with gusto; Mors Kochanski, the northwoods wizard, master bushman, and teacher of bushcraft who taught me that there is science behind the art of camping; Garrett and Alexandra Conover, who were the first contemporaries to write about the value of our camping traditions as more than quaint novelties to be thought about during bouts of nostalgia, but were viable and vital skills that deserved to be conserved and once again honed to perfection; Paul Petzoldt and Tap Tapley, who brought the idea back to America that camping was something, when mastered, could make us better people, and that those who fostered this thinking could actually make a living at teaching it; Bill Mason, who merged the art of camping with the beauty of the outdoors on film and in print, and drew many of us toward a new view of our camping heritage and the values derived from *Camping in the Old Style*.

Finally, I also need to thank my editor, Gail Yngve, who kept my feet to the fire when I just wanted to relax and sit next to it, and designer, Tadd Peterson, who shared the vision on how the book should be presented.

Horace Kephart, Dean of American campers—(ca. 1920)

PREFACE

The true masters of woodcraft are Ernest Thompson Seton (1892–1946) and Daniel Carter "Uncle Dan" Beard (1850–1941). Their writings and efforts at helping youth to appreciate the wild outdoors, thereby better understanding themselves, formed the footings for most of what we see now in the youth camping movement. Their thinking was responsible for development of the Sons of Daniel Boone, the Boy Pioneers, the Campfire Club, the Woodcraft Rangers, and ultimately the Boy Scouts, Girl Scouts, and Campfire Girls worldwide. They also made it legitimate for adults to engage in youthful activities, some saying their books were written for men but disguised for boys. You will notice in the quotes from both authors that woodcraft was taught for many more reasons than simply to make people better campers. Woodcraft was a metaphor used to help camping develop better people. Their skills, however, were no less accurate.

While perfection of detail and organization in the travelling camp is an essential, it makes no less for convenience and saving of time in the permanent one, so one may as well learn how the veteran does it from the start, for no experienced man will tolerate hardships and discomforts as part of the accepted regime of his camping out. He needs his strength for the toil of the trail and so requires a restful camp quite as much as does the man who merely wants to loaf in the woods and do it at a minimum of discomfort.
—Warren H. Miller, 1918

Horace Kephart, the so-called "Dean of American Campers," as well as contemporaries George W. "Nessmuk" Sears, Warren H. "Cap" Miller (editor of *Field and Stream*, 1910–1918), and countless others, heralded the golden age of camping. Most of them wrote regular columns for sporting journals and spent time field testing equipment for noted manufacturers, such as Abercrombie and Fitch, who made exceptionally fine gear from the late 1800s until about 1975, forming a fraternity of outers and establishing themselves as the masters of camping in the old style.

It is to these writers we turn to glean valuable knowledge and experience that we might otherwise lose if it is not conserved. Sources of information regarding techniques and technologies of our camping heritage are all but gone from the oral traditions.

Anyone who can remember camping in the early 1900s would be hard pressed to recall the exact details of how it was done, and those with the experience and knowledge who served as teachers and guides are almost all gone.

Their texts, however, now in the public domain, remain as chronicles of what we call traditional camping, or camping in the old style. Our aim in this text is not to steal their thunder but to honor it by making sure that it keeps on rolling, ever rolling in the ears of those who have the capacity to hear. Not everyone will listen, and it's not for everyone to accept. But for those with an affinity for wandering the woods on its terms and fostering the traditions of these mentors, they will find the resurrection and conservation of these words and illustrations a treasure.

Among the other sources we have tapped to give us a better glimpse of camping in the old style are the photo archives. Through these incredible images we have been able to "live back" and become part of what was taking place. Through modern technology and computer imaging, we are able to actually enter the photograph and move around at will, taking a closer look at equipment, dress, transport gear, tools, foodstuffs, and more.

Along with the photos and text are the line drawings and engravings used to illustrate the early texts. Most of the works were original, but it's interesting to note how many of the same drawings were used by a variety of authors. Some drawings came from and were used by permission of equipment manufacturers. They were lent from their catalogs and used to promote their gear in either magazine articles, books, or both. Brand names were commonly used in all sources.

An interesting phenomenon takes place when viewing one of the old photos or reading the text. At the time these images were taken and words penned, it was the modern age. There are repeated references to the "modern man" and the "modern woman," and fashion was an important part of the camping scene, just as it is today. However, in our own time frame, it's easy to look back and discount what was going on and place the technologies and techniques of those times in the categories of quaint and primitive as compared to today's standards, patting ourselves on the back for how far we've progressed. But if we take a close look at what was happening during the period of 1900–1930, we find uncanny similarities to today's modern man and woman, and one has to wonder just how far we have really come.

The sources for the quotes, line art, and photos contained in this book are listed below. These volumes were scanned for thoughts and information that would establish a foundation for those interested in becoming traditional campers. The book is arranged with quotes, photos and illustrations, a training regime, and new text in such a way as to present itself as a sourcebook for further experiential discoveries. *Camping in the Old Style* is a journal-like compilation of the best thoughts and resources of what makes the traditional style of camping so appealing to the modern outer or sport. It's like a scrapbook of notes, quotes, and images used to recapture the best of what traditional camping is all about.

PRIMARY SOURCES

Daniel Carter Beard
The Outdoor Handy Book (1900)
The Book of Camplore and Woodcraft (1920)

Ernest Thompson Seton
The Book of Woodcraft (1912)
The Birch Bark Roll (1927)

Warren H. Miller
Camp Craft (1915)
Camping Out (1918)

James Austin Wilder
Jack-Knife Cookery (1929)

Frank H. Cheley and Philip D. Fagan
Camping Out and Woodcraft
(two volumes in one, 1933)

Sitting far left is Daniel Carter Beard
and far right is Warren H. Miller.

CLASSICS CITED THAT REMAIN IN PRINT OR HAVE BEEN REPRINTED:

Horace Kephart
Camping and Woodcraft
(two volumes in one, 1917)
Reprinted by University of Tennessee Press

E. Kreps
Camp and Trail Methods (1910)
Woodcraft (1910)
Both remain in print from *Fur-Fish-Game: Harding's Magazine*

George W. Sears
Nessmuk–Woodcraft (1920)
Reprinted by Dover Publications

Bernard S. Mason
Woodcraft (1939)
Republished by Dover Publications as *Woodcraft and Camping*

We must also recognize the more recent contributions of Calvin Rutstrum. His *New Way in the Wilderness* (1958) and *Paradise below Zero* (1968) are considered modern classics.

Hundreds of books have been printed on the subject of camping that have yet to be rediscovered. The period of 1900–1930 was truly America's golden age of camping, and books and articles extolling the virtues of equipment and techniques were common. This book is based on only a few of the most widely available sources, and because of space considerations, only a small portion of the text and photos that were available could be included here.

We would be interested in additional titles missing from this edition. Books by W. H. Gibson, Edward Breck, Chauncey Evens, Stewart Edward White, Charles Stedman Hanks, John Gould, and Seneca are among the many printed. We have also taken quotes from the book *Camp and Trail* that is obviously from the same era, but it was a damaged copy and had no reference information available. Any information about it would be welcome.

There were also attempts in the '50s to bring traditional camping back, resulting in a few good texts from that era. Shortly after that, the era of nylon and down emerged, and the proponents of the light/cold camp did their best to proclaim "woodcraft is dead."

Fortunately, they did not prevail in convincing all of us, so for those of you who hold to the fraternity of outdoor traditions, let's load up our gear and go *Camping in the Old Style*.

The wilderness camp has limited conveniences but can still be made comfortable.

INTRODUCTION
Camping in the Old Style

When someone who is a true master teaches,
the process is a lot less painful and progress is assured.
A true apprentice never assumes common sense.

The reader will find a wide range, from the deluxe camping of the man who can afford a fine outfit and goes to the woods for rest and recreation, to the explorer's and hunter's camping, where getting into big game country or little-traveled lands far from the nearest railroad involves the utmost of comfort on the minimum of weight. Between the two lie many variations, such as the canoeist's trip, the lone hike, the automobilist's trek, the winter cruise by snowshoe and toboggan, the late fall camp where the tent stove becomes a feature, and the beach camp where sand and wind offer a new set of conditions requiring special solutions. Each kind of outdoor life offers its own special features, and, as nearly all of them will be tried by the enthusiast at one period or another in his development as a master camper, reading up on the subject before getting into the practice of it will well repay.
—Warren H. Miller, 1918

Camping in the Old Style is a journey through time, not only for the sake of nostalgia (although that is a legitimate reason for being here—a reverence for time-honored tradition is good enough), but also to bring the skills and techniques of our camping traditions back to life and blend them with our modern times for a more fulfilling future. We need to realize that maintaining a tradition isn't going backward. Unless one is doggedly holding onto the past for purely stubborn reasons, adopting traditional techniques can be very progressive, taking us a step forward. Blending the best of the past with the most appropriate of the present can create exciting possibilities.

As a first step on this journey, we need to look at camping as it was at the turn of the century, the golden age of camping, and see what made it so much a part of life. We also need to address some of the issues that we face today about the appropriateness of traditional camping methods and how they can once again be brought into full use.

It's a time of abundance and change. It's a time whose landscape is dominated by the ending of one era and the beginning of another. It's a time of fulfillment and frustration created by new technologies.

A temporary bark-tipi shelter.

Workers are coming into their own, and their efforts are being rewarded by management. Traditions of the past are discounted as old fashioned, while modern people are forward thinkers, ready to adopt anything new.

It's a time for making choices, some of which will sever connections with what is right and best, while best is replaced with newest. It's a time of short-term orientation, instant problems, instant solutions, and the solutions are ultimately tied to technology. Is it 1900 or 1999?

A camper/hunter comes home from a long expedition and is not able to buy anything because the method of purchase has changed. He or she can't repair his or her gear because not only the spare parts but the materials they're made of are no longer available. He or she is put on display because while away, clothing changed so much that what he or she is wearing has become collector's items. He or she packs a knife and hunting rifle and is castigated by people proclaiming "your days are done and there's no place for you here." Then he or she is approached by a soft-looking soul who wants to be taken out on expedition for the fun of it. Is it 1900 or 1999?

These scenarios are not far from what it must have felt like for indigenous people, or frontiersmen, coming east of the Mississippi in 1900. Whether a few months or nearly a lifetime of surviving on nature's terms, it was not recreation; it was living. Paddling a canoe or riding a horse were not fun (although they might have been pleasurable); they were transportation. Hunting and fishing, navigating, and chopping wood weren't grand diversions; they were work.

We can also apply these scenes to what it has been like watching the evolution of our modern social and camping practices. Of course, during our lives, camping has always been more recreation than work. But some guides are still amazed at how fast things are changing and how little of the real world their clients have experienced. Yet with the renewed interest in traditional camping, many people are looking for experiences that can reconnect them with themselves and the earth, and they are willing to spend the time and effort required to join the fraternity of woodsmen. *Camping in the Old Style* was written for them.

Most of the early camping movement was directed toward sports and outers looking for a break from the pressures of the workplace. They were urbanites with limited outdoor experience and discretionary cash, and an experienced guide was just what they needed. While the sport focused on his personal kit and outdoor clothing, the guide acquired the camp, food, furnishings, and transportation, and off to the wilds they went. In other cases, fine gents and ladies were taken to established camps, having all forms of pastime diversions, comfortable platform-tent cottages, and a lodge for eating and visiting.

When the automobile came on the scene, the weekend was created, and the masses began to enjoy what was previously available for only the well-to-do. Travel and camping were the most democratic of leisure pursuits. Guides, books, and articles began to appear on the benefits of camping and how anyone could plan for and acquire all they needed to join the life of the outers. Most authors directed readers to the latest gadgets and improvements—the ones the manufacturers gave them to write about. Others recognized the values of the old ways: the self-reliance gained from making gear and the dependability gained by buying only high-quality possessions—gear that was built to last, camping that was done with style.

After World War I, surplus military gear was available, and great camp kits could be put together inexpensively. Although the well-to-do sport had to have all the right gear from the right purveyors, the common man was satisfied with a tent that would keep him fairly dry, a pan that wouldn't burn his flapjacks, and a bit of road, trail, or stream to separate him from the masses.

Everything else came from know-how. We have a tendency to forget that a lot of our dependence on technology comes from lack of knowledge, but we never address the inverse; our lack of knowledge is directly related to our dependence on technology. Traditional campers knew that trap, and used their outings to rebuild ties of self-reliance through their favorite outdoor pastimes. Simplicity and a carefree life (even for a weekend) are the common traits displayed by the people who camped in the old style.

But as camping became a more democratic pastime, those who camped and those who knew wilderness living became more and more estranged. The popular press began to tell campers what they needed and how to do things. Books and articles were a poor replacement for the hands-on instruction of a trail-tested sourdough. The Chechako arrived on the scene, bringing with him a vast knowledge of things he had never experienced but was willing to try out because he wanted to be a woodsman.

While the numbers of campers increased and urban sprawl ate up local preserves and parks, more and more people had to compete for less and less space; the impacts created by the improper practices of the Chechako made the practice of traditional skills unacceptable. Not that the real skills were wrong, but the Chechako caused too much damage and took up more than his fair share of space. Now we know it wasn't the skills that were wrong but the irresponsible and inappropriate use of improperly applied skills that were the real cause of all the trouble.

So how do we get back to a place where we can once again learn and practice the skills that form the foundations of our outdoor heritage? How can we learn the best traditions, thereby learning the best values from the wild-wood ways?

Preconceived notions, especially when one is fairly brought up in their influence, are most difficult to shake off.
—*Camp and Trail*, 1920

COMMON SENSE

"That boy ain't got a lick o' sense" said the sourdough. "Nope," said his pard. "My mule's got more common sense than that young duffer."

People need to have something in common with each other in order to have a sense of what should be common knowledge between them. Common experience is the foundation, of course, and a knowledgeable guide is the best source for such training. But by the turn of the century, there were already a number of well-defined commons—the agriculturists, the industrialists, the urbanites, and those who remained as vestiges of the frontiersmen, trappers, and explorers from the previous century. Common sense between them was already a rare commodity.

The damage caused from assuming that there was still a common ground between the "ites" and "ists" and those people still reared in the ways of the commons, the wild outdoors, and frontier farmlands was generally limited to embarrassment. One was called a hayseed or commoner for wearing his hat indoors, using the wrong fork at the table, or staunchly praising the old ways as being "good enough for me." The other was loaded down with kit and plunder enough to spend a year on the dark continent when only outing for the weekend. He arrived in camp and promptly

The Wylie Permanent Camp in Yellowstone National Park, (ca. 1915).

CHECHAKOS, DUFFERS, AND CHUMPS

The terms greenhorn and tenderfoot, mixed with an assortment of local endearments, are well established in our lexicon of references to the beginner, especially in the outdoor setting. Here are a few more that pop up regularly in the old texts.

TYRO (ti´ro)—An inexperienced person; a beginner; a young soldier.

CHECHAKO—A term commonly used by Daniel Carter Beard to describe the uninitiated or novice camper, especially one who acts foolishly and refuses to learn from the experience of others—a know-it-all.

SAGEBRUSHER—Commonly used to describe the early travelers to the great western parks. Coming to visit in wagons and touring cars, their goal was sightseeing without the hardships of the camp.

DUDE—An easterner or city person visiting the West. Possibly a dandy, or what we call a "poser" today.

DUFFER—An incompetent or dull-witted person. "No one but a duffer and a chump will use another man's axe."
    —Daniel Carter Beard

CRUSTER—Nessmuk's obvious attempt to identify the duffer. He said, "And with kindness to all true woodsmen; and with malice toward none, save the trout-hog, the netter, the cruster, and the skin-butcher. . . ."

OUTERS—A fraternity of active campers who set the standards for what was an acceptable method and / or tool for the variety of camp styles available.

SPORTS—Those who seek the guided camp. Accommodations and services usually include cooked meals, set camps, transport of duffel from jump-off to camp, and assistance with hunting and fishing success.

GYPSIES (spelled gipsy in early texts)—Seekers of freedom on the open road. Their autos were packed to the gunnels, including running-board packs and camp trailers or auto tents. Camps may be set for the weekend or for months in a single location.

The auto tent was one of the most popular styles of camp in its day.

broke the handle on the camp axe when attempting to show his knowledge of woodcraft. Who, then, is lacking common sense?

He who knows not, and knows he knows not, is a student—teach him.
He who knows not, and knows not, he knows not, is a fool—shun him.
He who knows, and knows he knows, is a leader—follow him.
—Unknown

The problem with the duffer, chump, and chechako is that they are fools—knowledgeable from books and assumptions. But, knowledge without experience lacks wisdom. It is the wisdom of the wild woods that we seek here. What will be found here is information, but a mentor is needed for skilled experience. After, practice is necessary to gain wisdom.

Looking back at camping heritage with twenty-twenty vision, tapping the few great sources that still exist, blending them with the most appropriate options from the modern era, and then working with skilled mentors to master the art of camping, a tyro, with the right attitude and openness to learning, can come to a mastery of the art and science of camping relatively quickly from novice to journeyman, and then grow to become a master. However, there are no shortcuts. But when someone who is a true master teaches, the process is a lot less painful and progress is assured. A true apprentice never assumes common sense.

Afterall, it is an affair of common sense; but even common sense, when confronted by a new problem, needs a certain direction. The province of these articles is to offer that direction; I do not claim that my way is the only way, nor am I rash enough to claim it is the best way. But it is my way, and if anyone will follow it, he will be as comfortable and as well suited as I am, which is at least better than going it blind.
—*Camp and Trail*, 1920

IN DEFENSE OF WOODCRAFT

Woodcraft is dead—dead because modern equipment makes pioneer-style engineering unnecessary. Dead because nature-sensitive hikers have deeper, subtler pleasures than slashing and gouging. Dead because there are too many of us and too little undisturbed wild land for every would-be son of the frontier to be allowed full freedom to play with his toys.
—Harvey Manning, *Backpacking, One Step at a Time*, 1972

About 1970, the lightweight and minimum-impact camping came to the forefront. Paul Petzoldt was among the early innovators, but it was Harvey Manning who was the first to put it in print.

In order to accept Manning's proclamation, several assumptions need to be made: 1. Traditional skills are inherently bad and modern technology is inherently good; 2. People who practice traditional skills are not sensitive to nature and are out to destroy it; and 3. There is no place left to practice traditional skills. None of these assumptions are based on a sense common to anyone; they demand one wishing to camp traditionally to make an either/or choice, leaving no alternatives. Those who continue to practice traditional camping should either stop it, or they will be considered bad. The truth is, the promise of traditional camping in this era is that it provides an alternative with an ethically sound foundation, much more sound than the choices offered by Manning.

POINT NUMBER ONE:
TRADITIONAL SKILLS VERSUS MODERN TECHNOLOGY

It has been nearly thirty years, and there's no telling what kind of shape Harvey Manning is in, but camping in the woodcraft tradition is alive and well. However, it has taken thirty years to convince the chechako that his slash-and-gouge tactics are not appreciated and will not be tolerated. It is also conceded that the destructive practices of the duffers and chumps has left a physical scar that is just barely healing, and concessions have to be made to see to it that such practices don't take place in the future.

Looking back, we have to realize that everything we did wasn't perfect. Some of the practices that came to be known as common were creating impacts that were intolerable. The most glaring drawbacks were the misdeeds and damage created by the chechakos. Their attitude was that "there is always a new frontier" and "wilderness was meant to be tamed." This belief, although misguided and never taught by the early mentors, justified to them that whatever damage they inflicted, there was always going to be room enough for it not to matter.

We must make a note here. The early traditions of camping and woods lore were derived mainly from indigenous people. One fundamental belief that is shared by all people who live with their surroundings is that you must do so in balance. To make too much noise is to go without food. To be too obvious is to battle with an enemy. To waste or take more than your share is cold and hunger for others. To treat the earth with disrespect is death.

For every act there is a consequence. If the act is based on sound reasoning, the consequence will follow in the same fashion. If the act is faulty and out of balance, the consequence will be as well. Traditional campers trained in the woodcraft way live with their surroundings. They have to because their reliance on technology is limited to the most appropriate items. Knowing what to do at given times and how to live and minimize leaving tracks in the process have always been the best ways to camp. Blundering through the wilderness as a visitor who doesn't know his place, taking on the appearance but not the skill and judgement of one who is trained in the proper methods of wild-wood living, is off the mark. The resulting problem, and Manning misreads it, is not that practicing the old ways is bad, but that practicing the old ways badly is bad.

We must all understand this point. In fact, camping badly in any tradition is bad. Modern campers

The 1872 camps of the Hayden Expedition were home to some of the West's most notable guides.

SO YOU WANT TO BE A WOODSMAN

Master Woodsman—A man is skillful at woodcraft in proportion [to his] approach [to] balance . . . knowing the wilderness can be comfortable when a less experienced man would endure hardships. Conversely, if a man endures hardships where a woodsman could be comfortable, it argues not his toughness, but his ignorance or foolishness, which is exactly the case with our blatant friend of the drawing-room reputation.
—Camp and Trail, 1920

Mastery of camping techniques requires dedication, training, and practice. As a place to start, each chapter has a list of requirements that may help as well as providing a target to hit. Each activity requires that previous skills be learned in sequence, bringing the tyro closer to mastery of the newly applied skill. This is not a do-it-yourself list, as true mastery requires a mentor. The basis for this list was adapted from the old America Camping Association Campcraft scheme. The ACA has been the governing body of youth camping in America since 1910. In the mid-1990s they scrapped the Campcraft program in favor of a milquetoast environmental program, teaching their camp members that unless they provided their campers with access to cell phones and the Internet, they would not survive in the future. Even camping's leading organization has lost its way.

An APPRENTICE CAMPER has basic skills to stay alive in the wild outdoors for twenty-four to seventy-six hours. Survival training and outdoor basics are the focus in the knowledge that there always exists the possibility of a survival crisis developing in any trip.

SO YOU WANT TO BE A WOODSMAN
(Continued)

The JOURNEYMAN CAMPER's skills focus on what is required to camp comfortably for at least a weekend and up to one week's duration under prevailing conditions. The plan is to equip skilled campers with the know-how and practical information necessary to carry on such trips in a safe, enjoyable, and purposeful manner.

A JOURNEYMAN WOODSMAN possesses the skills needed to live one full season in the wild. Knowledge and experience go beyond camping to having a clear appreciation for one's surroundings and the ability to live comfortably while minimizing impact to the environment.

The MASTER WOODSMAN has the ability to live during each of the four seasons in the wilds with nothing but what nature provides. All gear can be replaced by improvised or handmade options. The Master Woodsman must also have a working knowledge of weather, geology, flora and fauna, and natural systems. The Master Woodsman is also a teacher who is able to instruct others in the wild-wood ways.

Master Woodsman Mors Kochanksi teaches what is known as the 3 X 10 Rule. A skill has to be demonstrated three times better than is needed so that the beginner's accomplishment is passable in the first try. A beginner should do the skill ten times under the supervision of the instructor to properly complete the learning process.

The traditional set-up at an encampment of the American Mountain Men, 1999.

have just as many duffers and chumps as the traditional ranks. The unfortunate thing is that our modern mentors continue to train people that the unbridled consumption of gadgets and gear will somehow make up for their lack of knowledge and skill. If one doesn't know how to forecast the weather, that's all right. They need only buy some new piece of gear, and they'll be fine.

A camp proper is a nomad's biding-place. He may occupy it for a season or only for a single night according as the site and its surroundings please or do not please the wanderer's whim. If the fish do not bite, or the game has moved away, or unpleasant neighbors should intrude, or if anything else goes wrong, it is but an hour's work for him to pull up stakes and be off, seeking that particularly good place, which generally lies beyond the horizon's rim.

Your thoroughbred camper likes not the attentions of a landlord, nor will he suffer himself to be rooted to the soil by cares of ownership or lease. It is not possession of the land, but of the landscape, that he enjoys; and as for that, all the wild parts of the earth are his, by a title that carries with it no obligation but that he shall not desecrate nor lay them waste.
—Horace Kephart, *Camping and Woodcraft*, 1917

POINT NUMBER TWO:
UNDERSTANDING LANDSCAPE—UNDERSTANDING OURSELVES

Not all methods and techniques work or are appropriate in all parts of the country equally well. We need to become native to our place. It has things to teach us about how to camp and how to enjoy its richness.

As stated in the preface, "Camping has two purposes: to make us acquainted with our own souls, and to renew our acquaintance with each other. To camp badly is to frustrate both." Camping with style includes camping with the natural world instead of in spite of it. Gleaning food, fuel, and shelter from it, or relying on knowledge and simple technologies that require campers to work with the environment are what truly bring us to this understanding. As another author once said, "No good feeling has ever been shared over the roar of a gas stove."

In 1964, the Wilderness Act made our culture the first to separate itself from the natural world by establishing

Classic wedge tent made from an 8 x 10-foot tarp and poles.

through law that wilderness "is a place where man himself is a visitor who does not remain." Such a noble effort has created a sense that the continuation of the over-consumption of resources to create consumer goods that allow us to pass through wilderness without changing it has no impact on wilderness. And manufacturers have done their utmost to convince us that the traditions and techniques of the early campers must now be replaced with these technologies, because the old ways were quaint but crude. The ones who persist in their use have an inferior camping ethic.

Manning's assertion that only those who camp lightly with modern gear have the capacity to be sensitive to nature is misguided. On the surface and at the time of its writing, it appeared a valid statement. Today, it is no less accurate than the assertion that those who choose to camp with traditional fashion and technique do so with an inferior environmental ethic. Traditional camping and woodcraft can be taught and used with low impact, and there is plenty of space for enjoying the comforts and pleasures of camping in the old style.

This conflict is a far cry from what any of the early proponents of camping, wilderness, and wood-craft ever intended. There is nothing wrong with woodcraft and traditional camping techniques when they are applied appropriately and responsibly. There are indeed, however, places where they are inappropriate. With traditional camping and modern camping, one is not better than the other; they are simply different by choice, and both must be applied with style.

Camping has no great popularity to-day, because men have the idea that it is possible only after an expensive journey to the wilderness; and women that it is inconvenient, dirty, and dangerous.

These are errors. They have arisen because camping as an art is not understood. When intelligently followed, camp-life must take its place as a cheap and delightful way of living, as well as a mental and physical savior of those strained or broken by the grind of the over-busy world.

The wilderness affords the ideal camping, but many of the benefits can be got by living in a tent on a town lot, a piazza, or even a housetop.
—Ernest Thompson Seton, 1921

POINT NUMBER THREE: SHORELINES AND OTHER BOUNDARIES

The classic Adirondack guide boat.

About the same time Manning's mantra, "Woodcraft Is Dead," gained popularity, alpine mountaineering boots and down-filled coats and vests became popular urban fashion. Today we have a similar phenomenon, with synthetic-clad sports dripping with fifty pounds of petro-chemical gear chanting the mantra of the manu-facturers, "Leave No Trace." Where do they think the resources for all those consumer goods came from? There's got to be a hole and a smoke-belching factory in somebody's yard.

Manning's ode to "modern gear" falls apart even more when we address the third assump-tion, "there's not enough room." In certain places on this earth, the conditions are not con-ducive to life as we know it—above timberline, underwater, in the stratosphere, and others. In order to live in those places, we must carry spe-cialized gear—high-alpine mountaineering gear for the mountains, scuba gear for beyond the shoreline, and space technologies that allow us to travel beyond the boundaries of our atmosphere. Equipment is made specifically to allow us to travel beyond our normal limits.

Since heroes are the ones who take the chances and use this gear to survive in those places, it is smart marketing for manufacturers to use them to sell the same gear to us. As a result, people who camp and never plan to assault Everest are sleeping in $300 subzero bags, cooking space-age foods on titanium stoves, sheltering inside $500 hurricane-proof tents pitched next to their cars. There are alternatives, but they know no better. It would be a pitiful chechako indeed who followed the same line of reasoning and showed up ready to live at the local KOA campground with a wet suit, spear gun, and flippers.

Tent camping is still the most popular and also one of the most inexpensive kinds of camping. Not all camping is done with a backpack, although the vast majority of all outdoor gear is developed

RESPONSIBLE TECHNIQUES
AND APPROPRIATE TECHNOLOGY

Many people may respond to the reintroduction of traditional methods and gear as a giant step backwards, suggesting that the use of these methods and gear is completely inappropriate for our times.

Use of technologies that depend on consumptive practices (for example, buying gear or building a fire) have to be done responsibly and appropriately. By responsibly, we mean that if one buys or makes gear, it should be done from renewable resources, or recyclable materials, such as wool, cotton, wood, army surplus, and tin cans. If the resources are not renewable, one should be honest about it and take responsibility for the impact they create. Camping gear that is handmade, that can be repaired in the field and / or refurbished at home, is not only functional but can also be beautiful and last for decades longer than any modern gear on the market, making gear a potential heirloom for one's children.

- A well-maintained canvas tent will last decades longer than a nylon tent and can improve with age.
- A nylon tent only degrades from the day it is made.
- That smell you get every time you open the stuff sac is your tent decomposing.

Those who choose to use wood as a fuel source need to make sure that fire is appropriate and permissible where they camp. In some areas, wood sources are depleted, requiring wood-fuel use to be curtailed, permitted, or otherwise highly regulated. One should obey regulations. In most cases fire use is restricted due to damage caused by improper fuel gathering, scars left by improper fire use, or tyros simply not cleaning up after themselves. Fire use is not a right; it's a privilege and one that must be earned. Creating unsightly messes and leaving charcoal chunks that will last for millennia is intolerable, and those who insist on continuing such behavior have made it impossible for the rest of the fraternity of traditional campers to be able to enjoy a campfire.

On the other hand, those who shake their fingers at fire users need to learn that buying, using, and discarding stoves made of fossil fuels and rare earth compounds may have as much or more impact if consumed with equal thoughtlessness. Minimizing impact is the key. There is no such thing as leaving no trace. To consume means to create waste in the harvesting (mining, refining, canning), using (transporting and marketing cartridges and canisters) and disposal of the product and byproduct (landfills).

Nothing is wrong with traditional or modern technology. It is the inappropriate and thoughtless use of either that creates the problem. We will address issues of concern, present updated options, or suggest concessions to appropriate technology in sections as they arise.

with the needs of the lightweight camper in mind. As a result, campers who buy gear that is adapted from this style of camping for styles that are better suited to traditional gear—campgrounds, winter camps, canoe and horseback trips—are provided shoddy gear. For example, a dome tent that is expanded to six feet tall and will accommodate a family of six, made of the same strength fabric and lightweight poles as its backpackable prototype, is no tent at all. It is a piece of gear marketed to people who know no better but want an image that the marketplace is willing to sell them:

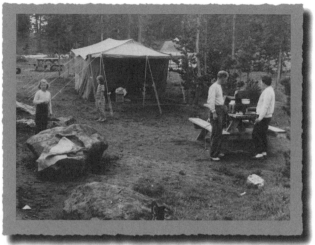

Taking the family afield.

The skills, technologies, and traditions of camping in the old style are experiencing a resurgence because people are realizing they are an appropriate alternative. They want quality gear that fits their needs and style. They don't necessarily need designated wilderness or absolute solitude to gain the benefits of tent camping, but traditional gear can be used there with no modification. We do need, however, to avoid the crowded roadside liveries of the modern developed campgrounds—cheek to jowl, one aluminum horseless hearse after another. Camping? Not a chance!

Pleasures can be sought in the quiet simple places such as the farm or backyard. Solitude and relaxation are not proprietary to wilderness. Skills can be honed where access is easy. The slash-and-gouge methods Manning referred to are often replaced with a few concessions to technology or simply planning ahead, such as a ground pad, cut and prepared poles for permanent use, a fire pan and a metal rack with imported fire wood. Axemanship can be demonstrated while preparing kindling. Quiet conversations by a welcome campfire, wood smoke, the soft noiseless glow of a kerosene lamp or candle lantern, and the patina of polished wood and brass fixtures are some of the pleasures of camping.

In many cases, the management of camping practices has been generated by guidelines needed to camp in designated wilderness settings or in response to areas receiving high impact from overuse. On the East Coast, from Maine to Maryland, there are slightly more than 200,000 acres set aside as wilderness, while a quarter of our population lives in close proximity. Only 5 percent of all wilderness lands lie east of the 100th meridian. We need to realize that these generalized guidelines come from sensitive lands that comprise less than 5 percent of the total lands in this country, and that not everyone seeks a wilderness setting to camp. The methods found in this text can be practiced with maximum comfort in the wild outdoors as well as established campgrounds with little change in technique, something nearly impossible with a Winnebego or nylon mini-cocoon.

A proper layout for a shanty tent.

MENTORS

A life in the open air calls for knowledge, which a very large number of human beings, because of their environments, cannot gain, except when the same is imparted by some more fortunate one who has learned it from experience.
—E. Kreps, 1910

The camp life is the climax of all woodcraft, and the man who leads us there—who blazes the trail, who teaches us the fords that grow less fearsome as we follow—is the heal-worker for our race.

Many a man and woman, I have heard say or imply, that they "would like to go camping, but they are afraid." Of what? Vague fears of animals? Unknown terrors? Or very definite fears or hardships that they believe are an essential part of it?

They are not well informed. The blue sky life is associated with some mighty benefits, and some real dangers. The wise aim at getting the first and avoiding the second. The benefits are beyond question—all the glorious purification of sunlight, the upbuild of exercise with the zest of pleasure, the balm of fresh air at night, the blessedness of sleep, the nerve rest, the change of daily life. The dangers are—rheumatism from improper beds, digestive trouble from improper meals, and minor troubles from insects or improper indulgence in sun-bath, or exposure to weather stress.

These are the real dangers (there is no danger from animals), and the man who shows us the simple, effectual, inexpensive ways of winning all the joys, and dodging all the sorrows, has done no small thing for his people.
—Ernest Thompson Seton, from Miller, 1915

When I was a boy I hungered beyond expression for just such information as I have tried herein to impart. It would be a great joy to me if I could reach and help a considerable number of such heart-hungry boys tormented with an insatiate instinct for the woods, and if I fail of this, I shall at least have the lasting pleasures of having lived through these things myself and of having written about them.
—Ernest Thompson Seton, 1912

FREEDOM OF THE HILLS

It's clear that camping was a requiem for the stressed masses of the workforce at the last turn of the century, just as it is today. The pressures of the workaday world and urban sprawl forced people to seek their simple pleasures and relaxation among the forests and glades of the wild outdoors. Camping allowed people to express themselves in a primal way that provided insights for them to learn more about and re-create themselves. The modern sport still seeks this solace in the freedom of the hills.

It does not mean that Herbert Spencer should cross the ocean to tell us we are an overworked nation; that our hair turns gray ten years earlier than the Englishman's; or, "that we have had somewhat too much of the gospel of work," and, "it is time to preach the gospel of relaxation." It is all true. But we work harder, accomplish more in a given time, and last quite as long as slower races. As to the gray hair—perhaps gray hair is better than none; and it is a fact that the average Briton becomes bald as

Fashion came in all forms, tastes, and traditions.

early as the American turns gray. There is, however, a sad significance in his words when he says: "In every circle I have met men who had themselves suffered from nervous collapse due to stress of business, or named friends who had either killed themselves by overwork, or had been permanently incapacitated, or had wasted long periods in endeavors to recover health." Too true. And it is the constant strain, without let-up or relaxation, that, in nine cases out of ten, snaps the cord and ends in what the doctors call "nervous prostration," something akin to paralysis from which the sufferer seldom wholly recovers.

Mr. Spencer quotes that quaint old chronicler, Froissart, as saying, "The English take their pleasures sadly, after their fashion"; and thinks if he lived now, he would say of Americans, "they take their pleasures hurriedly, after their fashion." Perhaps.

It is an age of hurry and worry. Anything slower than steam is apt to "get left." Fortunes are quickly made and freely spent.

Nearly all busy, hard-worked Americans have an intuitive sense of the need that exists for at least one period of rest and relaxation during each year, and all—or nearly all—are willing to pay liberally, too liberally in fact, for anything that conduces to rest, recreation and sport.
—Nessmuk, 1920

What can be more pleasant, and I will say, more profitable, to the tired, overworked business man, who has spent months in a stuffy office in the heart of some city, than to go away for a few weeks' vacation and camp somewhere in the solitude of the forest, on the bank of a babbling brook or the shore of a lake, with a few congenial companions, there to while away the days fishing, hunting, photography or some other out-of-door pastime; breathing the fresh, pure air and living close to Mother nature!

I venture to make the assertion that if anything is more pleasing it is just a little more of the same thing. Then too, there is a certain gain in these periodical outings. After a few weeks, or a month of this style of living, one can again return to the city feeling that he has a new lease of life. His general health is better, his muscles have become hardened and both himself and his friends are surprised at the change.

—E. Kreps, 1910

The many years spent as a member of the Board of Education in Flushing, Long Island, and as a teacher of art in New York, have impressed upon the author the importance of early training for children in the use of their hands. It is with the purpose of stimulating this sort of schooling that the author appeals to parents and boys to encourage the home production of kites, boats, and sleds, etc.; for the ingenuity and self-reliance thus developed are valuable qualities in a boy or man.

A brotherhood of weekend woodsmen.

Services include all the conveniences of home.

Moreover, a lack of the proper sort of play unfits a boy for the battle of life, and there is scarcely room to doubt that the most successful men of today in business, statesmanship, art, and science are those willing to undergo and capable of enduring the most severe and continued application; and as this power is dependent upon a robust physique and a strong, well-balanced mind, there is no doubt that well-directed boyish sport is the best school for attainment of such results.
—Daniel Carter Beard, 1900

Seriously, is it good for men and women and children to swarm together in cities and stay there, keep staying there, till their instincts are so far perverted that they lose all taste for their natural element, the wide world out-of-doors?

Granting, then, that one deserves relief now and then from the hurry and worry that would age him before his prime, why not go in for a complete change while you are about it? Why not exorcise the devil of business and everything that suggests it? The best vacation an over-civilized man can have is to go where he can hunt, capture, and cook his own meat, erect his own shelter, do his own chores, and so, in some measure, pick up again those lost arts of wildcraft that were our heritage through ages past but of which not one modern man in a hundred knows anything at all. In

cities our tasks are so highly specialized, and so many things are done for us by other specialists, that we tend to become a one-handed and one-idead race. The self-dependent life of the wilderness nomad brings bodily habits and mental processes back to normal, by exercise of muscles and lobes that otherwise might atrophy from want of use.
—Horace Kephart, 1916

This is a time when the whole nation is turning toward the Outdoor Life, seeking in it the physical regeneration so needful for continued national existence, is waking to the fact long known to thoughtful men, that those live longest who live nearest to the ground—that is, who live the simple life of primitive times, divested, however, of the evils that ignorance in those times begot.

Consumption, the white man's plague since he has become a house race, is vanquished by the sun and air, and many ills of the mind also are forgotten when the sufferer boldly takes to the life in tents.

Half our diseases are in our minds and half in our houses. We can safely leave the rest to the physicians for treatment.

Sport is the great incentive to Outdoor Life; Nature Study is the intellectual side of sport.

I should like to lead this whole nation into the way of living outdoors for at least a month each year, reviving and expanding a custom that as far back as Moses was deemed essential to the national well-being.

Not long ago a benevolent rich man, impressed with this idea, chartered a steamer and took some hundreds of slum boys up to the Catskills for a day in the woods. They were duly landed and told to "go in now and have a glorious time." It was like gathering up a netful of catfish and throwing them into the woods, saying, "Go and have a glorious time."

The boys sulked around and sullenly disappeared. An hour later, on being looked up, they were found in groups under the bushes, smoking cigarettes, shooting "craps," and playing cards—the only things they knew.

The weekend was created for the urban masses to re-create themselves.

Thus the well-meaning rich man learned that it is not enough to take men out of doors. We must also teach them to enjoy it.
—Ernest Thompson Seton, 1921

For brick and mortar breed filth and crime,
With pulse of evil that throbs and beats;
And men are withered before their prime
By the curse paved in with the lanes and streets.
And lungs are poisoned and shoulders bowed,
In the smothering reek of mill and mine;
And death stalks in on the struggling crowd—
But he shuns the shadow of oak and pine.
—Nessmuk, 1920

Thousands of people will go into the bush this summer to cut the high cost of living. A man who gets his two weeks salary while he is on vacation should be able to put those two weeks in fishing and camping and be able to save one week's salary clear. He ought to be able to sleep comfortably every night, to eat well every day and to return to the city rested and in good condition.

But if he goes into the woods with a frying pan, an ignorance of black flies and mosquitoes, and a great and abiding lack of knowledge about cookery, the chances are that his return will be very different. He will come back with enough mosquito bites to make the back of his neck look like a relief map of the Caucasus. His digestion will be wrecked after a valiant battle to assimilate half-cooked or charred grub. And he won't have had a decent night's sleep while he has been gone.

He will solemnly raise his right hand and inform you that he has joined the grand army of never-agains. The call of the wild may be all right, but it's a dog's life. He's heard the call of the tame with both ears. Waiter, bring him an order of milk toast.
—Ernest Hemingway, 1920

There is a dash of the gipsy in every one of us who is worth his salt.
—Horace Kephart, 1917

Yes, boys, we have won a great victory for boyhood! We have won it by iteration and reiteration, in other words, by shouting outdoors, talking outdoors, picturing outdoors, singing outdoors and above all by writing about the outdoors, and constantly hammering on one subject and keeping one purpose always in view. By such means we have at last, not only interested the people of

Camping teaches us about ourselves and our companions.

Music and enjoyment at the weekend camp.

the United States in the open, but stampeded the whole world to the forests and the fields. So let us all join in singing the old Methodist hymn:

Shout, shout, we are gaining ground,
Glory, Hallelujah!
The Devil's kingdom we'll put down,
Glory, Hallelujah!

The Devil's kingdom in this case is the ill-ventilated schoolrooms, offices and courts.

It is well to note that the work in this book was not done in the library, but either in the open itself or from notes and sketches made in the open. When telling how to build a cooking fire, for instance, the author preferred to make his diagrams from the fires built by himself or by his wilderness friends, than to trust to information derived from some other man's books. It is much easier to make pictures of impractical fires than to build them. The paste pot and scissors occupy no place of honor in our woodcraft series.

So, Boys of the Open, throw aside your new rackets, your croquet mallets, and your boiled shirts; pull on your buckskin leggings, give a war whoop and be what God intended you should be; healthy wholesome boys. This great Republic belongs to you.
—Ernest Thompson Seton, 1930.

To many a city man there comes a time when the great town wearies him. He hates its sights and smells and clangor. Every duty is a task and every caller is a bore. There come visions of green fields and far-rolling hills, of tall forests and cool, swift-flowing streams. He yearns for the thrill of the chase, for the keen-eyed silent stalking; or, rod in hand, he would seek that mysterious pool where the father of all trout lurks for his lure.

To be free, unbeholden, irresponsible for the once! Free to go or come at one's own sweet will, to tarry where he lists, to do this, or do that, or do nothing, as the humor veers. . . .

Thus basking and sporting in the great clean out of-doors, one could, for the blessed interval,

Forget six counties overhung with smoke,
Forget the snorting steam and piston-stroke,
Forget the spreading of the hideous town

—Horace Kephart, 1917

Camping is an American institution, because America affords the greatest camping ground in the world.
—Daniel Carter Beard, 1900

With a large majority of prospective tourists and outers, "camping out" is a leading factor in the summer vacation. And during the long winter months they are prone to collect in little knots and talk much of camps, fishing, hunting, and "roughing it." The last phrase is very popular and always cropping out in the talks on matters pertaining to a vacation in the woods. I dislike the phrase. We do not go to the green woods and crystal waters to rough it, we go to smooth it. We get it rough enough at home; in towns and cities; in shops, offices, stores, banks—anywhere that we may be placed—with the necessity always present of being on time and up to our work; of providing for the dependent ones; of keeping up, catching up, or getting left. "Alas for the life-long battle, whose bravest slogan is bread."
—Nessmuk, 1920

Escape the pavement and flee to the hills.

The charm of nomadic life is its freedom from care, its unrestrained liberty of action, and the proud self-reliance of one who is absolutely his own master, free to follow his bent in his own way, and who cheerfully, in turn, suffers the penalties that Nature visits upon him for every slip of

mind or bungling of his hand. Carrying with him, as he does, in a few small bundles, all that he needs to provide food and shelter in any land, habited or uninhabited, the camper is lord of himself and of his surroundings.
—Horace Kephart, 1917

Ages ago man was a savage, and though he has been under the restraining influences of civilization for centuries, the spirit of the savage is still strong within. Therefore, when he hears the "call of the wild" as one of the popular writers has so aptly expressed it, I would advise packing up the kit and hieing off to some secluded spot to spend a few weeks in close communion with Mother Nature.
—E. Kreps, 1910

Hidden in a drawer in the antique highboy, back of the moose head in my studio, there are specimens of Indian beadwork, bits of buckskin, necklaces made of the teeth of animals, a stone calumet, my old hunting knife with its rawhide sheath and—carefully folded in oiled paper—is the jerked tenderloin of a grizzly bear!

But that is not all; for more important still is a mysterious wooden flask containing the castor or the scent gland of a beaver, which is carefully rolled up in a bit of buckskin embroidered with mystic Indian signs.

The flask was given to me as "big medicine" by Bow-arrow, the Chief of the Montinais Indians. Bow-arrow said—and I believe him—that when one inhales the odor of the castor from this medicine flask one's soul and body are then and forever afterwards permeated with a great and abiding love of the big outdoors. Also, when one eats of the mystic grizzly bear's flesh, one's body acquires the strength and courage of this great animal.

During the initiation of the members of a Spartan band of my boys, known as the Buckskin Men, each candidate is given a thin slice of the grizzly bear meat and a whiff of the beaver castor.

Of course, we know that people with unromantic and unimaginative minds will call this sentimentalism. We people of the outdoor tribes plead guilty to being sentimentalists; but we know from experience that old Bow-arrow was right, because we have ourselves eaten of the grizzly bear and smelled the castor of the beaver!
—Ernest Thompson Seton, June 1920

SECTION ONE

Furnishing the Camp and Camper

[F]ield equipment is a most excellent hobby to amuse one during
the shut-in season. I know nothing else that so restores the buoyant optimism
of youth as overhauling one's kit and planning trips for the next vacation.

—Horace Kephart, 1916

PERSONAL GEAR

The same article that one declares is the most essential to his comfort, health, and happiness is the very first thing that another will throw into the trail. A man's outfit is a matter which seems to touch his private honor. I have heard veterans sitting around a camp-fire proclaim the superiority of their kits with a jealousy, loyalty, and enthusiasm they would not exhibit for the flesh of their flesh and the bone of their bone. On a campaign you may attack a man's courage, the flag he serves, the newspaper for which he works, his intelligence, or his camp manners, and he will ignore you, but if you criticize his patent water-bottle he will fall upon you with both fists.
—Richard Harding Davis, 1917

A personal camp kit, so far as details are concerned, is only gotten together, with any degree of satisfaction, after much experimenting and actual experience.

We can spend years arguing over gear and clothing. Everyone has his or her preferences and knows what works best for him or her. However, if we asked sourdoughs what their most important piece of gear might be, the responses would be divided along lines of experience, not hype, fashion, or fads. Marketing will never be a substitute for knowledge of what works in a given situation.

With clothing, in many cases the use of modern synthetics has replaced the use of natural fibers for no other reason than fashion. Their function is inferior, the quality is inferior, and they are non-biodegradable—once bought, they're around forever.

However, we should also avoid blind dedication to the past. Selection of gear needs to be based on utility and real need. Life in a luxury camp can get carried away with comfort and convenience common to all modern life, but the other extreme is rejection of anything simply on the premise that it is new—this makes no more sense than rejecting traditional gear simply because it's old. Some items of modern gear are simply better than their old counterparts, and we should make concessions for them. A lightweight sleeping bag has no rival when carried in the winter. But when weight and cold aren't as much of an issue, heavy woolen blankets can never be beaten by the nylon "fart sac." Modern ground pads will never match the comfort of a primitive bed, but when impact to fragile areas is the alternative, we need to consider their value and weigh the consequences of using either.

Of course, the prime essential of all personal equipment is that it be serviceable, that it meets your need, and that it keeps you comfortable. If it meets these simple conditions, it is well along toward a satisfactory personal camp kit.

Keep your kit simple, compact, and as light as possible. No doubt there are times when it would be nice to have a whole department store along, but in the long run it would prove very inconvenient. Be able to make a strong case for every single thing that is included, and you will need to argue the case over every time for every trip, for your exact needs will never be twice alike. One time you may be setting off on a go-light hike where you must carry every ounce of your own kit, and perhaps help some other fellows. . . . A few things are easier to look out for than many. Include essentials up to your weight limit, but leave non-essentials at home.
—Frank H. Cheley, 1933

TRADITIONAL CAMP FIXTURES

THE ULTIMATE WISH LIST

SHELTER AND ACCESSORIES
- Wall tent / tipi / campfire tent / pyramid or cone designs
- Canvas or Egyptian cotton
- Cotton ropes and wooden dog-bone sliders, whipped and spliced
- Copper-wrapped pole ends with iron pins
- Hardwood or iron pegs
- Stove and pipes
- Canvas fly and / or awning
- Sun visor / parasol
- Storage sacks

- Collecting tools—kill jar, plant press, and others
- Fire buckets and / or back pump
- Shaving horse

PACK / STORAGE
(one of the following)
- Wooden pack frame
- Pack bundle with diamond hitch
- Pack basket with tumpline
- Duluth pack
- Blanket, bedroll, and harness
- Trunks, shelves, or wanigans

TOOLS AND TACKLE
- Axe and leather sheath
- Bucksaw and scabbard
- Belt axe / hatchet with leather sheath
- Sheath knife
- Jackknife
- Files and whetstones
- Wooden toolbox
- Shovel
- Splitting maul and wedges
- Splitting froe
- Drawknife
- Small sledgehammer
- Hammer and nails
- Chopping blocks
- Bag of assorted ropes
- Shotgun or rifle—air rifle for children
- Fishing rod and tackle box / creel
- Bow and arrow / quiver— 35- to 40-pound pull

FURNISHINGS
- Folding wood-and-canvas stools, chairs, and cots
- Candle lanterns
- Candles and holders
- Solid or collapsible closet
- Kerosene lantern and fuel can
- Wooden stools
- Wooden storage boxes
- Wooden or metal folding table
- Wool blankets
- Straw / woolen tick
- Rope hammock or stretcher bed
- Collapsible water bucket
- Collapsible washbasin
- First-aid box
- Clothesline and pins
- Lap desk
- Storage baskets
- Steamer trunks
- Lap throws
- Flag
- Washbasin and stand
- Portable shower screen
- Toilet seat
- Camp torches
- Victrola
- Brooms
- Flyswatter

TRADITIONAL CAMP FIXTURES

THE ULTIMATE WISH LIST (CONTINUED)

KITCHEN FURNITURE
- Grub boxes
- Evaporative cooler
- Cast-iron ware—skillets, Dutch ovens, griddles or
- Sheet steel—skillets, griddles
- Enamel or stainless pots and pans
- Eating utensils—enamel plate, bowl, cup
- Flatware—bone or horn handles
- Cooking utensils: spatula, spoons, tongs, knives
- Coffeepot
- Teakettle
- Fire furniture—grate, crane, poker, tongs
- Glass jars—storage
- Fire kits
- Tin storage cans
- Dishcloths and hot pads
- Assorted cloth bags
- Fish plank—cutting board
- Reflector oven—folding or ridged
- Lashed shelves, tables, and other items
- Baskets
- Gourds—assorted functions
- Collapsible wooden dish rack
- Picnic basket
- Desert water bag
- Popcorn popper
- Ice-cream churn
- Pie irons

PERSONAL ITEMS
- Hiking staff
- Campaign hat
- Silk neck scarves
- Mackinaw vest
- Mackinaw and/or canvas coat
- Canvas anorak—for winter with sash

- Compass
- Whistle
- Flashlight (chrome metal)
- Sewing kit
- Notebook / journal and pencil
- Musical instruments—harmonica, guitar, dulcimer
- Mirror
- Pocketknife
- Shaving mug, brush, and razor
- Pocket tool kit
- Waterproof matchbox
- Haversack, ditty, or possibles bag

TRAVEL GEAR
- Snowshoes
- Cross-country touring skis
- Toboggan or pulk
- Wood / canvas canoe and paddles
- Wood / fabric baidarka
- Dog team and sled
- Horse and mule tack
- Fat-tire touring bicycle—beach cruiser
- Classic motorcar and pup trailer

TRAINING SKILLS FOR PERSONAL GEAR

APPRENTICE CAMPER
- *Make an item of individual gear.*
- *Select, pack, and carry suitable personal gear, including clothing and safety items for all day or an overnight trip.*
- *Make a list of all items chosen, including cost and weight of each item.*

JOURNEYMAN CAMPER
Demonstrate ability to:
- *Select individual gear to be taken on the trip and pack appropriately.*
- *Pack and carry personal gear for a week-long camping trip.*
- *Select proper footwear for the style of trip.*

JOURNEYMAN WOODSMAN
- *Select personal gear needed for a particular style of travel.*
- *Make a personal gear checklist for a specific seasons expedition.*
- *Demonstrate ability to maintain and make home and field repairs to all selected gear.*

MASTER WOODSMAN
- *Know the principles of dressing for long-term wilderness living.*
- *Demonstrate ability to maintain clothing, footwear, and gear for extended periods of wet and snowy conditions.*
- *Design and produce a quality item of specialized gear or clothing for four-season living.*

Regarding the quality of goods selected, I advise buying only the best. One does not like the idea of some much needed article giving out when far back in the woods, for such an occurrence may mean considerable annoyance and discomfort. Then, too, there is some satisfaction in the possession of a good outfit, while the cheaper goods always prove unsatisfactory. . . . There are many very complete camping outfits sold by the sporting goods houses, but they are not practical for the woodsmen, in fact, are not made for him, for the camp outfitters cater mostly to the city sportsman.
—*Camp and Trail Methods*, **1910**

TOLERATE ONLY QUALITY

When it comes to traditional camping, one has to wonder about the expense of setting up such an outfit. Unfortunately, many of the icons of the traditional style are now considered collectibles or antiques, and their purchase price is too high to press them back into service. However, most of these items have proven their worth so well, they are still manufactured to this day with little modification. There is also a resurgence of interest in traditional camping to the point that many manufacturers are reissuing old designs or reproducing items that haven't been made for years. And, of course, the best place to find many of the basic items is at secondhand and army-surplus stores.

When comparing a traditional camp to a modern camp (including clothing, personal gear, and common camp and trail furnishings), a complete high-quality traditional camp outfit can be put together for about $2,500. This is gear that, if cared for, will last for generations and is easily repaired and maintained. Compare this to a light / cold camp setup that will easily exceed $3,000 for gear that cannot compete in durability, long-term utility, or coziness.

If this is too much, it may be best to start with a few essentials. The kind of camp desired—light and mobile, permanent, rough, luxurious and comfortable—will dictate the items needed to get started. If the item can't be handmade, it should be bought from good craftsmen, and the quality will likely be costly but worth the expense. It will repay for the initial investment many times over. Our contemporary outdoor industry is rife with self-repair gizmos and lifetime-guarantee products, none of which can be repaired in the woods, nor can they fend off swarms of bloodthirsty pests until they can be returned to the manufacturer for a replacement. Built-in quality will outlast a guarantee any day.

That hits directly at the weak point of the sporting catalogues. Every once in a while an enthusiast writes me of some new and handy kink he is ready to swear by. It is indeed handy; and if one could pluck it from the nearest bush when occasion for its use arose, it would be a joy and a delight. But carrying it four hundred miles to that occasion for its use is a very different matter. The sporting catalogues are full of very handy kinks. They are good to fool with and think about, and plan over in the off season; but when you pack your duffel bag you'd better put them on a shelf.
—*Camp and Trail*, 1920

There are not so many of these accessories all told, so it is well worth the effort to strain the financial rigging a bit and get them of the best quality. A belt-axe that costs you less than about two simoleons is just no axe at all, merely a poor heavy thing whose edge and head alike are always coming off. The knife that will really serve you when it comes to skinning out a tough old hide is no cheap iron affair with hilt and handle all wrong for real work; it is rather an extra fine bit of steel, with a handle that has been evolved out of the needs of hunters who follow the art as a daily occupation, and it will set you back not less than one dollar and fifty cents. No matter where one hits the list of accessories the same rule holds good—there are two kinds of them, the sort that always has something out of order and do not somehow fit, and the kind that are always "all there," good and plenty, with something left over for extra hard duty.
—**Warren H. Miller, 1915**

PLANNING WHAT TO TAKE

Carry only essentials: but the definition of the word is not so easy. An essential is that which, by each man's individual experience, he has found he cannot do without.

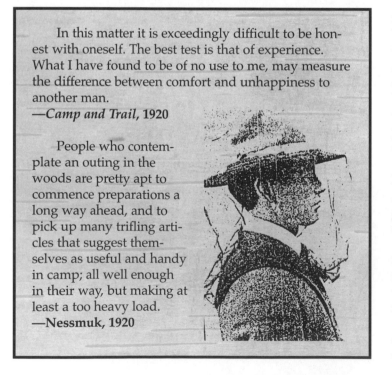

In this matter it is exceedingly difficult to be honest with oneself. The best test is that of experience. What I have found to be of no use to me, may measure the difference between comfort and unhappiness to another man.
—*Camp and Trail*, 1920

People who contemplate an outing in the woods are pretty apt to commence preparations a long way ahead, and to pick up many trifling articles that suggest themselves as useful and handy in camp; all well enough in their way, but making at least a too heavy load.
—**Nessmuk, 1920**

How to determine that? When you have reached home after your trip, turn your duffel bag upside down on the floor. Separate the contents into three piles. Let pile No. 1 include those articles you have used every day—or nearly that often; let pile No. 2 comprise those you have used but once; and pile No. 3 those you have not used at all. Now, no matter how your heart may yearn over the Patent Dingbat in No. 3, shut your eyes and resolutely discard the two latter piles.

Naturally, if you are strong-minded, pile No. 1 will be a synonym for your equipment. As a matter of fact you will probably not be as strong-minded as that. You will argue to yourself somewhat in this fashion:

"Yes, that is all very well; but it was only a matter of sheer chance that the Patent Dingbat is not in pile No. 1. To be sure, I did not use it on this particular trip; but in other conditions I might need it every day."

So you take it, and keep on taking it, and once in a great while you use it. Then some day you wake up to two more bits of camp

What to one is a necessity, to another may be excess.

philosophy which you formulate to yourself about as follows: An article must pay in convenience or comfort for the trouble of its transportation; and substitution, even imperfect, is better than the carrying of special conveniences. Then he hurls said Patent Dingbat into the nearest pool.
—*Camp and Trail*, **1920**

In discussion of the details of equipment, I shall first of all take up in turn each and every item you could possibly need, whether you intend to travel by horse, by canoe, or on your own two feet. Of course you will not carry all of these things on any one trip. What is permissible for horse traveling would be absurd for a walking trip; and some things such as a waterproof duffel bag—which you would need on a foot tramp, would be useless where you have kayaks and a tarpaulin to protect your belongings.
—*Camp and Trail*, **1920**

When packing, remember that a partly filled bag is easy to pack, easy to carry on one's shoulders; but a tightly filled bag is a nuisance on the trail.
—**Daniel Carter Beard, 1920**

PERSONAL ITEMS
❏ Matches and safe
❏ Pocketknife
❏ Sheath knife
❏ Compass
❏ 2 bandanas
❏ Sporting outfit
❏ Duffel bag
❏ Soap and case
❏ Crash towel
❏ Bath towel
❏ Toothbrush
❏ Tooth soap
❏ Shaving set in oiled silk
❏ Medicines and bandages
❏ Fly dope and head net
❏ Needle and thread
❏ Waxed thread
❏ Piece of buckskin

CLOTHING LIST
❏ 1 Felt hat
❏ 1 Silk kerchief
❏ 1 Waistcoat, buckskin shirt, and sweater
❏ 2 Gray woolen flannel shirts
❏ 2 Woolen undershirts, 3 drawers
   (includes one suit you wear)
❏ 1 Trousers and belt—buckskin over khaki
❏ 4 Pairs woolen socks
❏ 1 Pair boots
❏ 1 Pair camp slippers or
❏ 1 Pair oil tanned moccasins
❏ 1 Slicker
❏ 1 Pair gloves and leather cuffs

FIELD GEAR
❏ Silk tent (sometimes)
❏ Tarpaulin
❏ Rubber blanket
❏ Blanket
❏ Comforter
❏ Small pillows
❏ Canvas bucket
❏ Canvas wash basin
❏ Canvas wash tub
❏ Candle lantern and candles
❏ Pocket axe
❏ 3 pound axe
❏ File and whetstone
—*Camp and Trail*, 1920

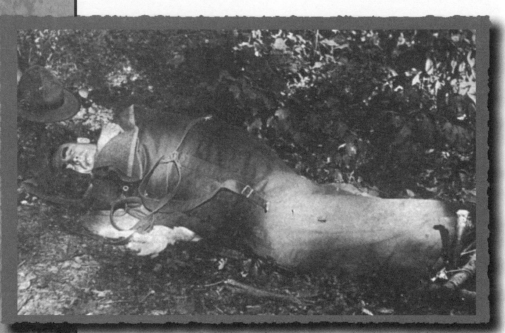

Early sleeping bags were converted pack-sacs with blanket liners.

GO-LIGHT CAMPING

The wild life is not to test how much the human frame can endure although that often enough happens—but to test how well the human wits, backed by an enduring body, can answer the question of comfort. Comfort means minimum equipment; comfort means bodily ease. The task is to balance, to reconcile these apparently opposing ideas.
—*Camp and Trail*, 1920

If one is going far back into the wilds he cannot take such an outfit as the ordinary camper would select, and the list must be weeded down until there is not one article that is not absolutely needed.
—E. Kreps, 1910

As I have said, the average man, with the best intentions, will not go too light, so I have laid especial emphasis on the necessity of discarding the unessential. But there exists a smaller class who rush to the opposite extreme.

We all know the type. He professes an inordinate scorn for comfort of all sorts. If you are out with him you soon discover that he has a vast pride in being able to sleep on cobblestones—and does so at the edge of yellow pines with their long needles. He eats badly cooked food. He stands—or perhaps I should say poses—indifferent to a downpour when every one else has sought shelter. In a cold climate he brings a single thin blanket. His slogan seems to be: "This is good enough for me!" with the unspoken conclusion, "if it isn't good enough for you fellows, you're pretty soft."

The queer part of it is he usually manages to bully sensible men into his point of view. They accept his bleak camps and voluntary hardships because they are ashamed to be less tough than he is. And in town they are abashed before him when with a superior, good-natured, and tolerant laugh he tells the company in glee of how you brought with you a little pillow-case to stuff with moss. "Bootleg is good enough for me!" he cries; and every one marvels at his woodsmanship.
—*Camp and Trail*, 1920

[W]hen season, weather and law combine to make it "close time" for beast, bird and man, it is well that a few congenial spirits should, at some favorite trysting place, gather around the glowing stove and exchange yarns, opinions and experiences. Perhaps no two will exactly agree on the best ground for an outing, on the flies, rods, reels, guns, etc., or half a dozen other points that may be discussed. But one thing all admit. Each and every one has gone to his chosen ground with too much impedimenta, too much duffel; and nearly all have used boats at least twice as heavy as they need to

have been. The temptation to buy this or that bit of indispensable camp-kit has been too strong, and we have gone to the blessed woods, handicapped with a load fit for a pack-mule. This is not how to do it.

Go light; the lighter the better, so that you have the simplest material for health, comfort and enjoyment.
—**Nessmuk**, 1920

There is more danger that a man take too much than too little into the wilderness. No matter how good his intentions may be, how conscientiously he may follow advice, or how carefully he may examine and reexamine his equipment, he will surely find that he is carrying a great many pounds more than his companions, the professionals at the business. At first this may affect him but little. He argues that he is constructed on a different pattern from these men, that his training and education have developed in him needs and habits such as they have never known.
—*Camp and Trail*, 1920

Rustic camps can fit in a basket but provide trainlods worth of benefit.

WHAT TO WEAR

I t is said that "fashion is—or reflects—a form of behavior accepted by most people in a society." And, while fashion may be introduced, traditions are handed down. Fashion remains popular for a few months or years before being replaced by another trend or fad. The traditions of dressing for the outdoors are founded in the use of natural fibers for protection and insulation, with trail-tested designs dating back perhaps centuries. Clothing is in fashion when a large segment accepts it as desirable, but when the majority no longer accepts it, it is old-fashioned. Tradition, on the other hand, is not dependent on popular opinion or adoption; it survives by needing only a select few who are dedicated to keeping it alive.

The casual nature of our current fashion is indeed reflected in our behavior. Traditional dress reflects a more formal time, with values of durability and longevity at its roots. The way we treat each other, lacking simple courtesies and respect, are indicative of our short-term approach to acquaintances and the anonymity we assume by avoiding eye contact, a friendly greeting, or other traits that encourage familiarity.

We live at a time in which readdressing some of the values found in the old style might do us some good. The history of who we are and how we arrived at our present state of affairs may help us create a better map for our future. If fashion truly is a reflection of who we are, a little added formality and a look back at our roots may be in order. The roles created by gender may be a sticky issue, and some of the following quotes may seem old-fashioned or offensive to some, but reestablishing a respect for each other may be a good place to start.

Why natural fibers? Because they are time-tested renewable resources that are available within a reasonable amount of refining. The fibers are readily available and may even be homegrown. They lend themselves to hard work under field conditions and take a fair amount of abuse before failing. The only things that synthetics can offer are a slimmer profile when layered and greater compressibility when packed.

Natural fibers are better suited to life near an open fire or stove, as they don't melt, and if damaged, they can be easily repaired. They are not prone to degrading as they get dirty and do not lose as much loft with age. Natural fibers can be dyed in gaudy colors like synthetics, but who wants to spoil their inherent beauty. The range of designs that can be developed for their use may be somewhat limited to the ones used in the past, but that's the point.

Dressed to the nine's and seated on rustic camp furniture.

You will desire, to begin with, to look well and properly dressed when taking your outing; to look the part, so to speak, so that you will command respect in place of derision wherever you may be. Good camping clothes are becoming both for the male and female of the species, and your backwoods yokel recognizes them at sight and tips his hat to you instead of visiting contumely upon you as he surely will if you appear before him in a gypsy assortment of odds and ends of old clothes. Your camping togs should withstand wear, rain, briars and scraggs, mud and swampy duff with equal impunity.
—**Warren H. Miller, 1918**

As a general rule I will say adopt the style of clothing which is most generally worn in the particular locality where you intend going.
—**E. Kreps, 1910**

CLOTHING—FABRICS PRIMER

The dapper camper as well as the seasoned trail hand knew the value of quality clothing for a safe and comfortable outing. Since natural fibers were the only alternative (rayon was the first synthetic fiber, invented in 1910, but not common to the scene until 1924), outdoor clothing during the golden age of camping consisted of sturdy, well-made designs of wool, cotton, hemp, silk, buckskin, and fur. Outer clothing was made from dense, polished fabrics, while loft and insulation were created by layers of thick, brushed, and knitted fabrics. With the exception of such specialty terms, like loden or forestry cloth, all of the following fabrics are still available. These are the fabrics that took early explorers to the highest, coldest, and most remote spots on earth and served outdoorsmen well for hundreds of years. They are the matrix from which we weave our traditional style.

Corduroy I would not have as a gift. It is very noisy, and each raindrop that hits it spreads at once to the size of a silver dollar. I verily believe an able pair of corduroys can, when feeling good, soak up ten pounds of water.

Good moleskin dries well, and until it begins to give out is soft and tough. But it is like the one-hoss shay: when it starts to go, it does the job up completely in a few days. The difficulty is to guess when that moment is due to arrive. Anything but the best quality is worthless.

Khaki has lately come into popularity. It wears relatively well, dries quickly, and is excellent in all but one particular: it shows every spot of dirt. A pair of khakis three days along on the trail look as though they had been out a year. The new green khaki is a little better.

—*Camp and Trail*, 1920

WEAVE

- Plain Weave (cotton / wool)—the weft or fill (crosswise) yarns are woven into the warp (lengthwise) yarns in a simple over one and under one pattern, forming a flat cloth.
- Twill Weave (cotton / wool)—the wefts cross over two, three, or four wefts, creating a diagonal pattern to the weave. The cloth is very strong and tightly woven. Denim is a common twill.
- Felt—fibers of wool, fur and / or hair are matted together through agitation under moist heat and pressure. Felt is made thicker by adding fibers as the process proceeds.
- Knits—looped yarns are linked together, creating a cloth that is very elastic compared to woven materials
- Worsted—compactly twisted yarn from long stapled fibers. Used to create very "hard" or "polished" windproof fabrics such as gabardine and serge.

FABRICS

- Bobinet (also spelled Bobbinet)—fine mesh fabric used as protection against mosquitoes and flies.
- Buckskin (also called Braintan or Smoketan)—deer hide (moose and elk hide are similar, but are not called buckskin) that has been tanned using brains as the tanning agent, and then smoked to keep the hide pliable after wetting. Very soft, breathable, and durable. Chemically tanned hides are not as good for clothing, gloves and footwear.
- Corduroy—cotton or cotton blend fabric with raised ribs of varying widths, from wide wale to pin-wale (narrow).

- Felt—fabric made by matting wool fibers together with moist heat and pressure. It is not woven and comes in a variety of weights, thicknesses, and values.
- Flannel—a soft, warm fabric made from cotton, wool or cotton / wool blends. One side is brushed or "fulled" to create a fuzzy surface. Fabric of pure cotton is properly called flannelette.
- Forestry Cloth—specialty wool fabric mentioned in old articles and catalogs made for forest ranger's clothing. Treated to be water-repellant. Olive drab.

Well chosen natural fibers in clothing and bedding make camp a comfortable place to relax.

- Gabardine—the closest woven (worsted), finest appearing cotton or wool twill—windproof. Resists rain, wind, snow, and sleet. Comes in tans, grays, and neutrals shades. Used today by the British Military.
- Jersey—plain knitted fabric of wool, cotton, or synthetics. Cloth may be smooth or napped.
- Khaki—a fine yarn, closely woven, twilled cotton or wool. Available in a variety of grades and qualities. Used by militaries throughout the world for rugged work. Fabric is named after the color, which ranges from olive to light tan.
- Loden—thick, heavily "fulled" waterproof fabric, also called "Loden Green" from the deep olive green color of the fabric.
- Makinaw—the toughest and most durable woolen material. Soft, rough, and wooly, very similar to heavy blanketing. Very warm for the weight, and very waterproof. Available in solids and plaids.
- Moleskin—fuzzy cotton fabric used mainly for shirts and collars for over 200 years, today known as chamoix.
- Paraffin Cloth—closely woven duck, filled with paraffin to make it waterproof.
- Tweed—rough, heavy woolen cloth, usually woven in two or more colors. May be woven in a plain, twill, or herringbone twill pattern. Favorite cloth for sports clothing.
- Whipcord—very hard, dense weave that has a polished finish. Fabric is very durable, windproof, and water repellant.
- Wool—fabric made primarily of yarns spun from the fleece of sheep (fibers may also include camel hair, goat, alpaca, angora, and others). Wool fibers are known for their low moisture absorption, and result in a fabric that remains warm even when wet. Mention is made of Scottish and Icelandic wool as fine products, and bats made from Australian wool for bedding.
- Worsted Wool—a smooth, shiny, strong wool yarn, spun from long wool fibers that have been combed. Fabric looks smooth and hard—poplin and serge are worsted materials.

OUTDOOR CLOTHING

[N]o city dweller brought up in proximity to laundries and on the firm belief that washing should be done all at once and at stated intervals can be convinced that he can keep clean and happy with but one shirt; or that more than one handkerchief is a superfluity.

Yet in time, if he is a woodsman, and really thinks about such affairs instead of taking them for granted, he will inevitably gravitate toward the correct view of these things. . . . In a similar manner he will realize that with the aid of cold-water soap the shirt he wears may be washed in one half hour and dried in the next. Meanwhile he dons his sweater. A handkerchief is laundered complete in a quarter of an hour. Why carry extras, then, merely from a recollection of full bureau drawers?
—*Camp and Trail*, 1920

A coat is useless absolutely. A sweater is better as far as warmth goes; a waistcoat beats it for pockets. You will not wear it during the day; it wads up too much to be of much use at night. Even your trousers rolled up make a better temporary pillow. Leave it home; and you will neither regret it nor miss it.

For warmth, as I have said, you will have your sweater. In this case, too, I would, impress the desirability of purchasing the best you can buy. And let it be a heavy one, of gray or a neutral brown.
—*Camp and Trail*, 1920

Traditional dress reflects a more formal time, with values of durability and longevity at its roots. They lend themselves to hard work under field conditions and take a fair amount of abuse before failing.

My rig, winter or summer, has boiled down to a gray woolen suit, the coat of which was once of a standard double-breasted city suit, and the trousers are all-wool homespun, rather thin-cut lower down so that they will fold easily inside one's hunting-boots. I long ago discarded the army breeches; they are no good to sleep in, and the cuffs are a nuisance, particularly if you are wearing larrigans that come not much higher than your shoes. Going to the train I wear the above-described suit with the trousers pulled down outside my hunting-boots, sport a linen collar and shirt, a red leather four-in-hand tie presented to me by a cowboy friend, a Stetson hat and a green woven-wool skating vest. Except for the hat, I look about the same as any one else in city duds and attract no particular attention.

On leaving the train I shoulder the pack and hike for the nearest timber. A temporary stop is made here, trousers are tucked into the boots and refaced, the linen is taken off and stowed in a small bag in the pack and my flannel shirt comes out of the latter and is put on, also belt axe and hunting-knife. Using the same leather necktie, I am ready for the trail.

This rounds up all the trail clothing, except what to take for a change. One needs, of course, night socks and bed-slippers for the sleeping-bag, and a wool toque to pull over your head for a nightcap. With head and feet comfortable you can sleep soundly even if the bed is hard; without them cared for, no bed will bring sleep. I confess also to a little down pillow a foot square that always gets into my pack.
—Warren H. Miller, 1918

Few items in the woodsman's wardrobe speak so clearly of tradition. For many years, access to good brain-tanned hides was limited to those who traveled among the people of the bush, or those who were self-reliant enough to brain tan for themselves. The beadwork and finery that highlight them require skill and patience to perform, virtues that are part of the woodcraft way.

Brain-tan is the best natural clothing material, bar none. It breathes, repels water, remains cool in hot weather, but serves the user well when it's cold, holding wind and rain at bay. Buckskin can be made into boots, gloves, hats, shirts, bags, and almost any other required gear. It is a natural byproduct of the hunter's tradition and shows high regard for the life taken by using the entire critter for food, tools, clothing, and gear.

The best informed sources on how to learn brain tanning accurately have only been available for a few years. There are also a number of sources for quality brain-tan hides now available at reasonable prices.

Smoked buckskin and native beadwork create the bushman's coat

THE WOODCRAFTER'S BUSHCRAFT COAT

To my mind the best extra garment is a good ample buckskin shirt. It is less bulky than the sweater, of less weight, and much warmer, especially in a wind, while for getting through brush noiselessly it cannot be improved upon. I do not know where you can buy one; but in any case get it ample in length and breadth, and without the fringe. The latter used to possess some significance beside ornamentation, for in case of need the wilderness hunter could cut from it thongs and strings as he needed them. Nowadays a man in a fringed buckskin shirt is generally a fake built to deceive tourists. On the other hand a plain woodsman-like garment, worn loose and belted at the waist, looks always at once comfortable and appropriate. Be sure that the skins of which it is made are smoke tanned. The smoke tanned article will dry soft, while the ordinary skin is hardening to almost the consistency of rawhide. Good buckskins are difficult to get hold of—and it will take five to make you a good shirt—but for this use they last practically forever.
—*Camp and Trail*, 1920

A waistcoat is a handy affair. In warm weather you leave it open and hardly know you have it on; in cold weather you button it up, and it affords excellent protection. Likewise it possesses the advantage of numerous pockets. These you will have your women folk extend and deepen for you, until your compass, notebook, pipe, matches, and so forth fit nicely in them. As it is to be used as an outside garment, have the back lined.
—*Camp and Trail*, 1920

The outer shirt of your daily habit is best made of rather a light weight of gray flannel. Most new campers indulge in a very thick navy blue shirt, mainly, I believe, because it contrasts picturesquely with a bandana around the neck. Such a shirt almost always crocks, is sure to fade, shows dirt, and is altogether too hot. A lighter weight furnishes all the protection you need to your underclothes and turns sun quite as well. Gray is a neutral color, and seems less often than any other to shame you to the wash soap. A great many wear an ordinary cotton work shirt, relying for warmth on the underclothes. There is no great objection to this, except that flannel is better should you get rained on.
—*Camp and Trail*, 1920

The true point of comfort is, however, your underwear. It should be of wool. I know that a great deal has been printed against it, and a great many hygienic principles are invoked to prove that linen, cotton, or silk are better. But experience with all of them merely leads back to the starting point. If one were certain never to sweat freely, and never to get wet, the theories might hold. But once let linen or cotton or silk undergarments get thoroughly moistened, the first chilly little wind is your undoing. You will shiver and shake before the hottest fire, and nothing short of a complete change and a rub-down will do you any good.
—*Camp and Trail*, 1920

Soccer pants of whipcord or wool have always been worn by mountain climbers, "Tyroleans," Soccer, and Basket Ballers, and should be adopted by athletes in general (except Base Ball and Football players) as giving the knee a square deal—that is, room to work. They are cheap, too, and one pair of good stuff outlasts three pairs of long "pants."
—**James Austin Wilder, 1929**

The matter of trousers is an important one; for unless you are possessed of abundant means of transportation, those you have on will be all you will take. I used to include an extra pair, but got over it. Even when trout fishing I found that by the time I had finished standing around the fire cooking, or yarning, I might have to change the underdrawers, but the trousers themselves had dried well enough. And patches are not too difficult a maneuver.
    —Camp and Trail, 1920

Shirt—All wool. Wash it only in water almost too hot to hold your hand in, with soap shavings, by dousing it up and down in the suds. Rinse (don't wring it) in clean luke-warm water. Hang up to dry without wringing. When perfectly dry, iron with clean fry-pan filled with coals. For an ironing board fold your tent on a flat place and spread your towel over it. Don't economize on your shirt. Get the best. Two handkerchief pockets, one for compass, one for First Aid kit.
    —James Austin Wilder, 1929

Belt—Leather or woven, with two in-serted rings for knife and lanyard.
    —James Austin Wilder, 1929

HATS

The hat should be fine, soft felt with moderately low crown and wide brim; color to match the clothing. . . . The proper covering for head and feet is no slight affair, and will be found worth some attention.
—**Nessmuk, 1920**

Your hat should be stiff enough to fan your coals, shed rain. Mark in indelible ink inside, on the felt, with your name and address. No borrower can stand seeing that name forty times a day.
—**James Austin Wilder, 1929**

Long experience by men practically concerned seems to prove that a rather heavy felt hat is the best for all around use. Even in hot sun it seems to be the most satisfactory as, with proper ventilation, it turns the sun's rays better even than light straw. . . .

I have found the Stetson, of the five to seven dollar grade, the most satisfactory. If it is intended for woods travel where you are likely to encounter much brush, get it of medium brim. In those circumstances I find it handy to buy a size smaller than usual, and then to rip out the sweat band. The friction of the felt directly against the fore-head and the hair will hold it on in spite of pretty sharp tugs by thorns and wind. In the mountains or on the plains, you can indulge in a wider and stiffer brim. Two buckskin thongs sewn on either side and to tie under the "back hair" will hold it on, even against a head wind. A test will show you how this can be. A leather band and buckle—or miniature cinch and latigos—gives added

BANDANA

Inside the sweat band of your hat, or around the crown on the outside of your hat, carry a gut leader with medium-sized artificial flies attached, and around your neck knot a big gaudy bandana handkerchief; it is a most useful article; it can be used in which to carry your game, food or duffel, or for warmth, or worn over the head for protection from insects. In the latter case put it on your head under your hat and allow it to hang over your shoulders like the havelock worn by the soldiers of '61.
—Daniel Carter Beard, 1920

About your neck you will want to wear a silk kerchief. This is to keep out dust, and to prevent your neck from becoming reddened and chapped. It, too, should be of the best quality. The poorer grades go to pieces soon, and their colors are not fast. Get it big enough. At night you will make a cap of it to sleep in; and if ever you happen to be caught without extra clothes where it is very cold, you will find that the kerchief tied around your middle, and next the skin, will help surprisingly.
—*Camp and Trail*, 1910

Bandana—Should be two cubits square. This keeps your upper spine cool in hot weather, warm in cold. Some of its uses are: An arm, head, knee support bandage; Dress-suit Case; Table napkins; Mosquito and Fly bar; As a warning signal for deer hunters who have a way of banging at any moving thing in the woods. It should be used often, washed often and rinsed, as above. After ironing hang it in the sun.
—James Austin Wilder, 1929

"The proper covering for head and feet is no slight affair."

WATERPROOF—WATER REPELLANT—BREATHABLE

I am no believer in waterproof garments. Once I owned a pantasote outer coat which I used to assume whenever it rained. Ordinarily when it is warm enough to rain, it is warm enough to cause you to perspire under the exertion of walking in a pantasote coat. This I discovered. Shortly I would get wet, and would be quite unable to decide whether the rain had soaked through from the outside or I had soaked through from the inside. After that I gave the coat away to a man who had not tried it, and was happy.
—*Camp and Trail*, 1920

You will see many advertisements of waterproof leather boots. No such thing is made. Some with good care will exclude water for a while, if you stay in it but a few minutes at a time, but sooner or later as the fibers become loosened the water will penetrate.
—*Camp and Trail*, 1920

The age-old quandary of how to stay dry from rain as well as perspiration can be answered in only one way—regulate body heat by regulating insulation and exercise. If it's raining, one should don his or her slicker and relax for a spell. Heavy travel in a waterproof coat can get a person as wet as no coat at all. Water-repellant gear is great so long as it protects the insulation layer long enough to acquire shelter. If anyone tries to sell gear that is both waterproof and breathable, he or she is a snake-oil vendor of the highest order. There is no such thing. Such fabrics have some utility in rainy weather, allowing water vapor from perspiration to escape at a rate that keeps wearers relatively dry. But in the winter, one can open the same coat and find it coated with a solid layer of ice.

Camping with a tent and stove allows any campers to carry gear that will keep them warm even when wet and will dry quickly in the peak of the tent. Natural fibers can be exposed to heat without worry of melting, are inexpensive compared to the modern wonder junk, and are adequately water repellant and breathable to be dependable under almost all conditions. People of the northern ice and bush still use natural fiber insulation even though they have access to space-age technology. We should take a lesson from them.

security. I generally cut ample holes for ventilation. In case of too many mosquitoes I stuff my handkerchief in the crown.
—*Camp and Trail*, 1910

POCKETS, POKES, & DITTIES

THE DITTY BAG

My great panacea for all emergencies is the ditty-bag. It is the first thing taken off and hung on a twig when a camp site is decided upon and the last thing put on when camp is broken. It has everything in it

COMPLETE OUTDOOR OUTFITTER   13

SLICKER GOODS

A BUCKSKIN MAN'S POCKET

When we speak of his pocket that includes all of his clothes, because on the inside of his coat, if he wears one, are stuck an array of safety pins, but usually the pins are fastened onto his shirt. A safety pin is as useful to a man in camp as is a hairpin to a woman, and a woman can camp with no other outfit but a box of hairpins. One can use safety pins for clothespins when one's socks are drying at night, one can use them to pin up the blankets and thus make a sleeping-bag of them, or one can use them for the purpose of temporarily mending rips and tears in one's clothes. These are only a few of the uses of the safety pin on the trail. After one has traveled with safety pins one comes to believe that they are almost indispensable.

In one of the pockets there should be a lot of bachelor buttons, the sort that you do not have to sew on to your clothes, but which fasten with a snap, something like glove buttons. There should be a pocket made in your shirt or vest to fit your notebook, and a part of it stitched up to hold a pencil and a toothbrush. Your mother can do this at home for you before you leave. Then you should have a good jack-knife; I always carry my jack-knife in my hip pocket. A pocket compass, one that you have tested before starting on your trip, should lodge comfortably in one of your pockets, and hitched in your belt should be your noggin carved from a burl from a tree; it should be carried by slipping the toggle underneath the belt. Also in the belt you should carry some whang strings; double the whang strings up so that the two ends come together, tuck the loop through your belt until it comes out at the other side, then put the two ends of the string through the loop and the whang strings are fast but easily pulled out when needed; whang strings are the same as belt lashings. A small whetstone can find a place somewhere about your clothes, probably in the other hip pocket, and it is most useful, not only with which to put an edge on your knife but also on your axe.

—Daniel Carter Beard, 1920

for repairs, accidents, emergencies of all kinds. Canoe leaking? In the ditty-bag is a small stick of canoe glue, a heavy needle, and strong thread. Moccasin stitch out? You'll find a leather needle with a thread of moccasin twine in the d - b. Suspender button off? In that repository of repairdom is another button, a needle, and shoe thread. Sick? There is a medicine-kit in the emollient of emergencies which will cure anything you have, from fever to delirium tremens. Hurt? Right this way, we have it right here, surgical bandages, tape, stitch needle, antiseptics—can give you a whole new rubber neck on demand. Gun needs cleaning? The whole works are in the ditty-bag. Hungry? There are a dozen square meals lurking inside the covers of that— grab it from me—justly famous ditty-bag. Tackle frayed or lost? There are bass and trout fly-hooks, a dozen leaders, spoons, plugs, sinkers, swivels, hooks, spinners, guides, tips, and safety-pins floating at large in the confines of that capacious receptacle. Lost in the woods or in a fog on a lake? In the—well, you know—you will find a compass that will help some. Grommet pulled out of tent or tarp? We have it, a spare one or two; also nails, tacks, copper wire, and four pothook chains. Lost your fish-line? Never mind, in this tucket of trinkets we have 50 yards of No. 5 casting-line and 30 yards of E trout-line. 'Possum up a hollow tree? We have the exact specific for him, for here comes the crowning glory of the ditty-bag—a steel 'possum hook made from a bent file, sharp as the devil, will hold a ton, good for any use to which a stout hook may be put, from gaffing a fish to lassoing a runaway canoe!

—Warren H. Miller, 1915

FOOTWEAR

Those who are not used to wearing soft shoes or moccasins are likely to be troubled by sore feet. For such, soled moccasins are advised. . . . The Chippewa moccasin . . . is by all means the most desirable article for snowshoeing. They are made of moose, caribou, or deer skin, Indian tanned (pattern on pages 28–29).
—*Camp and Trail Methods*, 1910

The day's work outside was done. My camp mocs for snow weather are "moose-hide"; that is, not buckskin which gets wet if you walk out in the snow, but heavy oiled leather.
—Warren H. Miller, 1918

When dressing the feet, I advise the use of the ordinary woolen socks, and plenty of them. Never wear cotton, especially during cold weather.
—E. Kreps, 1910

I have yet to see the country that is too rough for the high cowhide or moosehide moccasin "larrigans," as they are called in the north. But don't mistake me; this is purely an opinion based on personal experience. A bigger and heavier man would no doubt find the cruiser moccasin or the hunter's boot more serviceable in the same country. . . . Midway between the boot and moc comes the popular cruiser, or shoepack.
—Warren H. Miller, 1915

Get heavy woolen lumberman's socks, and wear them in and out of season. They are not one whit hotter on the feet than the thinnest you can buy, for the impervious leather of the shoe is really what keeps in the animal heat—the sock has little to do with it. You will find the soft thick wool an excellent cushion for a long tramp; and with proper care to avoid wrinkles, you will never become tender-footed nor chafed. . . . The ideal footwear should give security, be easy on the feet, wear well, and give absolute protection. These qualities I have named approximately in the order of their importance.
—*Camp and Trail*, 1920

Absolute protection must remain a tentative term. No footwear I have succeeded in discovering gives absolute protection.
—*Camp and Trail*, 1920

THE C.C. FILSON CO.

In 1897, entrepreneur Clinton C. Filson opened the Pioneer Alaska Clothing and Blanket Manufacturers to provide specialized outdoor gear to the hordes of prospectors heading for the Yukon during Alaska's Great Klondike Gold Rush. Stories of survival and hardship made their way back from the north, and Filson began to manufacture gear to match the terrible conditions that were encountered.

Owning his own mill, he was able to manufacture Mackinaw clothing, blankets and knitted goods. In addition he sold the finest boots, "moccasins and sleeping bags specially designed for the frigid North. Filson kept in close contact with his customers, improving his goods to meet their specific needs. The stampeders depended on Filson. In that era, clothing wasn't a matter of choice, but of survival."

In 1914 Filson began to patent designs that are still selling well today. Much of what he made was for the logging and fishing industries of the Northwest, but he had a growing market in the sporting world as well. Today, Filson maintains the reputation as the premier outfitter for outdoorsmen.

"The goods we quote must not be confounded with the cheap and vastly inferior grade with which the market is over-run. Such goods are not only useless for the purpose for which they are intended, but the person wearing them would be better off without them."

—C. C. Filson, 1914

Two hip-pockets—Handkerchief in right one, note-book and pencil in left. Query, why? (Work it out—you'll see.) Two side pockets. Left contains small Kit bag: flat, with threaded needle, flat bobbin of stout thread. Piece of string. Bit of wax. Matches in Gillette Razor ease, etc. Right hand pocket for rubbish: such as one dead crab, two horrible "all day suckers" and purse, containing, if you're lucky, a quarter in nickels. Two deep watch pockets—left, whetstone. Right, a watch. What underwear? Light wool "athletics," even in summer. "Damp cotton underwear keeps the boys' graveyard full. (In winter wear long trousers with your light woolen underwear, heavy over-coat and muffler.)

—James Austin Wilder, 1929

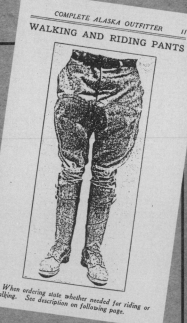

COMPLETE ALASKA OUTFITTER 11

WALKING AND RIDING PANTS

When ordering state whether needed for riding or walking. See description on following page.

One's personal outfit should be very complete, not in luxuries but in essentials. . . . There are quite a few minor essentials in wilderness equipment that do not loom up very large or very important in the beginner's eyes, but which have received quite as inexorable an evolution in the hands of the professional woodsman as the larger necessities, such as rifle, rod, tent, cook-kit, and sleeping-rig. I refer to those lesser, but equally needful, accessories, the axe, knife, compass, camp lamp, repair and cleaning outfits, sharpening-stone, match-safe and medicine-kit. Some of these things look superfluous to the inexperienced man—who is quite ready to borrow yours upon occasion—but there will surely come times when the wilderness will ask him personally for each and every one of these accessories, and there will be no old-timer around to lean upon and borrow from.
—Warren H. Miller, 1915

Ordinarily a cheap watch is good enough for the woods. . . . If you wear [eye glasses], carry a spare pair; the woods are hard on such items.
—Horace Kephart, 1917

Needle, thread, a waxed end, and a piece of buckskin for strings and patches completes the ordinary camp outfit. Your repair kit needs additions when applied to mountain trips.
—Camp and Trail, 1920

No camper, be he hunter, fisherman, scout, naturalist, explorer, prospector, soldier or lumberman, should go into the woods without a notebook and hard lead pencil. Remember that notes made with a hard pencil will last longer than those made with ink, and be readable as long as the paper lasts.
—Daniel Carter Beard, 1920

Every scientist and every surveyor knows this and it is only tenderfeet, who use a soft pencil and fountain pen for making field notes, because an upset canoe will blur all ink marks and the constant rubbing of the pages of the book will smudge all soft pencil marks.
—Daniel Carter Beard, 1920

Therefore, have a pocket especially made, so that your notebook, pencil and fountain pen, if you insist upon including it, will fit snugly with no chance of dropping out; also make a separate pocket for your toothbrush which should be kept in an oil-skin bag.
—Daniel Carter Beard, 1920

A piece of candle is not only a most convenient thing with which to light a fire on a rainy day, but it has ofttimes proved a life saver to Northern explorers benumbed with the cold.
—Daniel Carter Beard, 1920

Matches, knife, and a compass are the three indispensables. By way of ignition you will take a decided step backward from present-day civilization in that you will pin your faith to the old sulphur "eight-day" matches of your fathers. This for several reasons. In the first place they come in blocks, unseparated, which are easily carried without danger of rubbing one against the other. In the second place, they take up about a third the room the same number of wooden-matches would require. In the third place, they are easier to light in a wind, for they do not flash up and out, but persist. And finally, if wet, they can be spread out and dried in the sun, which is the most important of all. So buy you a nickel's worth of sulphur matches.
—Camp and Trail, 1920

The waterproof pocket safe is numerous on the market. A ten-gauge brass shell will just chamber a twelve-gauge. Put your matches in the twelve-gauge, and telescope the ten over it. Abercrombie & Fitch, of New York, make a screw top safe of rubber, which has the great advantage of floating if dropped, but it is too bulky and the edges are too sharp. The Marble safe, made by the Marble Axe Company, is ingenious and certainly waterproof; but if it gets bent in the slightest degree, it jams, and you can no longer screw it shut. Therefore I consider it useless for this reason.
—Camp and Trail, 1920

It is a comparatively easy thing to light a candle under the shelter of one's hat or coat, even in a driving rain. When one's fingers are numb or even frosted, and with the candle flame one can start a life-saving fire; so do not forget your candle stub as a part of your pocket outfit.
—Daniel Carter Beard, 1920

TAKING THE FAMILY AFIELD

I have once or twice alluded to ladies walking and camping. It is thoroughly practical for them to do so. They must have a wagon and do none of the heavy work; their gowns must not reach quite to the ground, and all of their clothing must be free and easy. Of course, there must be gentlemen in the party; and it may save annoyance to have at least one of the ladies well-nigh "middle-aged."
—**John Gould, 1877**

[A] few trips by trail and canoe will take the raw edge off all that; the angel becomes more tolerant and broad-minded, and you will find her the best camp-mate you ever took along.
—**Warren H. Miller, 1915**

As to the kind of trip to take, I believe a good down-stream canoe trip appeals more to the out-door girl than anything else. She will do thirty or forty miles of river a day and will enter every bit of rough water with squeals of delight. Do not rush her along too fast; stop to fish or hunt or loaf when you hit a particularly pretty camp site. Choose a really wild river—one with no farms along its banks.
—**Warren H. Miller, 1915**

GROUP GEAR

[T]hey should remember that we woodsman are all cranks and that their modes might seem as absurd to me as mine are to them.
—E. Kreps, *Camp and Trail Methods*, 1910

CHOOSING TRADITION

Those who choose to camp traditionally will encounter weight. If added weight is a concern, the best solution is to reduce gear. If doing that will force one to depend on what's at hand and live off the land, that choice has to be in balance with what the land can provide and what it will tolerate. The style and objectives of one's camp are also factors. If comfort and relaxation are the goal, all gear should be prepared in advance. If long-distance travel and roughing it are the objectives, reliance on natural resources may come into play. When this is the case, skill and knowledge may be substituted for gear—minimizing impact both at home and on the trail. Traditional camping should take its lumps for not policing out-of-control tyros in past eras. But with appropriate, responsible use, it is a solid alternative camping style and always has been.

The designs of traditional gear are far from old-fashioned. In fact, they are the models for all of our modern gear. Early gear catalogs and expedition photographs show four-man dome tents made from balloon silk, weighing less than ten pounds, in use as early as the mid-1800s. Wool clothing is still the best value and most dependable fabric available on the market, with available designs that date back to the turn of the century.

There has always been a tendency for writers of the day to lean toward modern developments. That's how they make a living. New developments are news, so they serve the manufacturer by selling the benefits of a new item of gear or improvements and accessories that "every woodland traveler needs." Choose your gear carefully and thoughtfully from a base of mentored experience.

I realize that I seem to be recommending this firm rather extensively, but it cannot be helped. It is not because I know no others, for naturally I have been purchasing sporting goods and supplies in a great many places and for a good many years. Nor do I recommend everything they make. Only along some lines they have carried practical ideas to their logical conclusion. The Abercrombie & Fitch balloon silk tents, food bags, pack harness, aluminum alloys, and reflector ovens completely fill the bill. And as they cannot be procured elsewhere, I must perhaps seem unduly to advertise this one firm.
—*Camp and Trail*, 1920

APPRENTICE CAMPER

- Share in selecting, packing, and carrying group gear for a one-day or an overnight trip.
- Make a list of all group items, including cost and weight of each item.
- Make an item of group gear.

JOURNEYMAN CAMPER

- Demonstrate ability to:
  - Share in the making or refurbishing of an item of group gear.
  - Select a pack for the type of trip to be taken.
  - Pack gear for a variety of forms of transport.

JOURNEYMAN WOODSMAN

- Select group gear needed for a particular style of travel.
- Demonstrate ability to make an improvised pack and / or travel gear.
- Make a group gear checklist for a specific season's expedition.
- Demonstrate ability to maintain and make home and field repairs to all selected group gear.

MASTER WOODSMAN

- Demonstrate ability to maintain group gear for extended periods of wet and snowy conditions.
- Design and produce with quality an item of specialized gear for four-season living.
- Demonstrate ability to improvise and / or make field replacements for all items taken into the field, using natural materials.

The beauty of camping, to me, is its never-the-sameness—never are two camps exactly alike, never are two locations in every way the same, and never are conditions similar.

For the mountain camp certain equipment would prove excellent, while for a trip to the burning summer sands of the Atlantic seaboard, considerable alterations in the duffel would have to be made. This for the simple reason that conditions are entirely different—it all depends where one intends to go and what one intends to do when arrived.
—F. Westevelt, 1933

PLANNING

I have found that nearly all who have a real love of nature and out-of-door camp-life, spend a good deal of time and talk in planning future trips, or discussing the trips and pleasures gone by, but still dear to memory.
—Nessmuk, 1920

Details of seat 5ft long

THE GROUP GEAR ULTIMATE WISH LIST

❑ BED

A warm, comfortable bed is an absolute essential. Animals can curl up in the lee of a great log, or under the protecting arm of an overhanging cliff, but not so the ordinary camper. Your bed is of more importance than your shelter, and should be cared for in advance, insofar as is possible. Seasoned campers that are used to the go-light trips become expert at making a one-night bed, with the aid of dry leaves, small brush and the like, along with their blanket, light sleeping bag, sweater, or combination of them all. Such beds are largely a matter of ingenuity and resourcefulness, and vary in details for every season as well as section.

If the camp is to be reasonably permanent, some permanent form of bed should be planned. The folding army cot is widely used and can be supplied by any outfitter. However, these are expensive and, unless great care is taken with them, do not last long. For certain sections at least, they are cold, and campers prefer to be on the ground.

—Frank H. Cheley, 1933

❑ STOVE

The main kitchen stove, if it is for a permanent camp, will likely be some type of a regular camp range, which can be secured in any desirable size; but in addition to this, there should be included in your equipment, regardless of the type of camp, at least some simple stove or camp grid for all-day trips or little journeys away from camp; for short cruises or for special outdoor suppers in connection with corn roasts and the like. These can be made, or purchased, just as you prefer. Some campers think there is nothing so good for the purpose as a piece of sheet steel that can be quickly adjusted to two logs or flat stones, and a fire built underneath it. An amazing number of fish or flap-jacks can be fried on such a stove in a little while. However, it is not suitable for all occasions because of its weight. Inexpensive camp grids can be secured from an outfitter, or easily made. If you have individual cooking kits, these grids are light and serviceable, and a great aid to cooking, especially if you do not wish to stop to build a standard cooking fire with dressed logs.

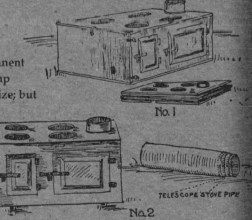

THE GROUP GEAR ULTIMATE WISH LIST

(Continued)

—Frank H. Cheley, 1933

❑ DUTCH OVEN

[T]he common Dutch oven . . . is simple to operate, and can be secured in various sizes and weights. Experienced campers with plenty of time on their hands and the inclination to get on with the absolute minimum of equipment, can often make a temporary Dutch oven by turning two kitchen pans together, taking care to have plenty of hot coals, and a simple shovel made of a tin container and a green stick, so that the coals may be replenished or removed at will. Most delicious camp dishes may be cooked in this manner.

—Frank H. Cheley, 1933

❑ BUCKETS

On a pack trip a pail is a necessity which is not recognized in the forest, where you can dip your cup or kettle direct into the stream. Most packers carry a galvanized affair, which they turn upside down on top of the pack. There it rattles and bangs against every overhead obstruction on the trail, and ends by being battered to leakiness. A bucket made of heavy brown duck, with a wire loop hemmed in by way of rim, and a light rope for handle carries just as much water, holds it as well, and has the great advantage of collapsing flat.

—*Camp And Trail*, 1920

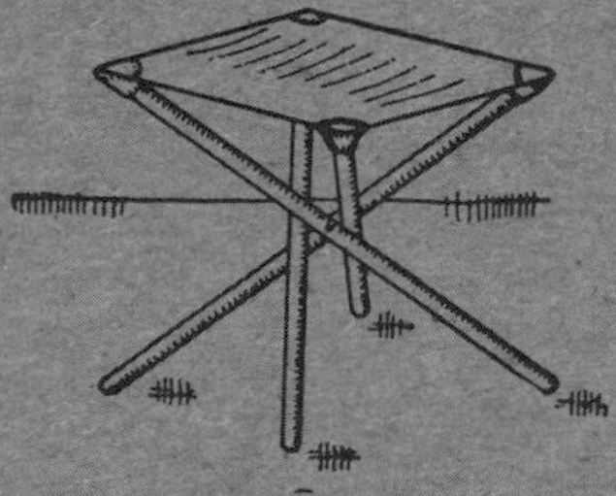

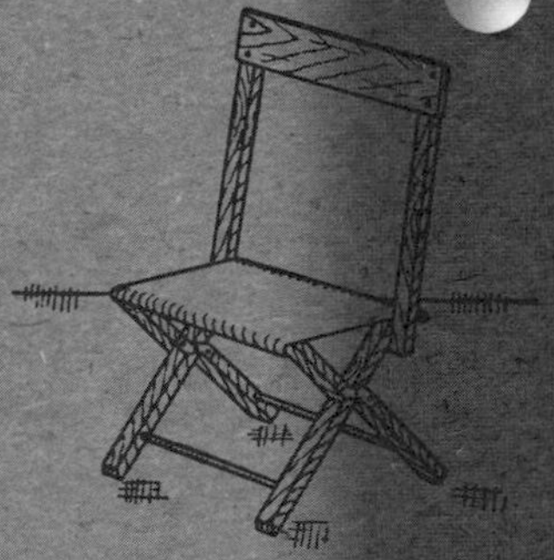

❑ CHAIRS

Have you even been in camp where there wasn't a blessed place to sit down. except a near-by old stump, or perhaps a log that nature was busy rotting away into plant food? Every grocery box has been turned into a part of the kitchen cabinet, the camp chests are doing duty in the mess tent, and—well, there simply isn't anything to sit on, unless you thought of that very contingency before you started, and included in your outfit a couple of durable, comfortable, folding camp chairs. Fortunately, such chairs are simple to make and cost little. . . . If you do not care to construct them yourselves, they may be purchased from camp outfitters at reasonable cost. Some boys prefer to make up the canvas parts at home and rig up the wooden parts in camp from crotches and poles.

—Frank H. Cheley, 1933

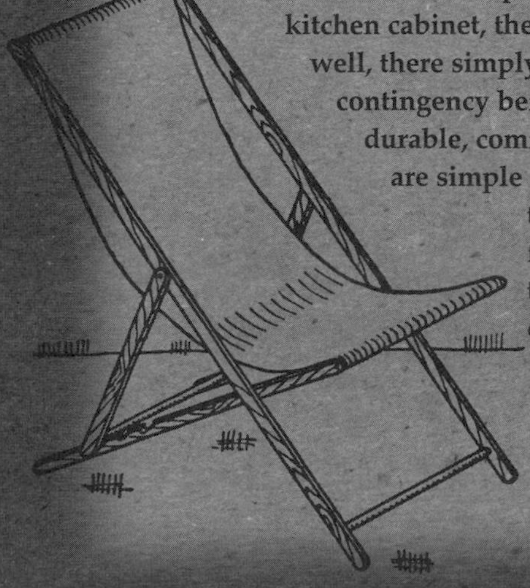

THE GROUP GEAR ULTIMATE WISH LIST

(Continued)

❑ TABLES

Unless your camp is a pack trip or a go-light hiking trip, you must plan some sort of a table. If your party is small, probably a table will be rigged from the tops of the camp chests, or from boards taken from packing cases. If your equipment is moved in a wagon, it may be worth your while to construct a light, durable, folding table, but for most purposes, it is most convenient, as well as economical, to build your table after you get into camp, either from common sheathing taken along for the purpose, or purchased at a near-by farm or sawmill.

—Frank H. Cheley, 1933

❑ CAMP BOXES

But what of the nomadic camps, such as on a down-stream canoe trip where no stop is made long enough to warrant any extensive construction? For this the outfitters have gotten up a wooden suitcase, made of the hardest and toughest veneers, light and strong and rendered water-proof by a rubber gasket running around the joint between the faces. Such a suitcase will be 5 inches deep by 30 by 16 in area and holds all the smaller provisions or sometimes a complete aluminum cook-kit of pots of the right height to fit inside it. When making camp, four stakes are cut and driven in the ground, the suitcase opened out flat, and at once you have a table 30 x 32 inches useful as a cooking table and bread-board while preparing the evening meal and later for setting the aluminum table-service upon.

—Warren H. Miller, 1915

❑ SHELVES

There is need in every permanent camp of a few simple sets of shelves for shaving purposes, for toilet articles, for books and magazines, etc. A small grocery box fastened to a tree will serve all purposes, or a set of folding shelves can be made of light wood and shipped in one of the camp chests. Smaller camp chests can easily be made, shipping them to camp full of equipment and supplies, and then converting them into a tree cabinet.

—Frank H. Cheley, 1933

LIGHTING CAMP
WITH A GLOW, NOT A GLARE

An interesting fact to consider is that a battery requires fifty times more energy to produce than it will ever return to the user. Once they are produced and used, they're off to the landfill, and more resources are mined to make more. It seems like a well-built fire would be the simplest and least damaging way to light the camp at night.

Along after dark in camp, another bodily infirmity makes its presence known, the inability to see things in the dark (and especially to find a lost belt-axe or salt-shaker). No man in the party should be without his own light-producing apparatus; carbide lamp, candle lantern, or electric flasher. The camp-fire and one or two carbides will just about supply enough working light for the cooks and firemen; meanwhile you have your share of the work to do, to get water or go skirmishing for dead trees in the dark and should have your own lantern. Personally I am never without both a flasher and a small carbide, the latter usually loaned for general illumination as soon as it can be filled and lit.
—Warren H. Miller, 1915

[C]andle lantern, [is] very popular for individual and tent lighting. It collapses flat in your pack and takes very little space and weight—9 ounces—and it has the advantage of being always ready to light and can be put out in a second, which the carbide cannot, so that one is loath to light the latter merely for some private errand of short duration, but rather it is held until after nightfall, when it is lit for its run of three hours and is then at the service of the whole party except when you need to borrow it for private purposes. Neither it nor the candle lantern can be blown out by any ordinary breeze, so that they are reliable and serviceable in rain, snow storm, or almost any weather conditions that obtain in the wilderness.
—Warren H. Miller, 1915

Every tent should have a light of some sort. A home-made lantern may be made of a tin can, and a candle that will often serve the purpose, but if used, great care should be taken against fire.
—Frank H. Cheley, 1933

Candles, lamps, and lanterns add to the luggage of a camper, and may be dispensed with, yet it often happens that you will need a light at night. If you do, remember that most any sort of fat or grease will burn. I have made a passable lamp of an old clam-shell filled with melted rancid butter and a twisted rag for a wick resting in the butter, and I have seen most dainty little candles molded in willow bark of tallow from the deer, with a wick of the inside bark of a cedar-tree. But such things are only made by guides for ladies, or as souvenirs to take home. A torch will answer all needs of camp life.
—Daniel Carter Beard, 1900

GEAR ON A SHOESTRING

[I]t is inconceivable that some folks might call it extravagant to pay thirty-five dollars for a thing to sleep in when you lie out of doors on the ground from choice, or thirty dollars for pots and pans to cook with when you are "playing hobo," as the unregenerate call our sylvan sport. . . .The best way is to make many of the things yourself. This gives your pastime an air of thrift, and propitiates the Lares and Penates by keeping you home at nights.
—**Horace Kephardt, 1917**

One of the hall-marks of the veteran woodsman is the way he contrives to make himself comfortable in camp, mainly by utilization of the forest materials ready to hand. He has gotten past the stage of unnecessary roughing it, knowing well that the hardships of the hunting trail will be quite enough without imposing any additional burdens in camp. . . .These who so suffer simply do not know the game, are inadequately supplied with either equipment or knowledge, or both, and richly deserve all the misfortunes that befall them or are heaped upon them. . . .
—**Warren H. Miller, 1915**

Elaborate camp equipments are all right to look at and dream about—and even use by parlor-car campers—but for the average young person they are out of the question, and he must learn from the beginning how to keep his outfit down to the minimum of bulk, and weight, and expense, and even how to get along very satisfactorily with only a small part of what he thinks he needs, if it becomes necessary. . . .

Even a party of a dozen boys can camp out with complete satisfaction with very simple equipment . . . leaving out quite completely "millionaire kits"; for the boy, or man either, who can camp that way, will not have to be bothered even with thinking of outfits and equipments: someone paid for the purpose will look after that for him, along with many of the other primary joys involved.
—**Frank H. Cheley, 1933**

Renting gear until you know your needs is a good option.

BEDS AND BEDDING

Bliss! Never have I slept more comfortably. This deponent is no man to endure discomfort if it can be remedied. . . .
—Warren H. Miller, 1918

"It is not he who praises Nature, but he who lies continually on her breast and is satisfied who is actually united to her."
—Olive Shriener, 1916

Proper bedding material is of the greatest importance, especially if you are to camp some time. Perhaps you will choose to live in woodsy shelters of some sort, instead of tents.
—Frank H. Cheley, 1933

The quality of bedding is determined by its ability to trap and hold warm air next to the user. However, a good sleeping system can be rendered ineffective if the tyro doesn't take into consideration all the ways that heat can be lost.

Heat is produced through eating, exercising, or shivering. External heat sources provide added warmth, reducing the amount of heat needing to be produced internally. Heat is lost through conduction, radiation, convection, respiration, and evaporation. The second law of thermodynamics states that heat is attracted to cold. Lying in contact with the ground will cause sleepers to lose heat uncontrollably through conduction. In fact, three times the amount of heat is lost to the ground as to the air. This means that three times more insulation is needed under sleepers than over them. Materials that reduce the conduction of heat and moisture may increase insulation efficiency. A good ground bed or pad can't be discounted.

Suspending bedding on a cot, hammock, or stretcher allows air to move freely around the body, convecting warm air away from the bed. Beds that suspend the body are notoriously cold, requiring almost as much insulation as one would use on the ground.

Bedding should also account for the fact that 40 percent of all heat loss from the body is radiated from the head and neck. The old adage, "If your feet get cold, put on a hat" is useful, telling us that the body will sacrifice extremities if heat is lost too easily in other areas. If feet and fingers get cold, too much heat is being lost from other sources. At night, this is usually from the head and neck. Wear a toque or keep bedding drawn up tight to reduce the escape of warm air.

Sleeping socks and/or slippers require the camper to remove socks worn during the day. Even if they feel dry, the amount of imperceptible moisture evaporating from them is enough to make toes frigid in the middle of the night. Have one pair of socks that are dedicated for night use only.

Breathing from the mouth at night liberates about a quart of water per person. If one's head is inside the bedding all night long, that moisture ends up in the insulation. Steffansen's research showed that clothing worn in winter without being dried, will last about four days before the moisture buildup is so bad they become worthless. The same goes for bedding. One should avoid adding unnecessary moisture to bedding by playing "turtle" at night. Wearing a hat allows for keeping one's face out of the blankets.

TRAINING SKILLS FOR BEDS AND BEDDING

APPRENTICE CAMPER
- Select the best sleeping gear for a one-day or an overnight trip.
- Demonstrate care and use of sleeping gear.
- Demonstrate knowledge of how to produce, conserve, and / or relieve heat.
- Discuss the importance of ground insulation systems.

JOURNEYMAN CAMPER
- Demonstrate ability to:
  - Identify characteristics of a warm sleeping system.
  - Improvise improvements for inadequate bedding.
- Discuss the importance of a restful sleep.

JOURNEYMAN WOODSMAN
- Demonstrate use and care of bedding while traveling.
- Demonstrate ability to:
  - Make a bivy bed in snowy conditions.
  - Maintain and make repairs on bedding.
  - Manage bedding during heavy rains.

MASTER WOODSMAN
- Demonstrate ability to:
  - Use natural materials for ground beds.
  - Build long- and short-term beds from natural materials.

[T]he veteran will roll out his sleeping-rig and see to it that it is comfortable before retiring . . . see that the bed site is level ground, particularly in the side-to-side direction, for sleeping sideways on a slope is one of the impossibilities of the outdoors. If using a very thin mattress, such as a skin or quilt, see that suitable hollows for hips and shoulders are scooped in the duff and filled with dry leaves, your aim being to distribute the area of your body as evenly as possible, so that all of it may be supported and not have the whole weight concentrated on hips and shoulders. And arrange some sort of windbreak, made of any available cloth or duffel bag, so that the prevailing wind will not sweep over you at night.
—Warren H. Miller, 1915

THE BOUGH BED

No camper is justified in "slaying" a young forest, merely to find a comfortable place to sleep. . . .

Unless you plan to bring beds of some description into camp, it will be very necessary for you to locate where there is an abundance of wild wood materials with which to make beds. If you are going to build browse beds, there should be large numbers of reasonably young trees handy. Only the lower limbs of these should be cut, and always with a sharp ax, and with the greatest care.
—Frank H. Cheley, 1933

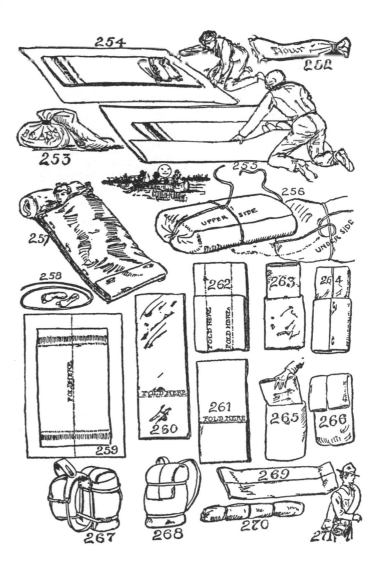

The experienced camper knows if and when a browse bed should be used. The tyro has no business applying this skill without supervision. The amount of damage that can be caused is significant enough to make bough beds a highly discouraged practice for general camp use. However, there are places on this planet where use is so sparse and resources so abundant that the browse bed is still commonly practiced without negative impact to the resource. In fact, some places have evergreens growing so densely that the use of boughs creates a thinning effect and is a positive thing to do. The woodsman's skills are stewarding his woodlands into a healthier state

On the other hand, the use of the browse bag has almost unlimited use with minimal impact. Ground litter such as leaves can be gathered in minutes, creating a soft warm bed, and then scattered in the morning, returning the woodland camp to its pristine status.

If neither practice is permissible or practical, a wide variety of good ground pads can be purchased at reasonable prices from an outfitter.

[A]n energetic clearing out of stubs, roots, rocks, and other offenders is in order, and then we go skirmishing for browse with the browse-bag.

Shades of Nessmuk and his beloved balsam! Balsam, pine, or any fresh green browse is too cold and too slow for me, a few inches of plebeian dead leaves or dry pine-needles are warmer and better.
—Warren H. Miller, 1915

If you are camping where there is an abundance of pine, spruce, fir, or balsam, probably the well-made browse bed is the thing you want. Do not be misled, however, into believing that a browse bed is merely a pile of green boughs upon which you sleep. One night on such a contrivance will convince you to the contrary. A real browse bed must be built with the utmost care and along certain lines. First, carefully clear the ground of all litter, sticks, stones and the like, and stake out a frame with four to six inch logs the size of the desired bed (3 by 6 feet for one person, 5 by 6 for two). Then with a shovel or sharp stick, dig a slight "hip hole" in the proper place. You are then ready to thatch your bed. Cut only the lower limbs of the trees, taking care not to damage them nor to cut any of them down. Lay smoothly one layer of the larger fans, convex side up, butts toward the foot, taking care to fill in clear to the edges all the way round. Now with smaller and more select boughs, thatch-in full and thick (breaking off all unnecessary stems) by thrusting the butt-ends underneath the layer already placed, in such a manner as to leave the fans-ends curved up and down toward the foot of the bed. Make it good and thick; and when completed, spread your poncho or tarpaulin over it, then your blankets, and you have a real bed. Boughs for beds should never be cut while wet, unless absolutely necessary, as they will hold the dampness and make a cold, uncomfortable bed.
—Frank H. Cheley, 1933

THE BROWSE BAG

A bag filled with dry leaves, dry grass, hay or straw will make a very comfortable mattress; but we are not always in the hay and straw belt and dry leaves are sometimes difficult to secure; a scout, however, must learn to make a bed wherever he happens to be.
—Daniel Carter Beard, 1920

The Browse Bag is a warm combination because the upper face of the browse-bag is of brown flannel with about 1/4 inch of Australian wool batting behind it. It is 30 inches by 72 inches, with 8-ounce duck, bottom face, and unbleached muslin upper face. It has a row of grommets 3 inches apart along each side and the foot, and a short thong of No. 36 tarpon line for lacing. It rolls up into a package 20 inches long by 3 inches diameter and weighs 2 pounds, with a 30-by-60-inch facing of army blanket sewed inside the bag. It goes into the pack on top of the tent, and there is room alongside it for a rubber floor-cloth, 2 feet by 4 feet 6 inches, a pair of socks, and camp mocks.
—Warren H. Miller, 1915

STICK BEDS

The use of a stick bed or woven mat can be done with surprisingly good results. The thin layer of material breaks contact with the ground just enough to overcome the effects of conduction. Mats made from woven bulrushes, cattail leaves, or grass can be made and carried on the trail, requiring the harvesting of materials only once. Simple willow-stick beds are no longer manufactured but can be made from simple materials and will last for a long time if cared for and properly maintained.

Every dealer in camp outfits can produce an array of different camp beds, cots, and sleeping bags, that shows how important it is to be dry and warm when you sleep.

The simplest plan is the oldest one—two pair of blankets and waterproof under sheet on a neatly laid bed of evergreen boughs, dry leaves or dry grass.

But there are few places now in eastern America where you are allowed to cut boughs freely. In any case you cannot take the bough bed with you when you move, and it takes too much time to make at each camp.

Sleeping bags I gave up long ago. They are too difficult to air, or to adjust to different temperatures.

Rubber beds are luxurious, but heavy for a pack outfit, and in cold weather they need thick blankets over them, otherwise they are too cool.

So the one ideal bed for the camper, light, comfortable, and of wildwood stuff, is the Indian or willow bed.
—**Ernest Thompson Seton**, *Book of Woodcraft*

The second proposal in getting away from browse is to adopt or modify the Indian stick bed. If you consider our woven-wire spring-bed you will have the principle of the stick bed, something flat and springy, upon which a mattress is to be laid, and on this your sleeping-bag or blankets. Out in Montana you can buy an Indian stick bed for eight dollars, with all its poles and trappings, highly decorated, made by the Blackfeet Indians. As they travel by pony and pack their goods on traverse poles, they have studied neither lightness nor compactness, for their beds are overwide and are truncate in shape, not rectangular. They are universally made of sticks of kinnikinnic, the sand-bar willow of the west, the sticks being some 3/8 inch in diameter and strung on cords just as close as they will go, I should say about 150 sticks for a 6-foot bed. To set up, just cut two short 6-foot poles of lodge-pole pine or white cedar and roll out the bed on them. Many a bivouac has been made on the prairie by scooping two hollows in the bunchgrass for hips and shoulders and rolling out the bed over these hollows. A deerskin or two forms the usual mattress. Mr. Ernest Thompson Seton, of the Camp Fire Club,

THE STRETCHER BED

If stretcher beds are to be built, then you will need ample supply of poles. If grass or brush are to be resorted then plan accordingly.
—Frank H. Cheley, 1933

The [stretcher bed] is sold in tan canvas, 6 feet by 3 feet, with pockets along each side to receive the stretcher poles; weight 3 pounds. Stretched taut and provided with any kind of a quilt mattress, it is comfortable, and I have slept night after night for weeks at a time in the canvas sailor's hammock, virtually the same thing as a stretcher bed, without ever wearying of it. In both hammock and bed, if hung like a bag, it will be impossible to stretch out arms and legs comfortably. The side poles should be amply strong so as not to spring in, and their ends are staked in place over two short cross-logs which form the foundation skids of the bed. Head and foot are secured by lashing the ends of the canvas to suitable cross-sticks on top of the side poles.
—Warren H. Miller, 1915

Warren Miller (center) and chums breaking camp. The chap on the right is rolling a commercial stick bed.

Bedrolls packed with tumps and broad bands.

BEDDING

To the one who has never done any camping, the question of bed and blankets is one that will set him to wondering and he will have doubts as to whether he will be comfortable with the outfits recommended by those who have been there.
—*Camp and Trail Methods,* 1910

To be really rested and get any benefit out of a vacation a man must get a good night's sleep every night. The first requisite for this is to have plenty of cover. It is twice as cold as you expect it will be in the bush four nights out of five, and a good plan is to take just double the bedding that you think you will need. An old quilt that you can wrap up in is as warm as two blankets.
—Ernest Hemingway, 1920

Quilts—ugh! . . . Cotton comforters are wholly unsuitable for outdoor use.
—Horace Kephart, 1917

The Hudson's Bay, the Mackinaw and the U.S. Army blankets are among the best. A wide single blanket is best, as one can lay on one half and use the other half as cover. Double bed blankets are not good. I have used a square horse blanket and found it very nice for camping.
—E. Kreps, 1910

has modified this bed for white man's use by making all the sticks uniformly 24 inches long, spacing them an inch apart, increasing the diameter to about 1/4 inch, and threading them through the strands of twisted hemp rope, tying fast with fine cord. He has retained the cloth binding of the edges of the bed universally used by the Indians, and, so fashioned, his bed rolls up into a package 8 inches in diameter by 24 inches long, and rolls out to make a 6-foot bed, weighing about 6 pounds. This bed, as stated above, requires a light mattress to make it comfortable and to take off the harshness of the sticks. A wool quilt or a thick deerskin or other fur will answer very well, and the combination makes a flat comfortable bed, fitting the contours of the body at all points and very pleasant to sleep on.
—Warren H. Miller, 1915

THE SLEEPING BAG

The camp bed that is generally unloaded on the unsuspecting tenderfoot is some form of sleeping bag. There may be good sleeping bags and it is possible that I am unduly prejudiced against this form of camp bed, for I have given only two styles a real tryout, but I can say emphatically that the kinds I used were no good.
—*Woodcraft,* 1910

BEDROLLS

Bedrolls and blanket packs have been used exclusively by the students and staff of Boulder Outdoor Survival School for the past thirty years. They are efficient for the warmer months and can be adapted for cold climates by simply adding a mat or another blanket. A heavy blanket is a trail companion that should never be left behind. They take some getting used to, and sleeping in one without drafts or cold spots is an art form.

Blankets require minimal technological interference and can be worked into a very serviceable pack that can carry gear and food comfortably. The Jet Pack, as it's called, is a thin profile pack that allows the user to hike, climb, or run unimpeded.

A variety of blanket-pack designs exist. The "jolly swagman" from the Australian tune "Waltzing Matilda" has been using one for years. Along with his billy can (tin-can cook pot), he was modeled from the Sundowners who still travel the outback with very little gear to hinder them.

A

B

C

E

D

Early sleeping bags were little more than canvas covers lined with blanket material. Some designs were fixed with grommets so the side could be laced up as a bag or as a packsack. Others had clasps (snaps) to hold them together so that they could be easily opened to air them out. These designs were lined with wool or double insulated with an eider or goose-down comforter and were called sleeping robes. The liners were removable for laundering and airing. Some outfitters custom-made bags for blankets that were sent in by clients.

Many of the early camping books spent entire chapters describing just what a sleeping bag was and how it could be made. Warren Miller's books were full of inventions that the author touted as state of the art. Weights ranged from four to twelve pounds. Bedding down under the weight of hides and woolen blankets generates a peace and comfort no down product ever offered.

Separate layers . . . no sleeping bag is worthy of serious notice unless its blankets or other lining can be removed quickly and spread out on a line to dry. A lining sewed inside a waterproof cover is an abomination.
—Horace Kephart, 1916

PACKS

One of the most indispensable articles for the outer is a rig of some kind for carrying or packing the outfit from place to place, and of the various articles for this use the most common and most satisfactory are the pack strap or "tump line," the pack sack and the pack basket. These three articles are intended for different kinds of work, and each is good for the work which it was designed, and practically worthless for any other.
—E. Kreps, 1910

The word "pack" itself is a joy to the outdoor man, for it is only outdoor men who use the word pack for carry and who call a bundle or load a pack. The reason for this is that the real wilderness man, explorer, prospector, hunter, trapper or scout, packs all his duffel into a bundle which he carries on his back, in two small saddle-bags which are carried by his husky dogs, or a number of well-balanced bundles which are lashed on the pack saddle with a diamond hitch over the back of a pack horse.
—Daniel Carter Beard, 1920

WEIGHT CONSIDERATIONS

For a long hike thirty pounds is enough for a big boy to carry, and it will weigh three hundred and fifty pounds at the end of a hard day's tramp. Heavy packs, big packs, like those shown in Fig. 223, are only used on a portage, that is, for short distance.

Remember that the weight of a load depends a great deal upon your mind. Consequently for a long distance the load should be light; for a short distance the only limit to the load is the limit of the packer's strength.
—Daniel Carter Beard, 1920

With a crowd on a canoe trip, at least half of them will be loaded up with a quantity of stuff that they are personally sure they cannot do without. Usually these are the wealthy members of the party, who have always hired guides to do their hard work, and their load is usually double that carried by the seasoned canoeists. What's to be done? . . . Load up the wealthy with their own plunder, put a tump line across each one's forehead, and take the residue of their stuff yourself, in addition to your own outfit. It's the only way to make progress!
—Warren H. Miller, 1918

KINDS OF PACKS—OVERVIEW

TUMPLINES

The straps are . . . cut about one inch wide
at the ends, which are fixed to the head band
and taper to about one-half inch at the free ends.
The entire length of the strap will be from
eighteen to twenty-two feet. The best kind have
the straps buckle to the head band. . . . When
properly adjusted, the part of the strap which
passes over the head should be of such a length
that it will not have a tendency to draw the head
back, and the pack should rest well up on the
back of the carrier. . . . To the uninitiated for the
first few days, this kind of work will be exceedingly tiring, the strain on the head and neck
being very severe, but it is surprising how soon
one will become accustomed to it.

It is a fact that a heavier pack can be carried with a head strap than with shoulder
straps, many of the northern Indians being able
to handle several hundred pounds on a short
portage, but when the nature of the goods is such that it may be arranged into suitable
packs, the majority of woodsmen prefer to make it up into lots of about seventy
pounds and on the short portages will take two packs, one on top of the other.
—E. Kreps, 1910

PACKSACK

[When] making long trips and carrying a light outfit, I recommend the use of the
pack sack. As the name implies, it is a sack or bag, made of duck, and fitted with both
shoulder and head straps. . . . When choosing a pack sack, beware of the kind having
gussets in the sides and bottom. This kind is sure to carry badly as one cannot make a

flat pack of such an arrangement and if the pack
projects too far from the back of the carrier, it has
a tendency to pull back hard on the head and
shoulders.
—E. Kreps, 1910

PACK BASKET

They are made in various sizes and grades,
the better quality being covered with cotton duck.
All that can be said in favor of the basket is that it
offers a great protection to the goods than does the
sack, but as an offset to this good quality it is
heavy and cumbersome . . . and brings the weight
of the goods too far from the back of the packer.
. . . it is nice for carrying frail articles.
—E. Kreps, 1910

BLANKET ROLL AND PACK

1 Spread out one of your blankets like this.

TOILET ARTICLES, VALUABLES AND POSSESSIONS WHICH MIGHT BREAK.

2 Roll up the blanket so the toilet articles etc. will be well padded and rolled into the center of the blanket roll.

3 With your other blanket or blankets wrap your grub, cooking tools, and any other articles into a package-like bundle. With leather thongs or light rope bind it like this.

4 Attach thong here.

6 Attach a pair of shoulder straps to the top of the pack.

5 Attach another thong here.

7 Bend your blanket roll over the top of your pack and secure it with the side thongs.

Correct position.

8 Bring straps over shoulders, cross them on your chest, then pass around your back, bring to front and tie at your waist.

On police, military, and western saddles just behind the cantle (or hind bow of saddle) are leather thongs or metal rings for tying on blanket roll.

9 When a pack is not needed a blanket roll is tied and carried like this.

10

J. Meagher

Straight Arrow was created by Nabisco as a premium that taught children about camping and woodcraft.

TUMP LINES

Like the birch-bark canoe, portages and packs have been with the native Red American since long before the white man came. Curiously, the original Iroquois pack, with its wooden frame, is the type which represents the survival of the fittest, for the latest pack of the present moment is of this type, after years of trial with pack baskets, harness, packsacks, and rucksacks, all of them white man's inventions. The Indian had just two carrying devices, the tump strap and its thongs, and the carrying frame. These two seem to have been universally distributed all over the country. . . . Two main natural principles of big weight portable by the strong neck muscles, and a frame holding the load off the small of the back and transferring its thrust to the brisket muscles, are the guiding motives in the design.
—**Warren H. Miller, 1918**

Tumplines allowed experienced woodsmen to carry in excess of 200 pounds.

WHY THE TUMP WORKS

For, while a load with shoulder harness is very limited—say, 60 pounds as a maximum—the amount that can be carried with the tump line and frame runs up into the hundreds of pounds. The reason why the shoulder harness has such a low limit is not the fatigue nor the disposition of the load on the shoulder blades, but the mere fact that constriction of the big arteries of the arms is produced by the pressure of the straps passing up from under the armpits over the breast muscles. Anyone who has carried a packsack much will recall that the first warning that the pack is too heavy is a numb and prickly feeling extending over the entire arm. If not relieved, the arm steadily gets worse and you have the same sensations of "foot asleep" as when that member is unduly sat upon. At what weight this takes place depends on the pack, the tightness and width of the straps, and the weight carried, but a limit of about 60 pounds is the general maximum.
—**Warren H. Miller, 1918**

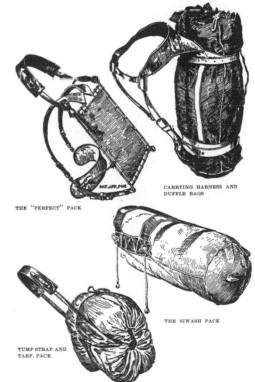

[Note:] There is no gainsaying the fact that, to the man unaccustomed to the tump line, the strain on the neck muscles which have never carried any such weight is very annoying and painful for a few days. Also, as one instinctively grasps the strap thongs up near his ears, to steady and ease the load, one has no freedom at all; in fact, tump line work is mere carrying, to be got over as soon as possible and nothing else is done or thought of when it is going on.
—**Warren H. Miller, 1918**

BROAD BAND AND HARNESS

The broad band [is] used by the men of the far north. The reader will note that the broad canvas bands come over the shoulders from the top of the pack; also that a broad breast band connects the shoulder bands, while rope, whang strings or thongs run through eyelets in the band and to the bottom of the pack. This is said to be the most comfortable pack used and has an interesting history; it was evolved from an old pair of overalls. There was a Hebrew peddler who followed the gold seekers and he took a pair of canvas overalls and put them across his breast, and to the legs he fastened the pack upon his back. The overalls being wide and broad did not cut his chest, as do smaller straps, thongs or whang strings.
—Daniel Carter Beard, 1920

A sort of first cousin to the tump strap is the Siwash pack, much used in the Northwest. To get around the fact that the shoulder strap of a packsack, if heavily loaded, will stop circulation in your arms, the Northwestern Indians transferred the pressure of the strap to the shoulder and back muscles, thus getting away from the big arteries and veins that pass up under the muscles of the breast. To do this a yoke crosses the chest, well above the swell of the breast muscles and two broad straps proceed from this yoke over the shoulders and around the pack. From their ends a couple of cords are led up under the armpits and tie with a slip knot in grommets or eyelets in the yoke. Thus no heavy breast muscles come under compression from any strap, and in case an instant release from the pack is wanted, simply pull the ends of the ropes, pulling out the slip knots and letting the pack fall off your back.
—Warren H. Miller, 1918

THE DULUTH PACK COMPANY

In 1882, Camille Poirier submitted a patent for the original Duluth Pack. One hundred and sixteen years later this same pack is available from Duluth Tent and Awning (Duluth, Minnesota) through their flagship retail outlet, Duluth Pack Store. The Duluth #3 is virtually the same as the original patent, except the umbrella holder has been removed (too bad—an umbrella adds style).

In the North Woods canoe country, the Duluth pack is standard issue for the canoe camper who needs a sturdy tote in which to pack the gear that will be portaged from lake to lake. Today's packs are made from rugged eighteen-ounce canvas with hand-hammered copper rivets and three-inch-wide leather straps.

The factory still stands at its original location. Just recently, a time portal was opened when catalogs from circa 1920 were found under the floorboards of the factory. Original ads for Coleman stoves, camp furnishings, auto camps, and a variety of tents and packs were included. Parts of these catalogs have been reproduced in this book through the kind permission of Duluth Pack. The title of one of the catalogs is "Camping With Comfort."

The Duluth Pack Factory storefront since 1882.

BLANKET ROLL

[The] blanket is rolled up in the poncho with pajamas, extra clothes and moccasins inside. Strapped up horseshoe shape the tent is jammed into the middle, the whole snugged with two long, soft leather thongs: chrome tanned are best. Then the shoulder straps! These are not on the market so you must make them yourself. Buy a strip of sail-cloth 18 inches long and 3 inches wide. Fold over into a hollow and sew. Turn inside out. Fold it over a strap (Strap 1) and fit it to your shoulders. See diagrams. This is very important, so pay attention. Some boys take a right angle, some an acute angle. (Diagram A.) You'll thank me some day after a long hike for all of this. These shoulder straps make a pack feel light, especially if lined with soft material like flannel. Strap one is a woven strap with buckle on which your pack hangs as it goes around and cinches your tent-bag near the top. Two "straw-size" sash cords, 18 inches long or longer and whipped carefully (B) go under your arms from the grommets or "eyelets" in your shoulder straps (C) . . . to strap No. 2 (which has two rings sewn or loops tied in it) fastened with a running half-hitch or even more loosely. You see, you might want to drop your pack in a hurry. One slight yank on a string should be enough. This is scientific!

Your blanket being rolled in your ground cloth (as in Diagram), you jam your tent bag into it. It must fit tight. Now tie all up snug with your long thongs, 1 and 2. (B) Pull the pucker-string of your Baby (food bag) through a strap (No. 1) and let it hang over so rain can't enter. Screw in your tent-poles, under all the straps and thongs and your dirk* (or axe, if you can't get a dirk)—under, and there you are! Looping cords 1 and 2 under the lower ends of the tent poles.

—James Austin Wilder, 1929

[NOTE: Non-folding knives with double-edged blades are now outlawed in most states. Today, carrying such a tool is a criminal offense—a felony—and punishable by arrest and imprisonment for five years. Know the laws in your state.]

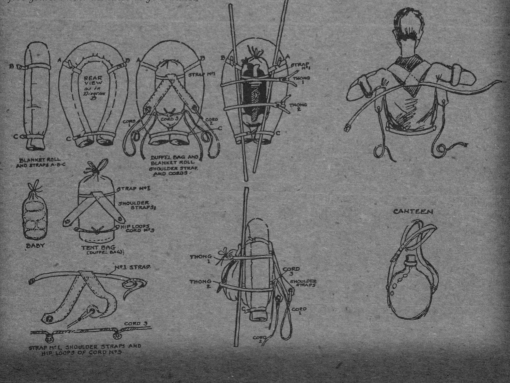

PACK SACKS

DULUTH PACK

There are two kinds of "packs"—the pack that you carry day after day on a long hike, and the pack that you carry when on a canoe trip and you are compelled to leave the water and carry your canoe and duffel overland around some bad rapids or falls. The first-named pack [Duluth Pack] should be as light as possible, say between 30 and 40 pounds, for on a long tramp every pound counts, because you know that you must carry it as long as you keep going, and there is no relief in sight except when you stop for your meals or to camp at night. But the last-named pack, the Portage Pack, the kind that you carry around bad pieces of water, may be as heavy as you can, with safety, load upon your sturdy back, because your mind is buoyed up by the fact that you know you will not have to carry that load very far, the work will end when you reach the water again, and strange to say—the mind has as much to do with carrying the load as the muscles. If the mind gives up you will fall helpless even under a small load; if the mind is strong you will stagger along under a very heavy one.
—Daniel Carter Beard, 1920

PACK BASKETS

People differ so in regard to how to carry a pack and what kind of a pack to carry, that the author hesitates to recommend any particular sort; personally he thinks that a pack harness hitched on to the duffel bags is the proper and practical thing. The portage basket is a favorite in the Adirondacks, but it is not a favorite with the writer; the basket itself is heavy and to his mind unnecessary.
—Daniel Carter Beard, 1920

This favorite of the North Woods weighs around seven pounds with a waterproof skin, and has the recommendation that it will carry articles not able to stand rough usage without breaking them, will hold a bushel of stuff, and carries well in the woods with tump strap and shoulder harness. It combines the stiffness of the frame pack with the carrying capacity of the large pack bundle, and is by no means to be sniffed at by those who live outside of the North Woods, its native home.
—Warren H. Miller, 1918

Don't be induced to carry a pack basket. I am aware that it is in high favor all through the Northern Wilderness, and is also much used in other localities where guides and sportsmen most do congregate. But I do not like it. I admit that it will carry a loaf of bread, with tea, sugar, etc., without jamming; that bottles, crockery, and other fragile duffel is safer from breakage than in an oil-cloth knapsack. But it is by no means waterproof in a rain or a splashing head sea, is more than twice as heavy—always growing heavier as it gets wetter—and I had rather have bread, tea, sugar, etc., a little jammed than water-soaked. Also, it may be remarked that man is a vertebrate animal and ought

to respect his backbone. The loaded pack basket on a heavy carry never fails to get in on the most vulnerable knob of the human vertebrae.
—Nessmuk, 1920

CAMP TRUNKS AND BOXES

Under the general head of packing come fiber and tough veneered wood cases for carrying camping outfits, also the pack baskets so popular in the Adirondacks, and, for permanent camps, a camp chest is worth mention. When you have a lot of truck and are going to stay a while and get there by team, the old camp chest is gotten out and packed with battle-worn duffel. . . . Arrived at the camp site, the chest is unpacked and made into a cupboard or table, and your stuff is all there, nothing smashed or torn. . . .The strong, light wooden suitcase is in the same class. It makes a fine camp table spread out flat over four stakes, carries a whole collection of breakable and bendable things.
—Warren H. Miller, 1918

HORSE PACKING

[In] the Rockies . . . the horse is about the only means of transportation, the canoe having but little water suitable for its use. . . . The standard western packsaddle has two sawbucks, rawhided or rivetted to wooden plates shaped to fit a horse's back. This constitutes the so-called "tree" to which the latigo straps, breeching and breast straps, and the two cinches are attached. This tree is the foundation on which you put from 120 to 200 pounds of load, so under it must go a pack blanket, usually hair filled padding. On it go two kyacks, panniers or alforjas, on opposite sides, with stout straps which hook over the cross-trees. The first of these carrying boxes is of fiber; the second is generally constructed of canvas with wood lining so as to in a measure protect the contents, and the alforja is a canvas saddlebag, no less, heavily stitched and leather reinforced and provided with stout leather loops to hang from the horns of the saddle. Which of these pack boxes are taken depends upon the material to be carried; a good outfit should have both panniers and alforjas, the former for canned goods, tinware, etc., and the latter for ordinary duffel that cannot be hurt with the rope pressure. When they are loaded and hung over the trees the sling ropes are next brought into play, the object of them being to not only tie the load together but to take the weight of the panniers off their straps as much as may be: they usually pass around the pannier, up over rear horn, down under the pannier, and end in a loop-knot tied in the part of the rope crossing in front of the pannier. This much is done as soon as the panniers are hung and before the rest of the pack is made up. The pack then is built up on the pannier tops, usually two duffel bags on top of the panniers on each side, a large central load like a tent in the center and some uneasy angular load on the cushion thus formed. The sling ropes for the panniers are then slung across the load and tied in the loop on opposite sides. So far so good, a tarp [manty] is thrown over the load, and then—in no two parts of the country will you find any one tying the same diamond hitch!
—Warren H. Miller, 1918

CAMP TOOLS

In the early days of American life the ax and the knife were the two indispensable tools. . . . With the knife they made spoons, brooms, rakes and bowls; trimmed the skins of the animals they caught, and made the smaller things needed in the cabin and around it.
—Phillip D. Fagans, 1933

In the temporary camps, a real camper can make his pocket or sheath ax serve him as a whole kit of tools, provided, of course, he keeps it sharp. In a permanent camp, however, or even a long-term camp, a few good quality common tools will always pay their way. There should be a common knock-about ax for the use of the "chumps" who insist on chopping down rock piles; and in addition, a good ax for the real camper. It should not be heavy, but of excellent quality, properly ground and, equipped with a stout leather muzzle-end, reserved for cutting wood only. This does not mean, by a greenhorn. [W}ith it should be a round carborundum stone, coarse on one side and fine on the other.

There should be at least one durable light-weight, long-handled shovel, a flat file to keep it in repair, and if space will permit, an extra handle will not come in amiss. Add to these a good claw-hammer, a medium log saw with extra attachable handle, and a saw file. A heavy canvas bag of assorted common nails, including a can of tacks, a few hooks and screw-eyes, will be many times a blessing. A stout brace with one-half, three-quarters, and a one inch bit, will serve a thousand purposes, if there is camp furniture to make.

The knife, axe, and saw are the backbone of the camp toolbox. Current efforts to discount the value of the axe and saw are poorly founded. The problem is not with the tool but with the lack of knowledge and experience on how to use the tool properly. Rather than discouraging their use, we should be actively educating people on how to use them properly.

Read carefully the notes on axe use. Traditional campers who are masters of the art are not hackers. Each tool carried into the bush has a specific task to accomplish, is designed for its task, and is maintained and used properly then stored away when done. Tool use is a hallmark of the woodsman and traditional camper. We have no tolerance for horseplay, wasted or damaged resources, or shoddy craftsmanship.

Just as in the old days, anyone wanting to use a camp tool had to pass a test from the mentor. Once they had the skill to use, care for, and maintain a tool, they were given a "toten chip" as badge of their proficiency. Maybe we need to nationalize such a program.

Then, of course, there will be a common eight-point saw and a sharp draw-knife, a pair of pliers, and, if possible, a medium cold-chisel. A good carbide lantern will be kept handy for emergencies, and a coil or two of extra rope for clotheslines, and a few bits of stout wire will come in handy. A strong iron rake will insure a cleaner camp, especially if there is much pine-needles and forest litter about.

All camp tools should be kept in a convenient, designated place, and should never be taken away without first signing up a simple tally arranged for the purpose, giving the initials of the borrower and the approximate time of day of the loan, checking each item off when the tool is returned.
—Frank H. Cheley, 1933

TRAINING SKILLS FOR CAMP TOOL USE

APPRENTICE CAMPER
- Select an appropriate knife for camp and trail use.
- Demonstrate ability to handle, care for, and store pocketknife.
- Discuss and display knowledge of:
  - Need for careful use of tools.
  - Proper use of tools.
  - Local regulations concerning tool use.
- Demonstrate ability to sharpen a knife.
- Demonstrate knife-handling skills by making a "try stick," displaying notches typically used in camp.

JOURNEYMAN CAMPER
- Select an appropriate axe and saw for camp and trail use.
- Demonstrate ability to:
  - Set up a chopping and sawing area.
  - Sharpen an axe.
  - Carefully use an axe and saw.
  - Saw a log into short lengths and split it for kindling.
  - Cut off and trim a tree limb where possible.
  - Make fuzz / feather sticks
- Work in a manner that reduces waste and is easily cleaned up.
- Use a knife to make simple camp tools, a spatula, spoon, and folk toys.

JOURNEYMAN WOODSMAN
- Demonstrate ability to:
  - Sharpen a saw and set the teeth.
  - Identify woods for various purposes.
  - Select vegetation for removal and use.
  - Make a handle and / or sheath for an axe and knife.
  - Select and use specialized tools for your kind of camping trip.
- Display ability to work and live by showing stewardship and minimal impact.
- Build a saw frame from natural materials.
- Use a knife to make netting needles or carving projects.

MASTER WOODSMAN
- Select, use, and maintain specialized tools used for woodcraft:
  - Spoke shave
  - Rasp
  - Froe
  - Shaving horse
  - Drawknife
  - Crooked knife
  - Adze
  - Maul or beetle
  - Wedges
  - Awl
  - Scraper
  - Gouges and Chisels
- Build a wooden toolbox or portable canvas storage pouch for tools and sharpening gear.

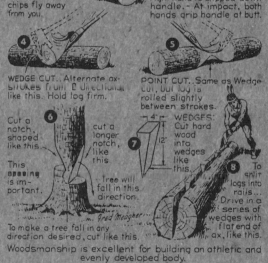

WOODSMANSHIP

Many useful things can be built from the trees in the woods but since an ax is a very dangerous tool be sure to get your PARENT'S PERMISSION before using one.

1. Always cut small limbs on a chopping log. Stand as shown above and be sure to cut away from your legs.

Stand so chips fly away from you.

Ax is lifted, like this. Right hand near ax-head. — Left hand near handle-butt. During chopping stroke, right hand is slipped down handle. — At impact, both hands grip handle at butt.

4. WEDGE CUT.. Alternate ax-strokes from 2 directions like this. Hold log firm.

5. POINT CUT.. Same as Wedge Cut, but log is rolled slightly between strokes.

6. Cut a notch shaped like this. cut a longer notch, like this. This spacing is important. Tree will fall in this direction.

7. WEDGES: Cut hard wood into wedges like this.

8. To split logs into rails... Drive in a series of wedges with flat end of ax, like this.

To make a tree fall in any direction desired, cut like this.

Woodsmanship is excellent for building an athletic and evenly developed body.

CAMP TOOLS

SHEATH KNIFE

One of the most useful articles in the hunter's, trapper's, camper's or prospector's outfit is the sheath knife, and I am sorry to say there are some who condemn this very useful tool. . . . I prefer a rather small knife, having no guard, and a deep sheath from which only the end of the handle projects. . . . The length of the knife overall is 9 inches, blade 4-1/2 inches, cutting edge 4 inches, thickness on the back about 5/32 inch, with a straight bevel from near the back to the edge.
—**E. Kreps, 1910**

A word as to knife, or knives. These are of prime necessity, and should be of the best, both as to shape and temper.
—**Nessmuk, 1920**

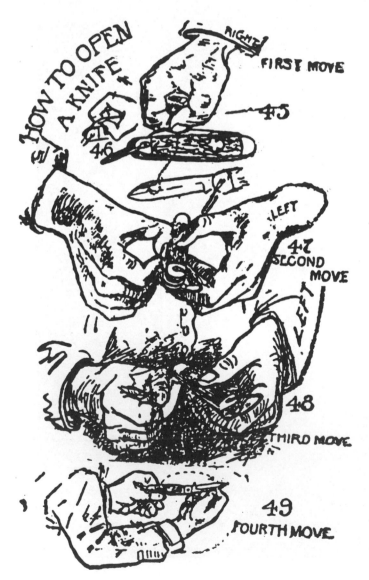

JACKKNIFE

Many hunters do not carry sheath knives, saying (and it is quite true) that a common jackknife will skin anything from a squirrel to a bear.
—**Horace Kephart, 1917**

"Where are the Barlows of yesteryear? City boys know them not."

How many city boys own a jackknife? Back in the country they all do, but in the cities it seems that most of them chew their school lead pencils when they have to be sharpened or use their mother's sewing scissors. Apparently, not even their fathers carry a veritable pocket-knife, as a general rule. Yet, it is only a few years—a generation at the most—since the jackknife was a great American institution.

Owning and carrying one was the boy's first symbol that he had reached the age at which he could be trusted with the first of the perquisites of his sex—a knife, the primal tool for the carving out of his career.

The old jackknife with a man's blade is as different from the city knife of today as the soldier's saber was from the courtier's rapier of a bygone age. It was made for work, and its work compassed the full scope of that American pioneer era which brought it into being and gave it vogue. . . . A man would no more think of leaving home in the morning without his jackknife than he would of adventuring fate without his galluses. The mechanic used his knife constantly, the farmer would have been helpless without it.
—**Phillip D. Fagans, 1933**

ETIQUETTE OF THE AXE

- An axe to be respected must be sharp and no one who has any ambition to be a pioneer, a sportsman or a scout, should carry a dull axe, or an axe with the edge nicked like a saw blade. It may interest the reader to know that the pencil I am using with which to make these notes was sharpened with my camp axe.
- No one but a duffer and a chump will use another man's axe without that other man's willing permission.
- It is as bad form to ask for the loan of a favorite axe as it is to ask for the loan of a sportsman's best gun or pet fishing rod or toothbrush.
- To turn the edge or to nick another man's axe is a very grave offense.
- Keep your own axe sharp and clean; do not use it to cut any object lying on the ground where there is danger of the blade of the axe going through the object and striking a stone; do not use it to cut roots of trees or bushes for the same reason. Beware of knots in hemlock wood and in cold weather beware of knots of any kind.
- When not in use an axe should have its blade sheathed in leather or it should be struck into a log or stump. It should never be left upon the ground or set up against a tree to endanger the legs and feet of the camper.

—Daniel Carter Beard, 1920

PROPER AXE USAGE

The way to learn chopping is to go slow, give all your attention to making every blow tell just where it is needed, and don't strike too hard.
—Horace Kephart, 1917

Having secured either your own ax or permission to use another's, what's next? You have heard of the man who was all dressed up but had no place to go? Quite frequently this happens when a boy gets hold of an ax. Consequently, he is very likely to hack at every thing in sight, perhaps ruin trees, fences, and lots of valuable material or objects, simply because he has an ax in his hands and must use it. Such actions are certain to brand any boy as a "greenhorn."

Don't hack. Don't blaze or chop trees that are not to be cut down. Don't do anything with the ax that will harm, or scar, or destroy property. When a "goop" gets loose with an ax, you can tell for years afterward what happened. Don't be a "goop."

Do something definite. Try to make something, using only an ax. If you are cutting camp wood, try to improve your axmanship. See how accurately you can hit, or how big chips you can make with how few strokes, or how smooth an end you can leave after your chopping. If you cut stakes, do it in a workman-like way, making the top end square and the pointed end foursided.

Never swing your ax until you are sure you have a free swing. Before starting, swing the ax carefully at full arm's length to see whether there are any twigs or branches to interfere with you as you chop. Just a slight touch is exceedingly dangerous. It may deflect the blow of the ax and cause serious damage to yourself or an innocent bystander.

Get a solid footing. Don't chop at a log or stick that is likely to slip or move as the ax is in the air.

Hold your ax securely. When using the two-handed ax, the hand away from the end slips up and down the handle as you chop but the other hand makes sure that the ax doesn't fly out of your hands.

Never take any chances with an ax when the head is loose, particularly when other

people are near you. There is no more dangerous missile than an ax thrown from an ax handle. Don't procrastinate; stop and fix it. Drive in a good hardwood wedge. Learn how to do it by doing it.

Always strike the wood at an angle. You will note that when striking the wood at right angles to the grain, the ax does not cut very much, and that there is a backward bounce due to the resistance of the wood. If you strike the grain diagonally, the ax will cut deeply and there will be no backward bounce.

If you are cutting small wood, use either a block or another log to chop or split upon.

Keep your ax out of the dirt. Look out for stones. Don't cut on the ground, even if you see no stones. Dirt isn't particularly good for sharp edges, and where there is dirt there are stones.

Avoid all knots if you can. Above all things don't put a sharp ax into a hemlock or balsam knot—they are particularly hard and are almost certain to ruin your ax.

If you use the ax in very bitter weather, it may be worth remembering that some woodsmen warm the blade with mittened hands before starting to chop, so as not chip it. Chopping always keeps an ax warm.

When you are not using your ax, sink the blade into a stump. Don't leave the ax just lying around. You may lose it, break its helve, or someone may cut himself badly by stepping or falling over its sharp edge.

Remember that the chief and only purpose of an ax is to cut wood. In order to do this, it must be sharp. The average camp ax reminds one of the old stone hatchet days. It would wear the wood away if you hit hard enough and often enough, but do very little effective cutting. Keep your ax sharp.

Don't pound stone or metal with your ax. Never drive another ax into a log as a wedge. Stop and cut wedges if you have no metal ones.

Don't throw your ax—it may hit a stone, break the handle, or hit someone. Always hand an ax to another party handle first.

In short, remember that a good ax is a fine tool to be handled with the greatest of respect.

—Phillip D. Fagans, 1933

AXE EXTRAS

Annealing—If you want a well-made axe, you have two options: buy an old one that has been taken care of, or buy a new Swedish axe. The difference between these axes and the modern American axe is in the annealing process. All axes are forged, tempered, allowed to cool, sharpened to factory standards, and sold. Quality axe makers go one step further to control the cooling process in such a way as to add strength to the blade. Annealing is a lengthy process that adds cost to the finished product—cost that a tyro sees no point in paying for—but the true woodcrafter won't consider going without. Look for and stand for nothing less than quality.

Handles—A well-made handle should have a straight grain that runs the entire length of it. The grain should lie parallel to the head and should not twist or roll in the handle. "Running parallel" means that the grain should be on the same plain with the head. Grain that is perpendicular will result in an easily broken handle.

Heads—See to it that any iron wedges driven into the helve are at a 45-degree angle to the grain in the handle. The head should be set so that when the axe is rested on the edge of a flat surface, the tip of the handle and a point just shy of halfway up the bit should be all that is touching. If the bit touches above the halfway point, or toward the toe (top) of the blade, it is hung too low. If only the heel (bottom) of the bit touches, it is hung too high.

FELLING A TREE

If you want to learn to fell a tree, find a mentor. There are few books that can teach it well if at all. For the purposes of the camper, felling is a skill that is rarely required. For the woodsman, however, wood of a size that will provide for his needs can be obtained only by knowing how to fell safely.

For the campfire, we want trees of a small diameter that can be bucked to a desired length and easily split with a hatchet or two-pound axe. The trees that provide standing dead wood are easily pushed over without the need for an axe. Watch out for a trunk buckling and falling on your head. Push the tree over. Rocking it or shoving it will create a wave effect that might snap the trunk and drop the top of the tree right onto you.

Once the tree is down, a bucksaw is used to cut it to length. If a hatchet is what you have for splitting, lengths of about eight to ten inches will split easily. If you have a two-pound axe, lengths of eighteen to twenty inches with few branches or knots can be handled. Split all wood, but wood that is to be used on an open fire must be split to the size no larger than your wrist.

THE AXE

The northern forest traveler . . . may, to lighten his load, discard all of the articles in his outfit which are not absolutely essential, but never by any chance is the axe among those cast aside, because this tool is the most necessary and the most useful article used by the bushman.
—*Woodcraft*, 1910

In all the crafts of the outdoorsman there is nothing that can be developed into an art more readily than handling the ax. Kephart says that if one is to become a real ax-man, he must begin to handle the tool at eight and, I suppose, literally grow up with the ax in his hands. Lincoln did, Grant did, as did many other Americans, so that, when they became young men, they could not only fell a tree so accurately as to drive a given stake as the tree came down, but from it could split clapboards, dress timbers, or shave shingles, as the case might be.
—**Phillip D. Fagans, 1933**

Even more useful and more necessary than the knife is the hunting axe, in fact, an axe of some sort is indispensable to the trapper and camper, and it should be selected with care, especially when one is going into the wilderness on a camping trip, and must depend on fire for comfort at night.
—**E. Kreps, 1910**

On a hiking or toboggan trip in winter the Hudson Bay axe takes the place of the three-quarter axe (although again a sharp belt-axe alone would answer), because with the light, keen head and long handle of the Hudson Bay axe one's swing radius and cutting power are enormously increased, and, as there is a lot of night wood to cut, it meets the requirements admirably.
—**Warren H. Miller, 1915**

HOW TO MAKE A CHOPPING BLOCK

After you have cut the crotch and trimmed it down into the [proper] form, you may find it convenient to flatten the thing on one side. This you do by hewing and scoring; that is, by cutting a series of notches all of the same depth, and then splitting off the wood between the notches, as one would in making a puncheon. (A puncheon is a log flattened on one or both sides.) With this flattened crotch one may, by sinking another flattened log in the earth and placing the chopping block on top, have a chopping block. Or one may take the crotch, spike a piece of board across and use that, and the best chopping block or crotch block is the one with the puncheon or slab spiked onto the ends of the crotch. In this case the two ends of the crotch should be cut off with a saw, if you have one, so as to give the proper flat surface to which to nail the slab. Then the kindling wood may be split without danger to yourself or the edge of the hatchet.
—**Daniel Carter Beard, 1920**

HOW TO SPLIT KINDLING

When splitting wood for the fire or kindling, make the first blow as in Fig. 346, and the second blow in the same place, but a trifle slanting as in Fig. 347; the slanting blow wedges the wood apart and splits it. If the wood is small and splits readily, the slanting blow may be made first. These things can only be indicated to the readers because there are so many circumstances which govern the case. If there is a knot in the wood, strike the axe right over the knot as in Figs. 348 and 349.

If you are chopping across the grain do not strike perpendicularly as in Fig. 350, because if the wood is hard the axe will simply bounce back, but strike a slanting blow as in Fig. 351, and the axe blade will bite deeply into the wood; again let us caution you that if you put too much of a slant on your axe in striking the wood, it will cut out a shallow chip without materially impeding the force of the blow, and your axe will swing around to the peril of yourself or anyone else within reach; again this is a thing which you must learn to practice.

In using the chopping block be very careful not to put a log in front of the crotch as in Fig. 340, and then strike a heavy blow with the axe, for the reason that if you split the wood with the first blow your axe handle will come down heavily and suddenly upon the front log, and no matter how good a handle it may be, it will break into fragments. . . . A lost axe handle in the woods is a severe loss, and one to be avoided, for although a makeshift handle may be fashioned at camp, it never answers the purpose as well as the skillfully and artistically made handle which comes with the axe.

—Daniel Carter Beard, 1920

THE HATCHET

The hatchet is to the axe as the pistol is to the rifle. Because of the compact nature of the pistol and hatchet, they are able to inflict damage to the thoughtless user with deadly speed. The length of the rifle and axe keep the working end farther from the user, making them less likely to be turned on oneself. We should not forget, however, that they are no less deadly when used without thinking, and the damage they can inflict can be more severe. So, even though they may be safer, in the long run they can cause more damage. Supervised instruction is recommended.

An axe with a two-pound head and twenty-four-inch handle will do all of the work of a hatchet and can be used for heavier work as well. Even in the light of comments by Nessmuk and Beard, perhaps the tyro may want to start out with the margin of safety that the larger axe provides.

A hatchet of 1 1/4 pounds is about the right size for general use.
—E. Kreps, 1910

The notion that a heavy hunting knife can do the work of a hatchet is a delusion. . . . A camper's hatchet should have the edge and temper of a good axe.
—Horace Kephart, 1916

And just here let me digress for a little chat on the indispensable hatchet; for it is the most difficult piece of camp kit to obtain in perfection of which I have any knowledge. Before I was a dozen years old I came to realize that a light hatchet was a sine qua non in woodcraft, and I also found it a most difficult thing to get.
—Nessmuk, 1920

The axeman with his woodcrafter's coat.

CARE OF CAMP TOOLS

Knicks and dull edges are abominations, so use knives and hatchets for nothing but what they were made for . . .
—**Horace Kephart, 1917**

To keep this edge you will carry a file and a water whetstone. Use your hatchet as much as possible, take care of how and what you chop, and do not wait until the axe gets really dull before having recourse to your file and stone. It is a long distance to a grind stone. Wes Thompson expressed the situation well. He watched the Kid's efforts for a moment in silence. "Kid," said he sorrowfully at last, "you'll have to make your choice. Either you do all the chopping or none of it."
—*Camp and Trail*, 1920

Axes, as they come from the factories, have a decided bevel near the edge and a new axe is of no account until it has been well ground. The proper way to grind an axe is to start well back on the blade and grind it out to the edge, or until all of the bevel has disappeared then it should be well whetted with a small, smooth stone. The thickest part of the blade should be not exactly in the center, but somewhat towards the outside corner, that is, the corner that is farthest from the axeman when the tool is in use. An axe so shaped will spring the chip nicely and will not bind in the wood.

For keeping the axe sharp when in the woods, I carry a small, flat, mill file of six or eight inches in length and a small axe stone. A carborundum stone with coarse and fine sides is best for the purpose.
—E. Kreps, 1910

SECTION TWO
The Traditional Canvas Shelter

There is a large variety [of tents], each of which is suited for special
needs and conditions. You should be familiar with all the standard shapes,
advantages and disadvantages, and then select the one you think best suited for your
particular purpose. But if at all possible, be sure to camp in a tent. Cabins, shacks,
and shanties have their attractions and place, no doubt, and should not be
belittled, but for a real camping out in the summertime, a tent.

—Frank H. Cheley, 1933

CANVAS TENTS

The principle function of a tent is to make a real "woodser" of you. A shack or a log cabin, located in the heart of the woods, will shelter you from the elements and put you in reasonable touch with the sights and sounds and smells of the wilderness, but you are not of it, not in the real heart of the wild life, nor will a year in a cabin be as beneficial to your health as thirty days in a tent. The reason is that, day and night, there is a constant seepage of the fresh ozone of the forest through the texture of the tent wall, neither draft nor stagnation, but a constant change of air. The fresh, fine woods aroma is not barred out by log or clapboard, nor yet does it blow over you in chilling drafts as in an open-air bivouac or under a single sheet of shelter cloth. I never regarded the latter as anything but an unnecessary outdoor hardship, and the cabin I have always considered as anything but a luxury when there was a possible choice of a tent to sleep in.
—Warren H. Miller, 1915

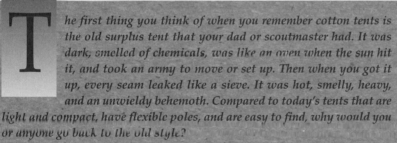

The first thing you think of when you remember cotton tents is the old surplus tent that your dad or scoutmaster had. It was dark, smelled of chemicals, was like an oven when the sun hit it, and took an army to move or set up. Then when you got it up, every seam leaked like a sieve. It was hot, smelly, heavy, and an unwieldy behemoth. Compared to today's tents that are light and compact, have flexible poles, and are easy to find, why would you or anyone go back to the old style?

Living in a cotton tent that is heated by a wood stove has no match for comfort, aesthetics, or style. When viewed from the outside, the simple lines of the tent, with smoke gently rising from the chimney and the whole structure lit to a warm glow with candles or lanterns, speak of the true wildwood home. This icon of traditional camping has earned its place in your choice of how to camp. It hasn't outlived its usefulness as you might think of many old-fashioned ways. Once you come to understand its value and beauty and make a choice (rather than being sold on the style of camping you would like to do), the traditional wood-and-canvas tent has no rivals.

The size of the tent and the material it's made from determine just how portable it will be. It's also a self-limiting factor. Most tents consist of wooden or metal poles or frame with a fabric covering. In the case of traditional camping, the fabric is some form of cotton—ten-ounce canvas and Egyptian cotton being the most common for mobile camps.

The variety of tent sizes and designs is limitless. The World Book Encyclopedia sets the number at a half million. In fact, it's said that all of the old outdoor outfitters left their legacy on the sport by designing a tent and hanging their name on it. Why a tent? Why not a pack stove or knot? Most tents are a variation on otherwise-sound geometry. Modification isn't always an improvement.

Tents can be had in all sizes, but the number of people staying in the tent and helping to move it should determine its size. There is, however, a point of diminishing return. A two-person tent is optimal for size and material. If more than two people will inhabit it, size and weight can be divided among the campers. For winter, a 10 x 12-foot is likely as large as anyone need go. If more room is needed, it's preferable to get a second tent.

A tent is merely a windbreak. It provides no "R" or insulation value, but temporarily holds a bubble of warm air in place for a short time. The stove keeps generating heat to offset the loss of warmth through the tent fabric. The use of cotton allows the stove to be used safely indoors.

TENT GEOMETRY

The triangle is the most stable structural form, and most tents are designs derived from the triangle. The wedge, or the A tent, is the most obvious triangle. It is suspended with a ridgeline or poles. The steepness of the walls allows weather to shed quickly, but reduces living space dramatically. The stability of the wedge is testament to why they were used as high-altitude tents for so many years.

Chop off the back or tilt the front of this same wedge tent, and the Explorer, Blizzard, Ranger, and Hudson Bay designs take shape. If the triangle has walls attached to the bottom of each side, it becomes taller, and the useful amount of interior space is greatly enhanced. The wall tent is said to be the most efficient use of interior space of all closed tents. If the wall is added and the ridge stays the same height, the roof gets flatter. If the angle gets to less than thirty degrees, it will allow pooling of rain, and a snow load will collapse it. A 35-degree slope is an improvement but the closer one gets to 45 degrees, the better. The relationship of the wall and ridge are critical, but a tent that is too tall requires working harder to keep it warm.

If the original triangle shape is suspended at one point with a pole instead of having a ridge, it becomes a pyramid or canoe tent. If short walls are added all around, it becomes a miner. The pyramid shape is easy to erect: it takes few stakes and guylines, a strategically placed tree can replace the pole, and a single line can suspend the whole tent. By adding a simple frame and expanding the headroom of this same design, an umbrella effect is achieved.

Eliminating the corners and making the tent round instead of square, creates the cone or Sibley design. Rounded sides allow wind to move by without the sail effect stressing the structure. By adding a tripod with multiple poles and opening the apex, the tipi comes to life—the ultimate icon of America's historical camping tradition. We have intentionally left it out of the scope of this book.

By tipping the original wedge tent over, a lean-to with a floor is created—an open tent. If sides are folded down, destabilizing the original form, the campfire/Baker tent allows a fire to be built in its open side.

All of the above forms are based on the triangle. "You can break it, but you can't bend it."

TYPES OF TENTS

I feel a little diffident about talking tents, being somewhat of a tent crank myself, so that I look on all other designs with a yellow and a jaundiced eye. There are, however, other tents that I take off my hat to.
—**Warren H. Miller, 1918**

Styles, sizes, and materials of tents vary greatly according to the climate, number in the party, and transportation possibilities. Every different style going has its own best kind of tent, and this in its turn is modified by temperatures, wood supply, and available time for camp-making.
—**Warren Miller, 1915**

The proper shape for a tent is a matter of some discussion. Undoubtedly the lean-to is the ideal shelter so far as warmth goes. You build your fire in front, the slanting wall reflects the heat down and you sleep warm even in winter weather. In practice, however, the lean-to is not always an undiluted joy. Flies can get in for one thing, and a heavy rainstorm can suck around the corner for another. In these circumstances four walls are highly desirable.

On the other hand a cold snap makes a **wall tent** into a cold storage vault. Tent stoves are little devils. They are either red hot or stone cold, and even when doing their best, there is always a northwest corner that declines to be thawed out. A man feels the need of a camp fire, properly constructed.

For three seasons I have come gradually to thinking that an **A** or **wedge** tent is about the proper thing. In event of that rainstorm or those flies its advantages are obvious. When a cold snap comes along, you simply pull up the stakes along one side, tie the loops of that wall to the same stakes that hold down the other wall—and there is your lean-to all ready for the fire.
—*Camp and Trail*, **1920**

You can break a triangle, but you can't bend it.
—**Peter Marques**

TENTS FROM A SINGLE SHEET

If you will cut out a sheet of stiff notepaper twice as long as it is wide and experiment with it by creasing and setting up, you will find that the following six well-known tents can be shaped of that one sheet of cloth: Lean-to (no back wall and one-third of canvas wasted); Miner (no wall); pyramid; Arabian; cone; and canoe tent.

Only three of these will be any good for practical camping, as the others are either too small for their shape or involve considerable waste canvas. Of these three, the Baker lean-to and the Miner will cover both forest and prairie. To get your square of canvas: Most country stores and city department stores carry 8-ounce and 10-ounce duck canvas in the standard 30-inch width at about 18 and 22 cents a yard. The wide sizes, all in one piece, such as are used for motor-boat cabin decks, etc., can only be obtained from ship chandleries or the cotton goods manufacturers. In any event, a tent is much like a sail in the wind stress it has to carry, and is better seamed and gored with a fold in the middle of each 30-inch width. Out of this piece of canvas a passable lean-to can be

folded by losing about a third of the material in sod cloth. More floor space can be covered by using it as an Arabic rectangle tent, but the angles are so flat that there is little real head room in it for your 15 yards of cloth. Used as an A-tent or a wall tent it has no back or front—a trifle draughty—and, folded into a pyramidal form, again a third of it is lost in sod cloth, while the resulting tent is tiny. Tent shapes are just like gambrel roofs—you can get much more living room under that shape than in a straight gable roof for the same spread of canvas. And, as soon as you give it two slants from ridge pole to tent peg (as in the wall tent) you must have specially cut ends for it.
—**Warren H. Miller, 1918**

Fig. 309 shows some of the ordinary forms of tents, the wall tent, the Baker tent and the canoe tent. Fig. 310 shows a tent with a fly extending out in front, thus giving the piazza, or front porch. In the background is a tepee tent. Fig. 311 shows two small Baker tents in the background, and the Dan Beard tent in the foreground. These comprise the principal forms, but the open-front tents to-day are much in vogue with the campers. A mosquito netting in front will keep out the insects and allow the air to come in freely, whereas the old-fashioned way of closing the tent flap stops circulation of air and makes conditions as bad as that of a closed room in a big house, and the air becomes as foul as it did in the little red school houses and does now in the Courts of Justice, jails and other places of entertainment.
—**Daniel Carter Beard, 1920**

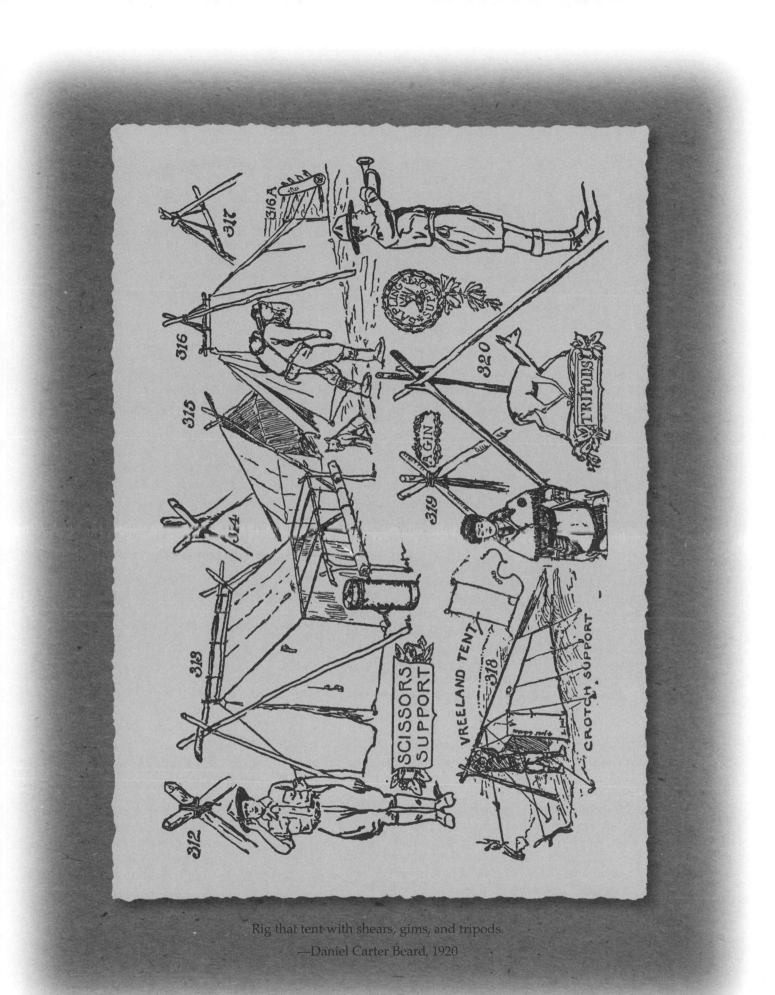

Rig that tent with shears, gims, and tripods.
—Daniel Carter Beard, 1920

TREATMENTS

FIRE RETARDANT

No tent is fireproof. Fire-retardant chemicals are placed on loom-state fabrics to slow the action of fire if the fabric is exposed to sparks or flame. Fire retardant stops sparks from spreading. Treated canvas will burn but only when an open flame is held to the fabric; otherwise, it should self-extinguish. So in tents, one must be careful of sparks damaging the tent roof. One must also be cautious that all pipes are secure and the stove is stable to prevent introducing an open flame into the tent. Stoves should also be as air tight as possible so they can be "damped down" if they become too hot. Unregulated temperature inside a tent can create a flash-point condition in which the canvas can combust.

WATERPROOFING

Whereas fire retardant weakens the fabric, water repellant does not, but it does add weight. Modern waterproof chemicals alleviate the age-old problem of touching the canvas. In the old days, when wet canvas was touched, it broke the surface tension, and the tent began to leak. New additives eliminate this problem. Sunforger, the modern treatment, makes canvas water repellant and mildew resistant—the two major drawbacks to canvas in the early days of camping.

- Mill or loom state—fabric as it comes off the loom. No chemicals or additives have been applied. Fabric is strongest and most breathable at this state and is preferred by many traditionalists for its authenticity. Any treatment added to the fabric after it leaves the loom has a weakening effect on the weave.
- Preshrinking—prewashing and preshrinking of loom-state materials. This process eliminates the problem of tents changing shape when wet and shrinking to the point of pulling stakes and ripping seams as cited in many old texts.
- Water-repellant versus waterproof—a tent should not be waterproof. At its best, it may be water-repellant, which still allows breathability. Sunforger (formerly known as Vivatex) is a factory process in which the chemical is baked into the fabric. This makes the canvas mildew-resistant and eliminates the old problem of a tent leaking when touched due to lost surface tension. Water-repellant yet breathable.
- Nik-wax—a new water-based waterproofing being used to treat loom-state material used on garments and Egyptian-cotton tents.
- Flame-resistant versus fireproof—fire-retardant treatment is referred to as CPAI-84. Fire-retardant fabrics for tents are mandated by many states, all federal reserves, and Canada. A fire-retardant fabric must be self-extinguishing if sparks land on it. However, any fabric will continue to burn if exposed to a constant open flame.

In many sections of the country you will need a tent, even when traveling afoot. Formerly a man had to make a choice between canvas, which is heavy but fairly waterproof, and drill, which is light but flimsy. A seven by seven duck tent weighs fully twenty-five pounds when dry, and a great many more when wet. It will shed rain as long as you do not hit against it. A touch on the inside, however, will often start a trickle at the point of contact. Altogether it is unsatisfactory, and one does not wonder that many men prefer to knock together bark shelters.

A FIBER AND FABRIC PRIMER

TERMS

- Fibers—slender filament or strand; plant or animal

- Yarn—fibers twisted together

- Thread—two or more small yarns twisted together

- String—same as thread, but using larger yarns

- Strand—two or more large yarns twisted together. Yarns are laid up with a left-hand twist to make a strand.

- Cord—several threads twisted together

- Rope—several strands twisted together. Strands are laid up with a right-hand twist to make a rope.

NATURAL FIBERS

- Cotton—used for both fabric and guy ropes. Imported fabric of exceptionally long staples is called Egyptian cotton.

- Flax—plant fiber used to weave linen. Thirteen-ounce linen was used to make tents.

- Hemp—soft fibers used for both fabric and guy ropes. Historically imported only from Asia, a new Romanian product is now available at reasonable prices.

- Jute—soft fibers used to weave burlap or twist string.

- Manila—a hard fiber taken from the leaf stems of the abacá plant (a member of the banana family), grown in Ecuador and the Philippines. Most widely used in rope-making as it is strong and resistant to rot from wind, rain, and sun.

- Sisal—comes from the leaves of the sisalina plant, which grows in Haiti and Africa. It is a harder fiber, but has only 80 percent of the strength of manila. Fibers can be twenty to fifty inches long. Used primarily to twist binder twine.

- Silk—threads made from fine lustrous fibers produced by a silkworm.

A FIBER AND FABRIC PRIMER
(Continued)

MATERIALS

- Duck/Canvas—a coarse fabric that is closely woven in a variety of ways from cotton, hemp, or flax. It is referenced by either weight or number. The common weights are 10, 12, and 14 ounces (some packs even use 16- and 18-ounce). Weight refers to weight per square yard. Numbered canvas is rated similar to a gauge system of reference. The numbers 2, 4, 6, 8, 10, and 12 refer to the thickness of the material—the larger the number, the lighter the fabric. Fabric is bleached or dyed yellow, brown, or dull green. Ten ounce is necessary for tents—eight ounce for flies—minimum.

- "Fill"—a subcategory that refers to the weave of the fabric.

- Single fill (cheap, coarse fabric)—fabric woven with one-thread warp (lengthwise) and weft (crosswise).

- Double fill (close weave, best for summer use)—fabric that is woven with two threads twisted together; woven the same as single fill.

- Army Duck I—woven to military specifications with smaller double fill that has twisted threads at a higher count (threads per square inch).

- Drill/American drilling—a very lightweight canvas woven in a twill-like diagonal pattern. Look at denim to see what it looks like.

- Egyptian cotton—fabric woven from exceptionally long fibers (staples). Fiber length allows fabric to be lighter with same fill as heavier weights. Balloon Silk, Tent Silk, or Silkoline are old references for what is truthfully Egyptian cotton. It is tightly woven with a shiny look and hand that feels silk-like. Available in weights from 3 to 8 ounces, with a common fabric weight for tents of 4.8 ounces, making them exceptionally light, but having some inherent drawbacks. Best used as a material for winter tents.

- Gauze—refers to mosquito netting used on windows and doors. Bobinet (also bobbinet) is the term often used.

- Japanese silk—rarely referred to as a tent material. Genuine silk appears to have been used but was on a very limited basis. Even historically the cost and fragile nature of the material would dictate the limits of its use.

- Muslin—very light and cheap cotton fabric. Available as bleached or unbleached fabric.

- Waterproof flax—a fine, tightly woven, light-colored fabric. Fine grades of flax fabric are called linen.

- Cheesecloth—a coarse, loosely woven cotton gauze.

Ten- to twelve-ounce canvas will be found the best economy, with a ten-ounce fly, unless standard government khaki can be secured. This is somewhat lighter in weight, but is of the very finest grade of cotton goods, and will wear like iron, if taken care of. In addition, it has the advantage of being cooler, more restful to the eye and less conspicuous than a white tent. Tests have proven that insects, especially mosquitoes, dislike the interior of khaki tents. Its very color saves it from showing the ordinary wear and soiled spots that are inevitable. (Canvas or duck used in tents is designated according to the number of ounces by weight to the yard.)

—*Frank H. Cheley, 1933*

Nowadays, however, another and better material is to be had. It is the stuff balloons are made of, and is called balloon silk. I believe, for shelter purposes, it undergoes a further waterproofing process, but of this I am not certain. A tent of the size mentioned, instead of weighing twenty-five pounds, pulls the scales down at about eight. Furthermore, it does not absorb moisture, and is no heavier when wet than when dry. One can touch the inside all he wishes without rendering it pervious. The material is tough and enduring.

I have one which I have used hard for five years, not only as a tent, but as a canoe lining, a sod cloth, a tarpaulin, and a pack canvas. Today it is as serviceable as ever, and excepting for inevitable soiling, two small patches represents its entire wear and tear.

Abercrombie & Fitch, who make this tent, will try to persuade you, if you demand protection against mosquitoes, to let them sew on a sod-cloth of bobbinet and a loose long curtain of the same material to cover the entrance. Do not allow it. The rig is all right as long as there are plenty of flies. But suppose you want to use the tent in a flyless land? There still blocks your way that confounded curtain of bobbinet, fitting tightly enough so that you have almost to crawl when you enter, and so arranged that it is impossible to hang it up out of the way. The tent itself is all right, but its fly rigging is all wrong.

—*Camp and Trail*, 1920

TENT SPECIFICS—*Closed Tents*

WALL TENTS

It is not the object of this book to advertise, or even advise the use of any particular type of outfitting apparatus other than the plain, everyday affairs with which all are familiar. What we want to do is to start the reader right, then he may make his own choice, selecting an outfit to suit his own taste. There are no two men, for instance, who will sing the praise of the same sort of a tent, but there is perhaps no camper who has not used, and been very comfortable in, the old style wall tent. It has its disadvantages, and so has a house, a shack or a shanty. As a rule, the old wall tent always on hand, is too heavy to carry with comfort and very difficult for one man to pitch alone unless one knows how.
—**Daniel Carter Beard, 1920**

No asthmatic or consumptive patient ever regained health by dwelling in a close, damp tent. I once camped for a week in a wall tent, with a Philadelphia party, and in cold weather. We had a little sheet iron fiend, called a camp-stove. When well fed with bark, knots and chips, it would get red hot, and, heaven knows, give out heat enough. By the time we were sound asleep, it would subside; and we would presently awake with chattering teeth to kindle her up again, take a smoke and a nip, turn in for another nap—to awaken again half frozen. It was a poor substitute for the open camp and bright fire.
—**Nessmuk, 1920**

The closed types of tents offer a fascinating field for study and experiment. An open tent requires an all-night fire in severe weather, and such a fire one can get with an hour's work with a camp-axe, cutting twenty 5-inch logs 3 feet long, and building a Nessmuk fire with backlogs and andirons. But on hunting trips, where every hour of daylight is used in the pursuit of game and you come home too tired to do more than cook supper, to chop a supply of night wood is out of the question.
—**Warren H. Miller, 1915**

THE WALL TENT

The added space provided by the dining fly makes camp life less congested.

WEDGE TENTS

[A] wedge tent can be used much as a wall tent. It can be pitched upon poles cut in the wilderness, or with a stout rope sewed into the ridge. Where weight and bulk are a consideration, it is a desirable shelter. Sometimes it is made in two halves, much as a shelter tent is, each half being carried by a camper and laced together into a tent at night.
—Frank H. Cheley, 1933

This "blizzard" tent weighs just 3 pounds, and packs into a parcel 3 inches diameter by 20 inches long. It is made of a light, oiled-silk fabric, given me by Abercrombie on one of our trips. Along one side goes the stick bed, with room for a bunky beside me, at the rear end the duffel and grub, and in the front end the stove. I have since added a bobbinet ventilator up in the rear peak, as I found the tent breathy after a night in it closed up, whereas the Forester is always sweet and full of forest ozone.
—Warren H. Miller, 1915

The blizzard tent is in no way to be compared to the Forester for general roominess and healthfulness, but in thick weather, either rain or snow, it does possess the advantage that one can cook in it, and with the addition of one of those small briquet burners, or the briquet itself burned in the tent stove, same giving out quite a noticeable heat for ten hours after igniting, it would be comfortable at very low temperatures. These briquets weigh 7 1/2 pounds to the dozen, or enough to last a week of cold nights, at a weight of 4 pounds.
—Warren H. Miller, 1915

When you get your tent made, have them insert grommets in each peak. Through these you will run a light line. By tying each end of the line to a tree or sapling, staking out the four corners of your tent, and then tightening the line by wedging under it (and outside the tent, of course) a forked pole, your tent is up in a jiffy. Where you cannot find two trees handily placed, poles crossed make good supports front and rear. The line passes over them and to a stake in the ground. These are quick pitches for a brief stop. By such methods an A tent is erected as quickly as a "pyramid," a miner's, or any of the others. In permanent camp, you will cut poles and do a shipshape job.
—*Camp and Trail*, 1920

I am not in the least averse to experimenting in new fields with tents, and never yet was wedded to any of my own inventions; so in this case I set to work to devise a new "blizzard" tent, for one or two men, that would weigh 3 pounds. The illustration shows the result. It is, in effect, a modification of the well-known Hudson Bay tent, in that the ends are pyramidal instead of circular, so that only two more pegs are needed than with the ordinary wedge-tent, and no poles at all are required. This tent sets up 5 feet wide by 6 feet long on the straight faces, with the addition of the pyramidal triangles at each end, which make it 9 feet long from peg to peg. In the rear pyramid is room for duffel and a side-opening food-bag, hung up on two short stakes. The door is in the front pyramid, which is also the space sacred to a small tent-stove. This is something that I have always wanted for snow work, for if run right it will keep you warm and comfortable and cook breakfast or supper for you while the gale is roaring outside.
—Warren H. Miller, 1915

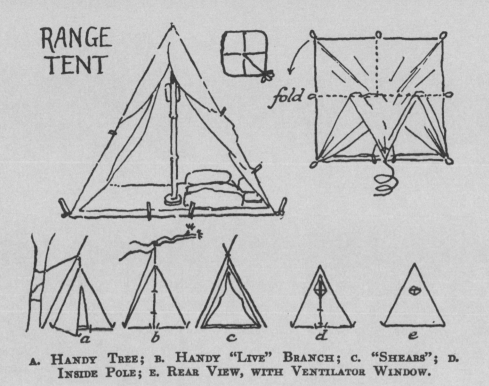

RANGE TENT

A. HANDY TREE; B. HANDY "LIVE" BRANCH; C. "SHEARS"; D. INSIDE POLE; E. REAR VIEW, WITH VENTILATOR WINDOW.

LOCKED UP

FOLD

THE RANGE TENT.

This is not in any catalogue that I have but any Awning and Tentmaker will make it for you. Eight feet high, pyramid, with stout sewed-in ground canvas, 7 by 7, with a bug or snake fence across the door. This sheds torrential rain and flaps of the door tie up. Dog proof.

Has a rear window for ventilation, made mosquito proof by pinning netting over it. Goes up in many ways, as you see. Made of Egyptian it would be almost light enough to "tote"; meanwhile it is just the thing for an auto or pack mule trip. 10 lbs.

This is the most comfortable one or two man tent I ever used. On pegging down over browse or hay your bed is under the floor . . . minus the beetles, ants and other crawling bed-fellows. Goes up in all sorts of ways, quick as a wink. Outside shears, outside gin or tripod, inside or outside four-pod and inside single pole. For the latter you must guy against the wind. In a storm rig the inside four-pod, cut to fit the inside angles of the pyramid. This stops all flapping, usually that boresome snapping of fire crackers that you hear when camping on the reef in the Trade Wind belt.

Folding up the Range Tent. Begin by letting down your poles, or striking poles, as the saying is. Then, with tent-pegs still in the ground, fold as in the cut, page 95, getting your edges tucked in all square. Take up front tent-pegs, stow them in your rope bag, to save your tent from getting dirty, and then pull up your back pegs. Fold over with an eye to having only the under side of the ground-cloth exposed. Your tent will stay white for a long time.

—James Austin Wilder, 1929

"A" Tent Pitched as Shelter.

"A" Tent Pitched Between Two Trees.

"A" Tent Pitched on Treeless Ground.

Method of Tightening Rope.

The Ranger Tent

The Ranger Tent must have poles—long ones, for the outside, but only one for the inside. Sometimes you do not need any. It was raining cats and dogs, but that troubled us not, for our shirts and their breeches were of electrically waterproofed wool and it never penetrated. The electric current acts by osmosis, not to put the waterproofing between the fibers as in ordinary dip solutions, but right into the fibers. Consider what happens when a drop of water falls on cloth. The fibers take it up and become wet. When they are full the interstices take up water and also become wet, and then the water communicates itself to the undergarments and a capillary action is set up by which every drop is passed on in to wet still more cloth. With the fibers themselves waterproofed this does not happen, nor do you get the closeness of rubber where the interstices are filled with rubber and there is no porosity to pass off sweat. With electro-waterproofed fiber the raindrop is simply rejected—it stays outside like dew on grass and falls harmlessly to the ground.
—**Warren H. Miller, 1918**

PYRAMID TENTS

MODIFIED PYRAMIDS—*Hudson's Bay, Snow Tent*

To my mind the best tents of this type are the Hudson Bay, Snow, and Miner's. The weights in modern tent fabrics run: Hudson Bay, 4 x 7 feet, 4 pounds; Snow, 6 x 7 feet, 5 pounds; Miner's, 7 feet 4 inches by 7 feet 4 inches, 7 1/4 pounds; Frazer, 8 feet 9 inches by 8 feet 9 inches, 10 1/4 pounds. These tents have the further advantage that one can stand upright in them, or sit down in camp-chairs or on cots during "enforced indoor weather" (whatever that may be), and are all the better for a bobbinet tent window in the back wall to afford a view.

The so-called Snow tent resembles a Miner's, except that it has a short ridge which is held by a club and bridle outside. It thus has steep snow-shedding slopes, and considerable headroom, a desirable feature when one wishes to work indoors skinning and mounting specimens, making and labeling scientific collections, etc. It is best put up with two pairs of shears, supporting the club to which the ridge is taped. In Japanese silk, a 7 x 8 x 8-foot headroom tent will weigh about 6 pounds.
—Frank H. Cheley, 1933

The Miner's Tent seems to be standard for cold, snowy countries, where timber is scarce or wanting. Peary's parties used them throughout their expeditions, only abandoning them for the warmer Eskimo igloo during the long winter night. They used alcohol-lamps for warmth, and found the tent good down to about 30 below zero. Below that the igloo! It uses a single 7-foot jointed pole in the center, and some manufacturers call for 24 stakes, which seems considerable of a hardship. The Miner's come in four sizes, from 6 feet 6 inches by 6 feet 6 inches up to 10 feet 3 inches by 10 feet 3 inches; heights 7 to 9 feet, and weights 7 1/4 to 12 1/4 pounds. The floor space is not particularly available, the headroom is restricted, and I should regard them more as a special cold-weather tent for special territories.
—Warren Miller, 1915

Peary used this type in his Arctic work because one or two walrus oil fires á la blubber-and-wick sufficed to keep the tent within reasonable temperatures below zero.
—Warren H. Miller, 1918

MINER'S AND CANOE TENTS

[A] pyramid or miner's tent, [may be made] both with and without walls. This is a one-pole tent, or can be conveniently put up by equipping it with a stout manila rope, sewed at the apex. This rope

MINER'S TENT

—Warren H. Miller, 1918

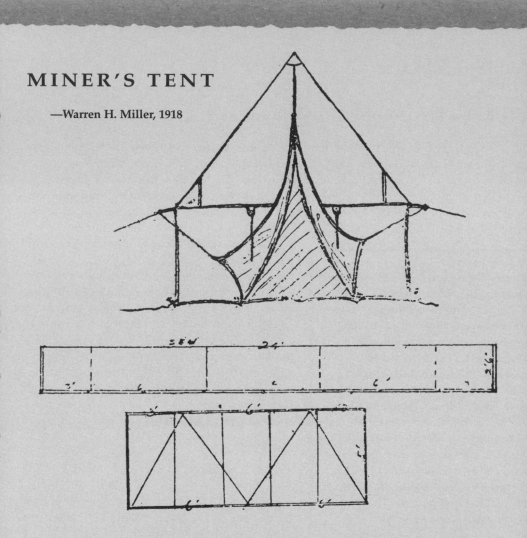

may be thrown over a convenient limb, or fastened to a tripod of poles erected on the outside. It is a very satisfactory two-man tent (7 x 7) or a four-man tent (9 x 9). It is light, easily set up, and roomy. A clothes hanger can conveniently be dropped from the apex inside, upon which wearing apparel can be hung at night.
—Frank H. Cheley, 1933

The canoe-tent is of much the same shape and uses a front pole with its rear corners guyed to high stakes. Its front pegs out round, but enough of the entrance flap can be thrown back to admit the fire heat-rays. Smallest size, 6 feet 6 inches by 4 feet 9 inches, floor area, with 2-foot back wall, weight, 6 1/2 pounds. It requires no front guy, as does the automobile type, because the pegs taking the front slope of the tent produce the necessary forward strain to counteract the rear guys. It takes 16 pegs.
—Warren H. Miller 1915

TENT SPECIFICS—
Open Tents

And now I wish to devote some space to one of the most important adjuncts of woodcraft, i.e., camps: . . . There are camps, and camps. There are camps in the North Woods that are really fine villas, costing thousands of dollars, and there are log houses, and shanties, and bark camps, and A tents, and walled tents, shelter tents and shanty tents. But, I assume that the camp best fitted to the wants of the average outer is the one that combines the essentials of dryness, lightness, portability, cheapness, and is easily and quickly put up. Another essential is, that it must admit of a bright fire in front by night or day.
—**Nessmuk, 1920**

On the whole, for all kinds of weather, the shanty-tent is perhaps the best style of camp to be had at equal expense and trouble . . . it is the best form of close-side tent I have found. It admits of a bright fire in front, without which a forest camp is just no camp at all to me. I have suffered enough in close, dark, cheerless, damp tents. . . . The worst ones are the A and wall tents, with all closed camps in which one is required to seclude himself through the hours of sleep in damp and darkness, utterly cut off from the cheerful, healthful light and warmth of the camp-fire.
—**Nessmuk, 1920**

CAMPFIRE DESIGNS

For such is the open-camp tent. Not a bivouac, but a forest home. Not a cold, chill canvas box into which you retire, to creep into an icy mountain of blankets, which you will be hours warming up, but rather—far rather—a bright, cozy retreat, with the warmth of the camp-fire penetrating to its farthest recesses; a place of jollity and good fellowship; a place where you can dream over the fire flames in comfort. To me the open tent with the backlog fire is the acme of forest life.
—**Warren Miller, 1915**

The "Camp Fire " or "Dan Beard " tent is practically a wall-tent with one side sheared off about 2 feet beyond the ridge. The place of this side is then taken by a veranda flap, which can be closed down or else guyed out horizontally, permitting an open camp-fire in front. It has the advantage of plenty of headroom, besides being rain-proof. It is put up with two pairs of shears, ridge pole, and high stakes for the wall guys. The smallest size made is 6 1/2 feet by 4 1/4 feet, weight 5 1/2 pounds. A larger size is 8 feet by 6 1/2 feet, weight 10 pounds.
—**Warren Miller, 1915**

For a hunting party of four men, I should consider a 7 x 9 Baker Shelter-tent, weighing 12 pounds in balloon silk, to be a good investment. It has become standard for north woods and Canada hunting and fishing parties.

Even though drafty, cold, hard to put up, hard to keep insects out of without a bulky roll of bobbinet big enough to cover the entire front, it has much to be said for it. Its front veranda makes a night fire in front a long-distance proposition, and to trench it properly is not an easy matter on the average wilderness camp site; yet, with these known ailments, it has the undeniable advantages of quickly and easily sheltering four men and their duffel, with headroom enough to stand up in or sit down in on camp-chairs (if you insist on that kind of comfort); it does reflect the camp-fire heat-rays, and if it rains you can rig out the front fly and have a comfortable sort of porch to lounge under. In a snow-storm unless some one keeps the snow from accumulating, it will soon get you into a variety of troubles, due to the weight of the snow on the roof.
—**Warren Miller, 1915**

[T]he Amazon tent, which is a great favorite, [looks and pitches just like a Mason campfire]. The extra front makes a capital lounging place or mess tent for a small party, and will serve nicely, when properly adjusted, to throw heat from a small outside fire into the inside of the tent. It is easily pitched, is roomy, and is very generally used for camps that are moved every few days. It differs from the lean-to, light-pack tents, by being larger, with a complete front wall in the form of tightly fitting flaps.

It is a good idea to have the protruding fly made separate, and a row of brass grommets put in along both ends and the ridge of the tent, as well as one side and one end of the fly, in order that it may be conveniently laced into position as a fly, or as a wind-break at either end, to better facilitate warming the interior from the night fire.
—**Frank H. Cheley, 1933**

The Forester Tent

[T]he sportsmen's tents [are] used especially for canoe trips, automobile trips, hiking trips, and pack trips. For these purposes, any of them are probably superior to the wall tent. They are easily pitched on poles that can be cut in any thicket, or even pitched with ropes tied to trees, and have the advantage of making possible an all-night fire, the canvas backs catching the heat rays and reflecting them upon the sleeping occupants. They should always be made with generous sod cloth, and as thoroughly fire-proofed as it is possible to make canvas. They are so simply made that every camper should own one and keep it in readiness for short trips. Made from the lighter fabrics, the weight can be reduced to a very small figure.
—**Frank H. Cheley, 1933**

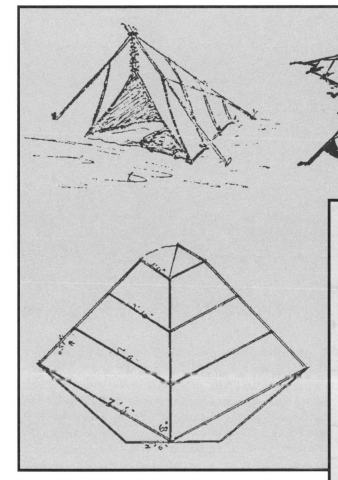

THE FORESTER

The Forester is the lightest and warmest of them all. I designed it ten years ago as a protest against the draftiness and lack of coziness of the sheet lean-to. I wanted something in which all the walls of the tent would reflect the fire heat-rays down on the occupant.
—**Warren Miller, 1915**

To put up the Forester requires 8 pegs and 3 poles—a ridge-pole and a pair of shears. The ridge should be about 12 feet long and reasonably straight, the shears 10 feet and as crooked as you please. I never saw yet, in the U. S. A., a country where these 3 poles could not be had in any thicket in five minutes, and I have been camping steadily in the original Forester for over

FORESTER/VREELAND

The old chief [Dan Beard] and the writer once camped out in a villainous Nor'easter that filled the woods with wetness for a week. Did we close the flap and shiver in gloom inside? We did not. We spent the entire week before an imperishable Nessmuk fire, sitting in our shanty-tent in a continuous orgy of poker playing, cooking and eating, varied only by periodic clubbings of a hound that would try to purloin our ham.
—Warren H. Miller, 1918

Among the special forms of light camping-tents [that] may be mentioned [are] the canoe-tent with ridge-pole, the Vreeland tent, and the Camp Fire tent. The ridge type of canoe-tent is, in effect, an extension of the old style, the addition consisting of about a yard of material running up to a ridge instead of a peak. This ridge is held up by a short club by means of tapes, and a pair of shears is put up over the tent, with a short rope to hold up the ridge. The forward strain of the front face of the canoe-tent and the rear strain of its rear guy-ropes react on the club and shears to form a triangular strain which holds the tent up. It has somewhat more available space than the older form and considerably more headroom. It is made in sizes from 6 1/2 feet by 4 1/4 feet up to 8 feet by 6 1/2 feet, with weights from 6 1/2 to 10 pounds. Sizes do not include circular ends.

Vreeland's tent is developed evidently from the Nessmuk shanty-tent. It is made in one size, 8 feet deep by 6 feet wide; height in front 6 feet, back 2 feet. It will sleep three men easily. It uses a ridge-pole and pair of shears, and the sides are guyed out by ropes, making the side walls very steep.
—**Warren Miller, 1915**

I have devoted this much space to the Forester because any one can make it of ordinary department store 8-ounce duck, sewed up on a domestic sewing machine, and get a service-able, strong, weatherproof tent, weighing 6 pounds with the hood and covering a triangular floor space 7 feet 8 inches on a side. It takes 13 yards of canvas, and the angles are tan. 15 and tan. 8 for peak and foot. The height at the ridge and shears should not exceed 5 feet 6 inches when set up. I gave this tent to the outdoor fraternity over nine years ago. It is free to all, and I have no financial interest what-ever in any of the various makers who are now selling it—in fact, only one of them has been man enough to even credit me with being its designer.

While it is true that an astonishing variety of tent forms can be made of a single rectangular sheet of canvas, say 8 by 16, and provided with suitable rings at strategic points, it is also true that the strains in a tent run up the lines of the folds from the tent pegs to the point of support. As canvas stretches more across the bias than up and down the weave, such a tent will neither take nor hold its true shape unless the lines of strain are reinforced with gores and bolt-ropes, or, in very light material, strong tape. Remember that each wall or slope of your tent must hang or draw from some stout fixed edge, such as a hem or a seam or a rope, along which the strain that holds the tent in shape must travel. Any attempt to make this stress travel through the weave of the canvas itself will result in an almost indistinguishable edge and a weak and formless tent.

—Warren H. Miller, 1918

nine years. The ridgepole passes down inside the tent and out through a small hole in the rear peak. You thrust this end into the ground and rest the other in the shears, peg out the sides, and the tent is up. Time, ten minutes. Some of the outfitters furnish it with tapes so that the ridge-pole can go outside. I do not fancy this as it destroys the stanchness and rigidity of the tent; there is nothing to tie your mosquito-veil to inside and no way to spread the tent inside in case two men are using it. In case I have a guest, I cut a hickory switch a yard long and slip it under the ridge-pole, and then turn it at right angles so that it will make a spreader, up about where your head will come. So arranged, there will be plenty of room for two sleeping-bags. The mosquito-bar is a 3-foot triangular piece of bobbinet with a canvas edge along each side. It weighs 4 ounces and takes up about as much room as a sock. I fasten the peak of this on each side of the ridgepole, about 4 feet from the rear peak, and peg down the canvas edges so that they fit snugly along the tent walls. The bobbinet has a gore let in the center so that there is plenty of freedom to lift it up and then tuck it around the sleeping-bags after you are inside. Many's the night I have dozed off to sleep with a howling chorus of insects buzzing around just out of reach of vulnerable points of attack, with that little bobbinet triangle all that intervened between peace and misery! With the ridge-pole outside it would puzzle you some to work this scheme.

Attached to the front edges of the Forester is a hood which can be laced up at night. It does not entirely close in the front of the tent, as there is still a low opening for the fire heat to strike in, but

it does prevent rain driving in and saves you turning the tent around or cutting leafy branches to prevent a driving storm reaching you, as I often did before the hood was thought out. It also holds the heat in the tent where formerly a steady flow of heat went out along the ridge. Some of the manufacturers have added a sod-cloth. Why have this extra weight, bulk, and fussiness? Surely it's no trouble to bank up a few leaves or pine-needles along the sides after pegging down, not forgetting to throw on a branch or two to keep them from blowing away. Never carry anything into the woods that you can easily make with the materials ready to hand.
—**Warren Miller, 1915**

The logical outcome of all this is that, for the most roomy and light forms of tents, a rectangle of canvas will not do. It is better to choose the style that suits you best, decide on the size which fits you and your chums, and make a real tent.
—**Warren H. Miller, 1918**

For a summer camp, however, I have finally come to prefer the simple lean-to or shed roof. It is the lightest, simplest and cheapest of all cloth devices for camping out, and I have found it sufficient for all weathers from June until the fall of the leaves. It is only a sheet of strong cotton cloth 9 x 7 feet, and soaked in lime and alum-water as the other. The only labor in making it is sewing two breadths of sheeting together. It needs no hemming, binding, loops or buttons, but is to be stretched on a frame as described for the brush shanty, and held in place with tacks. The one I have used for two seasons cost sixty cents, and weighs 2 1/4 pounds. It makes a good shelter for a party of three; and if it be found a little too breezy for cool nights, a sufficient windbreak can be made by driving light stakes at the sides and weaving in a siding of hemlock boughs.
—**Nessmuk, 1920**

TARPS

Often, however, you will not need to burden yourself with even as light a tent as I have described. This is especially true on horseback trips in the mountains. There you will carry a tarpaulin. This is a strip of canvas or pantasote 6 x 16 or 17 feet. During the daytime it is folded and used to protect the top packs from dust, wet, and abrasion. At night you spread it, make your bed on one half of it, and fold the other half over the outside. This arrangement will fend quite a shower. In case of continued or heavy rain, you stretch a pack rope

between two trees or crossed poles, and suspend the tarp over it tent wise, tying down the corners by means of lead ropes. Two tarps make a commodious tent. If you happen to be alone, a saddle blanket will supplement the tarp to give some sort of protection to your feet, and, provided it is stretched tightly, will shed quite a downpour.

A well-designed and constructed tent will serve you well.

The tarp, as I have said, should measure 6 x 16. If of canvas, do not get it too heavy, as then it will be stiff and hard to handle. About 10-ounce duck is the proper thing. After you have bought it, lay it out on the floor folded once, as it will be when you have made your bed in it. To the lower half and on both edges, as it lies there, sew a half dozen snap hooks. To the upper canvas, but about six inches in from the edge, sew corresponding rings for the snap hooks. Thus on a cold night you can bundle yourself in without leaving cracks along the edges to admit the chilly air.
—*Camp and Trail*, 1920

CHOOSING A TENT

Outdoor life calls for a shelter of some kind and the canvas tent is the thing to use for all ordinary hunting, prospecting, fishing and trapping trips, lasting for a few days to a month; . . . for a greater length of time I advise the use of a log cabin. This for the North, but for the trapper and outer of the central, western, and southern states, a good tent with a sheet iron camp stove will make a good home for the entire season.
—**E. Kreps, 1910**

As a rule, not more than four persons should occupy one tent. Two in a tent will get along better; for camp life is very intimate in any case.
—**Horace Kephart, 1916**

THE VERSATILE TARP SHELTER

Listed here are eight methods for pitching a tarp. A 10 x 10-foot tarp is roomy yet small enough to easily pack away. Reinforce the edges with strong webbing or sew a cord into a hemmed edge. Loops or grommets can be added to the edges and field of the tarp, or small pebbles can be tied as shown. Cut a piece of paper into a square and try the variety of forms shown below.

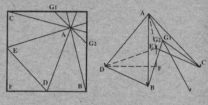

- Tipi—For a tent 6 1/2 feet high with a 5 x 7-foot base peg, down B, C, D, and E into a square base. Raise A as high as possible either with a pole or suspend from a tree branch. Pull G-1 and G-2 together and attach a guy line. Then fold D, E, and F inside to form a partial floor.

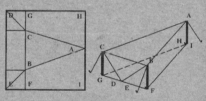

- Mountain Pod—Attach point A to a tree or suspend on a 5-foot pole. Pull out points B and C and suspend on 2 1/2 foot poles. Stake points F and G at the base of the poles, and stake point H or I at the base of the A pole. If guylines are used, pull point A straight out front, and pull points B and C out at 45-degree angles to the back wall. Pull points D and E to the middle of the rear wall and stake them tightly.

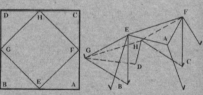

- Adirondack—Either attach points E and F from a line strung between trees or support them on 5-foot poles. If using poles, guy the sides out at a 90-degree angle and connect a guy line at A and attach loosely. Pull out points G and H and stake out so the roof is taut. Attach points B and C to the base of their nearest poles.

- Forester—This is one of the most popular tent designs. It pitches similarly to the tipi but has a larger floor area and sloping roofline. The height of the pole establishes the profile of the shelter. Use a long pole in summer and a shorter pole in winter. Moving point A back along the ridgeline provides more material for a lower door as well. When suspending the tarp from a tree, a single rope can be run from point A to D to add support.

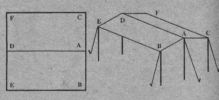

- Dining Fly—Use six poles, four of one length and two of another length. Stakes and guys must be securely attached as this shelter is susceptible to wind gusts. Guys should have toggles or taut-line hitches to keep the shelter adjusted. Guys should be long enough to pull out from the shelter at 45 degrees from the point of attachment to the ground.

THE VERSATILE TARP SHELTER
(Continued)

- Wind Shed—This can be set up with four poles, but is much more stable with two upright poles and one ridgepole. Points C and D are moved farther forward and the poles at A and B are removed and the guys pulled out farther. Also, shears can be lashed to replace the C and D poles, making the whole shelter very stable.

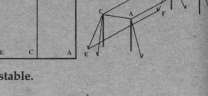

- Diamond Fly—Tie a rope to a tree at point B and stake it to the ground at point C. The wedge is tied at B and C along the rope, staked at points A and D, creating a simple, stable, and dry shelter.

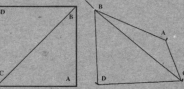

- A-Frame—Throw the tarp over a ridge created by poles or a rope. Points A, B, C, and D are either staked out or guyed for a taller shelter. Guys should have toggles or taut-line hitches to keep the shelter adjusted. An A-frame can also be lain on its side to make a lean-to tent with a floor.

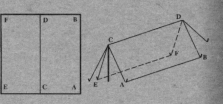

POINTS TO CONSIDER
during the seasons you will be camping:
- Is firewood readily available and allowable for use?
- How many poles and stakes are required for setup?
- How much will the tent weigh if it gets wet or frozen?
- Do you have room to thoroughly dry the tent before storing it?
- How many people will be staying in the tent?

Back to basics never sounded so good. It is futile to promote the virtues of the high-tech method of camping to a group of guests who have just exited a modern bivy snow pit with the best nylon shelter cover and its ultimate mate, the lightweight gas stove, cranked to the max. The stove generates just enough heat to boil water and take the edge off of the 44-below temperature flooding through the fabric, keeping everyone in a comfortably frigid condition. The team exits the cold camp and crawls into a traditional native shelter, the quinzee—a shelter common to low-snow conditions above and below treeline. The dome of metamorphosed snow captures a bubble of air that is easily generated by candles, and on severely cold days with adequate ventilation, a gas stove can bring it to positively balmy conditions—classic melding of traditional and modern technologies.

An open shelter with a simple lean-to and back-fire setup is next. The fire is huge by today's comparisons, and cold is constantly held at bay by the roaring fire. To stay warm, it's a constant contest to locate just the right distance from the fire and outwit one's shelter mate by claiming the spot that provides the best heat with the least smoke invasion. Traditional and democratic in design and access, such a setup creates potentially high-fire impact without equal return on effort and desire for comfort. With apologies to Nessmuk and Bill Mason, the open-shelter tent maintains the romance of the woods but lacks many of the requisite characteristics needed for a shelter set against the cold.

It is a short distance to a small thicket that provides adequate fuel and break from the wind. Just beyond is a tent. Its soft glow and gently rising chimney smoke say "home." Inside is a camper's paradise. Dinner is simmering on the small stove while the team sips warm drinks (meals can be prepared more than one course at a time). The gear worn all day is hung from a clothesline along the ridgeline and is quickly dried in the radiating heat. Candles placed in strategic locations light the entire lodge, and soft beds allow the team to lounge and read or talk about the day. When it's time for bed, they undress in the warmth, standing up, and slipping into beds that are already pre-warmed.

A supply of wood is stacked next to the stove so that a few sticks at a time can be added to the night logs. Sleep comes easily and rest is assured. Only camping in the old style can provide this.

For a nomadic moving camp, or one reached by canoe or pack tramp, the style of tent changes. You want something light—not over 5 pounds for a capacity of two or three men, and if there are six in the party, take two tents. These can be had in closed and open types, 7 x 7 feet and 9 x 7 feet being the popular sizes. Weights run from 3 to 11 pounds in modern tent textiles.
—Warren Miller, 1915

TRADITIONAL OR HOT-TENT CAMPING

When the night is clear and breezy, campers can sleep in the open air. Things such as pests and unpleasant weather force the camper to seek shelter. If the night is punctuated by the constant buzz and bite of unwanted guests at the hearth, the use of smudges, dopes, and nets help keep them at bay. How the screen is suspended or enclosure created still leaves room for a variety of shelter options. The camper's choice can be allowed a wide margin for personal preference and regional style.

Wind and rain narrow this margin by requiring more specific geometry and design in response to cold and wet conditions. In this case, the open shelter exposes far too much canvas to wind gusts and swirling smoke to justify its rustic charm. Even though the wedge has broad flat sides, the pitch of its walls sheds weather—as proven by its appearance in countless early high-altitude expedition photos. Its drawback is that it creates limited living space for the design, and living hunched over to avoid contact with the walls for days on end can be annoying and difficult.

If shedding weather is the goal, the steep-pitched roof is best suited. And if creating heat from wood fuel with limited resources while creating minimal environmental impact from harvesting fuel and creating waste, the closed stove has no peer. Whereas, if capturing heat is the goal, the benefit created by a closed structure is unmatched. To maximize living space and headroom while limiting weight, the short side wall must be included. And if ease in the ability to pitch, strike, and maintain tension while in use is a common characteristic of dependable tents, the camper needs to look carefully at a much more limited set of options.

TENT CARE AND USE

There are a number of things that every camper should know about the care of a pitched tent.
—**Frank H. Cheley, 1933**

And I do dearly love to face the tent to the northeast where the rising sun can stream in and warm me—lazy devil—before finally turning out for the day. It also brings the tent doorstep in cool shade during the sweltering 4 o'clock sun of the afternoon.
—**Warren H. Miller, 1918**

TIPS FOR TENT DWELLERS

CARING FOR A TENT—90 PERCENT OF A TENT'S LIFE IS SPENT IN STORAGE
- Dry the tent thoroughly prior to storing.
- Pitch and strike the tent using a tarp to protect the cover from getting soiled.
- Clean all dirt and debris from the tent after each use.
- Keep the tent mended and hardware repaired, and guy-lines in good shape.
- All ropes should be whipped and/or spliced, kept clean, and securely attached.

- Untie all knots that are not permanent after every use.
- Roll or fold the tent with the roof to inside for protection.
- Transport and store the tent in a sturdy bag.
- Keep extra lines and stakes in the tent bag as needed.
- Store the tent in a dry, cool, well-ventilated area free from bugs and rodents.

PITCHING A TENT—GENERAL GUIDELINES
- When properly set, you shouldbe able to bounce a quarter off of the tent cover.
- Avoid setting up a camp that requires ditching. But if you must, replace soil and reclaim the site before leaving.
- Clear and smooth an adequate area.
- Carry adequate stakes and poles or improvise from local dead materials.
- Use toggles or taut-line hitches on all lines to keep them adjustable.

- Set all anchors so that in a wind gust they fail before the tent tears.
- Set stakes at the proper pitch and angle to hold the tent taut and secure. Use deadmen anchors on soft campsites (for example, sand and snow).
- Pull out and stake all lines at 45 degree angles to all directions of pull. That is, lines from the tent should be long enough to form a 45 degree angle with the ground; at corners lines should be pulled out at 45 degrees to each side.

LIVING IN A TENT—GENERAL GUIDELINES
- Periodically lift the skirt and allow the sod cloth to dry out.
- Keep extra lines available for quick rigging of a storm set.
- Canvas shrinks and slackens with the weather. Keep all lines adjustable with toggles or taut-line hitches.
- There is a very fine line between a well-set tent and one that is too tight. Practice.

- You don't "put up" a tent, you pitch it—and you don't "take down" a tent, you strike it.
- Keep the base of the tent free of leaves and dirt. They will create rot and leaking.
- Suspend all open-flame light sources well away from walls and ceiling.
- Provide a doormat for guests and tenants to clean their feet before entering.
- Keep a broom near the door and use it regularly.

WATERPROOFING RECIPES

Rain invariably tightens a tent to a marked degree, especially if it is equipped with long guy ropes. Unless it is closely watched and loosened before a storm, very often the shrink of the rope will pull the eyes completely out of the tent, unless by chance some weak seam goes first. Keep your ropes just taut and examine them frequently.
    —Frank H. Cheley, 1933

Unless your tent has been very heavily waterproofed, it will drip at every point that is touched while it is wet. These ceaseless drips are very annoying, and should be avoided as far as possible.
    —Frank H. Cheley, 1933

Water-proofing . . . the following receipt will answer very well, and add little or nothing to the weight: To 10 quarts of water add 10 ounces of lime, and 4 ounces of alum; let it stand until clear; fold the cloth snugly and put it in another vessel, pour the solution on it, let it soak for 12 hours; then rinse in luke-warm rain water, stretch and dry in the sun.
    —Nessmuk, 1920

If you care to, you may render your goods mildew, water and fire proof before you make it into a tent (or treat the completed tent afterward, just as you please), by soaking it over night in a solution made of two bucketsful of tepid rain water, in which [you] carefully dissolve three pounds of sugar of lead and three pounds of alum. In the morning, remove the tent and hang it up to drip and thoroughly dry. Never try to waterproof a tent by applying any oily compound, for it invariably rots the fibers and makes a sticky, nasty odor in extreme hot weather.
    —Frank H. Cheley, 1933

That last word brings to mind the subject of weight in tents. Many good woodcraftsmen advise against any duck less than ten-ounce, and will even speak of twelve-ounce (which is good material for boards, bed bottoms and twenty-foot army tents). It is purely a matter of the slope. A wall tent with 45-degree roof must have a fly over it to keep out a pelting rain if of eight-ounce duck, or the tent will soon be full of a fine rain mist, which wilts everything inside. In a sharp A-tent this disappears and in all steep-sloped tents eight-ounce is plenty weight enough, and even American drilling, still lighter (almost four ounce) will do. Good waterproofing, however, is necessary in all tents. The alum processes are good and leave the tent still a piece of cloth, albeit somewhat dense as regards rain. Seton and Kephart both advocate the alum-and-sugar-of-lead process. I have always used Nessmuk's lime-and-alum recipe, published by him over twenty years ago. The chemical basis of both processes is virtually the same—the formation of an insoluble double salt of calcium and alum or lead acetate and alum.

This impregnates the fibers of the canvas and stays there. The tent gains from one to two pounds in weight, depending upon its size. I give Nessmuk's directions here: To ten quarts of water add 10 ounces of lime and 4 ounces of alum; let it stand until clear; fold tent and put it in another container; pour on solution and let it soak for twelve hours. Then rinse in lukewarm rainwater, stretch and dry in the sun, and the shanty tent is ready for use.
    —Warren H. Miller, 1918

After the tent is pitched true and straight with every peg in proper place and ditched, then turn your attention to the inside and make it as convenient as possible. Have a place for everything and keep everything in its place. Stretch a stout rope from upright pole to pole to hang clothes on. A tent hall tree can easily be devised for each tent that will aid materially in keeping things in place.
—Frank H. Cheley, 1933

I pitch my shelter at an angle of about 45 degrees, facing leeward.
—E. Kreps, 1910

TENT STAKES LINES AND ANCHORS

DEADMEN

In sandy or soft ground it often taxes one's ingenuity to supply anchors for one's tent; an anchor is a weight of some sort to which the guy ropes may be attached. Fig. 296 shows a tent anchored by billets of wood; these are all supposed to be buried in the ground as in Fig. 308, and the ground trampled down over and above them to keep them safe in their graves.

Fig. 297 shows the first throw in the anchor hitch, Fig. 298 the second throw, and Fig. 299 the complete hitch for the anchor. Fig. 308 shows the knot by which the anchor rope is tied to the main line. Figs. 300, 301 and 302 show the detail of tying this knot, which is simplicity itself, when you know how, like most knots. Fig. 308 shows the anchor hitch complete

Stones, bundles of fagots, or bags of sand all make useful anchors; Fig. 304 is a stone; Fig. 305 are half billets of wood, Fig. 306 shows fagots of wood, Fig. 307 a bag of sand. All may be used to anchor your tent in the sands or loose ground.
—**Daniel Carter Beard, 1920**

Tent pegs are necessary for almost any kind of a tent; you can buy them at the outfitter's and lose them on the way to camp; they even have iron and steel tent pegs to help make camping expensive, and to scatter through the woods. But if you are a real sourdough you will cut your own tent pegs, shaped according to circumstances and individual taste. [There are] two principal kinds: the fork and the notched tent pegs.
—**Daniel Carter Beard, 1920**

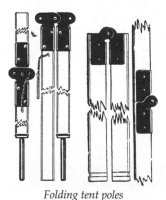

Folding tent poles

Pegs for each tent should be shipped in a stout bag. The angle iron peg is by far the most satisfactory, and costs little more than the wooden one. If you can't buy them, have a blacksmith make them for you. Fifteen inches is a good length, with the notches filed smooth, so as not to cut the guy ropes. Such stakes are wicked things to fall over, especially in bare feet or in the night. Wherever they are out in the open, a stout stake should be driven by them as a warning and protection. If they are driven flush with the ground as is often done, there is danger of rotting your guy ropes in a few seasons, and this is expensive.
—**Frank H. Cheley, 1933**

The method used in driving the pegs is of utmost importance. There is a right way and a wrong way. Sometimes pegs will not hold a tent at all because of the nature of the soil. In that event, various methods may be resorted to.
—**Frank H. Cheley, 1933**

If this is not convenient, and it isn't always, try anchoring all the ropes by placing on top of them just back of the stakes and full length of the tent a green log. This may even be further improved by anchoring the comer guy to a stout bundle of brush, or a stone.
—**Frank H. Cheley, 1933**

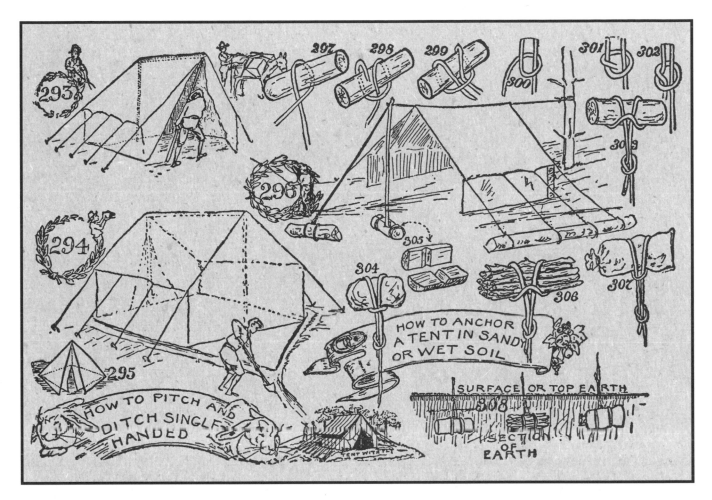

TENT POLES

For the wall tents one will need a ridge pole, and two forked sticks, or rods, to support the ridge pole; the forks on these should be snubbed off close so that they will not thrust themselves up against the canvas on the top of the tent and endanger the fabric; these poles should be of a proper height; otherwise if the poles are too long, the tent will not touch the ground at all, or if the poles are too short, the tent will wrinkle all over the ground like a fellow's trousers when his suspenders break.
—**Daniel Carter Beard, 1920**

Shears, Gins and Tripods are the names used for different forms of rustic supports for the tents. Fig. 312 (see page 83) shows the ordinary shears, Fig. 318 shows the tent supported by shears; you will also note that the guy ropes for the tent (Fig. 313) are made fast to a rod instead of to the pegs in the ground. This has many advantages, because of the tendency of the rope to tighten or shrink whenever it becomes wet, which often makes it necessary for a fellow to get up in the night to adjust the guy ropes and redrive the pegs. When the rain is pouring down, the thunder crashing and the lightning flashing, it is no fun to go poking around on the wet ground in one's nightie in order that the tent pegs may not be pulled out of the ground by the shrinking ropes, and the cold mass of wet canvas allowed to fall upon one's head. It is always necessary to loosen and tighten the guy ropes according to the weather; naturally the longer the guy ropes are the more they will shrink and the more they will stretch as the weather varies. To prevent this, lay a rod over the ends of the guy rope between the pegs

and the tent (Fig. 316A) and it will be an automatic adjuster. When the ropes are dry and stretch, the weight of this pole will hold them down and keep them taut; when the guy ropes shrink they will lift the pole, but the latter will keep the tension on the ropes and keep them adjusted.

The arrangement of Fig. 313 has the advantage of making a clothes rack for your bed clothes when you wish to air them, while the weight of the suspended log keeps the tension on the ropes equalized. Fig. 314 shows the shears made by the use of forked sticks. Figs. 315 and 318 show the ridge pole supported by shears, and the ridge poles supported by forked sticks; the advantage of the shears in Fig. 315 is that it gives a clear opening to the tent. Fig. 316 shows an exterior ridge pole supported by shears to which the top of the tent is made fast. Fig. 317 is the same without the tent. Fig. 318 shows the famous Vreeland tent; in this case the ridge pole is supported by a crotched upright stick, but may be equally well supported by the shears as in Fig. 315. Fig. 319 shows the gin or tripod made by binding the three sticks together. Fig. 320 shows the same effect made by the use of the forked sticks; these are useful in pitching wigwams or tepees.
—**Daniel Carter Beard, 1920**

HOW TO PITCH AND DITCH SINGLE-HANDEDLY

There is a right and a wrong way to pitch a wall tent, as well as an easy and a hard way. Learn to do it right the first time, and forever afterward it will be an easy, simple task.
—**Frank H. Cheley, 1933**

Spread out your tent all ready to erect, put your ridge pole and your two uprights in place, and then drive some tent stakes, using the flat of your axe with which to drive them, so that you will not split the tops of the stakes; drive the two end stakes A and B at an angle to the ends of the tent. After the tent stakes are arranged in a row, adjust the forks of the uprights two inches from the ends of the ridge pole, then make fast the two extreme end guy ropes A and B to the tent pegs; the others are unimportant for the present; after that is done, raise one tent pole part of the way up, then push the other part of the way up; gradually adjust these things until the strain is even upon your guy ropes. You will now find that your tent will stand alone, because the weight is pulling against your guy ropes. This will hold your tent steady until you can make fast the guy ropes to the pegs upon the other side, not too tightly, because you need slack to straighten up your tent poles.

Next see that the back guy pole is perpendicular, after which it is a very easy matter to straighten up the front pole and adjust the guy rope so that it will stand stiff as in Fig. 293 (page 81).

Remember, when you are cutting the ridge poles and the uprights, to select fairly straight sticks, and they should be as free as possible from rough projections, which might injure the canvas; also the poles should be as stiff as possible so as not to sag or cause the roof to belly.

—Daniel Carter Beard, 1920

CAMPSITE SELECTION

If you can locate where there is a safe and attractive place for swimming and boating, so much the better, but be very sure of the safety element. If not, you should seek something to take their place, such as hiking and mountain climbing, and above all, abundant opportunity to study nature in your own way. Go where the wild flowers riot in the meadows, bogs, and on hillsides; go where the wild birds live, and sing, and rear their young. Go where there are patches, at least, of "forest primeval," with the "murmuring pines and the hemlock." Go where shy wood-folk peep out of alder thickets, or around rotting stumps, or from carefully concealed tree homes; for unless your camping-out tremendously enlarges your wild-wood acquaintance, it has not been a real success—was not in the proper place. . . .

If you can remember these things, you will find camping out the biggest thing in your life, and you will return home each time with a body strong and more healthy, with a mind enriched, with an imagination immeasurably stimulated, and life enlarged. What more can you rightfully expect from any experience?

—Frank H. Cheley, 1933

CHOOSING A CAMPSITE

In selecting a good camp ground, the first thing is a dry, level place near good wood and good water. If you have horses or oxen, you must also have grass.

Almost all Indian camps face the east, and, when ideal, have some storm-break or shelter on the west and north. Then they get the morning sun and the afternoon shade in summer, and in winter avoid the coldest winds and drifting snows, which in most of the country east of the Rockies come from the north and west.

DITCHING

Just as soon as your tent is erected and you feel like resting, get busy on ditching; no matter how dry the weather may be at the time, put a ditch around the tent that will drain the water away from your living place. There is no positive rule for digging this ditch; it varies according to surface of ground, but the gutter should be so made that the water will run away from the tents and not to it, or stand around it (Fig. 294 on page 81).

—Daniel Carter Beard, 1920

NEW GUIDELINES
Ditching, just like fire building is no longer a welcome practice in the modern ethic—not because it has no value, but because it was improperly used for so many years by irresponsible users. If you must ditch, clean up after yourself and completely reclaim the site. No excuses!

APPRENTICE CAMPER
- Learn to locate a suitable site for the number of people camping.
- Show good conservation and safety techniques in selection of campsites.
- Consider all the functions you will need and set up a site to take best advantage.

JOURNEYMAN CAMPER
- Demonstrate complete knowledge of campsite selection requirements.
- List local/seasonal techniques for minimizing impacts for group and personal camping.
- Discuss techniques needed to minimize impacts from kitchen, fire, and sanitation setups.

JOURNEYMAN WOODSMAN
- Demonstrate skills needed to stabilize a fragile site or rehabilitate a damaged site.
- Conduct postseason service work on commonly used campsites.
- Rotate or modify use in areas showing obvious impacts.

MASTER WOODSMAN
- In some established or outpost sites it is best to use the same fire-scar, wastewater, and latrine sites all season. In such cases, leave them intact until the last use. Justify your decisions.
- Assess campsites and areas of use to determine proper techniques to be used for minimum environmental impact. Become a steward of your territory.

Sometimes local conditions make a different exposure desirable, but not often. For obvious reasons, it is well to be near one's boat-landing.
—**Ernest Thompson Seton, 1912,** *Book of Woodcraft*

Remember to choose the best camp site that can be found; do not travel all day, and as night comes on stop at any old place; but in the afternoon keep your eyes open for likely spots. . . . Halt early enough to give time to have everything snug and in order before dark.
—**Daniel Carter Beard, 1920**

Roughing it does not by any means demand that you ignore common sense. Primarily, you camp in order to enjoy "the pure air, the bracing and lung-healing power of the woods, the sun bath, its tonic exercise, the nerve rest, and the joy that comes from control of mind and body." Consequently you should avoid, in choosing the camp site, anything that would tend to neutralize these benefits.

There are a few absolute fundamentals that should always be considered, and in addition a larger number of desirable conditions, as many as possible of which should be sought, for each one adds its bit in its own way to the joy and worthwhileness of the experience. . . .

The go-light camper should invariably begin two hours before sundown to locate a suitable high and dry location on which to spend the night. In fact, the good woodsman is always on the

lookout for an ideal spot. Better lose an hour's time by stopping too soon, than to lose a night's rest by being caught in a storm in a bad location.
—**Frank H. Cheley, 1933**

First among the absolute essentials is a desirable place to pitch your tents. High, dry ground is of paramount importance, with careful consideration given to natural drainage. Wet, or even damp beds, muggy clothing, and mildew in camp belong only to tenderfeet, and are responsible for all sorts of colds, sore throat, rheumatism and the like. Then, too, summer storms are often very sudden in their origin and severe in their nature. Select a spot, therefore, that can never "drown out," no matter if it should rain all summer.
—**Frank H. Cheley, 1933**

Unless you plan to bring beds of some description into camp, it will be very necessary for you to locate where there is an abundance of wild wood material with which to make beds. If you are going to build browse beds, there should be large numbers of reasonably young trees handy. Only the lower limbs of these should be cut, and always with a sharp ax, and with the greatest care.
—**Frank H. Cheley, 1933**

THE FOUR W'S—
Wind, Wood, Water, and Widowmakers

Having decided to respond to the insistent call of the wild, and having gotten ready "so far as lieth in you," and having determined by the simple process of elimination the type and the approxi mate geographical location of your outing, the next logical thing to determine is the exact spot, if it is to be a permanent camp. If not, to carefully consider the important points of any good camp site, coming to understand them so well that you can apply them quickly and with wise judgment to any

number of locations that may come under consideration, for, in the long run, much of the lasting benefits of your camps will depend on how well you have chosen the spot.

There are a good many things about camping that are mostly good, but, on the other hand, there are also some dangers that should be carefully avoided. These have quite as much to do with where you camp as how you camp.
—**Frank H. Cheley, 1933**

WOOD

Fuel supply, also, is an important matter to consider in locating your camp. It is surprising how much wood it takes to supply a camp, even with reasonable economy. Of course, the go-light camper, the hiker, the packer and the like have very little difficulty with fuel, for their wants are simple.
—**Frank H. Cheley, 1933**

Squaw-wood, if there is no other kind, will keep them supplied, but before a permanent or even a long-term camp is finally located, the matter of quantity, quality, and accessibility of fuel should be looked into carefully.
—**Frank H. Cheley, 1933**

In this connection, it is well to know what sorts of wood, native to your section, are most satisfactory for cooking and night fire. Generally speaking, the various sorts of hard wood burn more slowly and give a more satisfactory bed of hot coals for cooking. For a quick, hot fire the soft woods will be better.
—**Frank H. Cheley, 1933**

The mere fact that there are quantities of trees near by with ëkinds" of down-wood does not signify that it is desirable camp fuel. You must have wood that burns well.
—**Frank H. Cheley, 1933**

Many family camps have found it an economy to purchase hardwood from a near-by farmer, rather than to cut the standing timber if this is the only kind accessible. . . . On Government Forest Reserves it is absolutely against the law to cut living trees without permission.
—**Frank H. Cheley, 1933**

WIDOWMAKERS

When choosing a camp site, if possible, choose a forest or grove of young trees. First, because of the shade they give you; secondly, because they protect you from storms, and thirdly, because they protect you from lightning.

Single trees, or small groups of trees in open pastures are exceedingly dangerous during a thunder storm; tall trees on the shores of a river or lake are particularly selected as targets for thunder bolts by the storm king. But the safest place in a thunder storm, next to a house, is a forest. The reason of this is

that each wet tree is a lightning rod silently conducting the electric fluid without causing explosions. Do not camp at the foot of a very tall tree, or an old tree with dead branches on it, for a high wind may break off the branches and drop them on your head with disastrous results; the big tree itself may fall even when there is no wind at all.

Once I pitched my camp near an immense tree on the Flathead Indian Reservation. A few days later we returned to our old camp. As we stopped and looked at the site where our tents had been pitched we looked at each other solemnly, but said nothing, for there, prone upon the ground, lay that giant veteran tree!

But young trees do not fall down, and if they did they could not create the havoc caused by the immense bole of the patriarch of the forest when it comes crashing to the earth. A good

scout must "Be Prepared," and to do so must remember that safety comes first, and too close neighborhood to a big tree is often unsafe.
—**Daniel Carter Beard, 1920**

See that the ground is comparatively level, but with a slant in one direction or another so that water will drain off in case of rain. Never, for instance, pitch your tent in a hollow or basin of ground, unless you want to wake up some night slopping around in a pool of water. Do not pitch your tent near a standing dead tree; it is liable to fall over and crush you in the night. Avoid camping under green trees with heavy dead branches on them. Remember the real camper always has an eye to safety first, not because he is a coward, but because the real camper is as brave a person as you will find anywhere, and no real brave person believes in the carelessness which produces accidents. Do not pitch your tent over protruding stones which will make stumbling-blocks for you on which to stub your toes at night, or torture you when you spread your blankets over them to sleep. Use common sense, use gumption. Of course, we all know that it hurts one's head to think, but we must all try it, nevertheless, if we are going to live in the big outdoors.
—**Daniel Carter Beard, 1920**

If the camp is small, there will be no difficulty in locating a spot where the sun strikes it a good part of the day, and the prevailing breeze gets a fair chance at it. If the camp is to be a large one, probably the best location will be a high prairie or plateau, with plenty of open ground for games and the like. Camp parties need plenty of room. If such a spot is chosen, it should be in close proximity to woods, or a considerable number of large trees. Avoid camping under old and decaying trees. They are very dangerous.

In case the tents are to be pitched in or near large trees, there are several matters that need special notice. Are the trees solid, safe, and deep-rooted in case of high wind? Keep a sharp eye out for dead limbs. In case of fire starting in the tents, could a general forest fire result, or in case of a general forest fire, would an escape be easy on short notice? I was in a camp one season where a boy narrowly escaped death from a huge falling limb, which crashed through his tent in the night, as a result of a heavy wind. I heard this past summer of a dozen boys who were compelled to break camp and pack-out in the wee hours of the morning because of an on-rushing forest fire. Both parties had chosen their camp sites without due regard to important matters.
—**Frank H. Cheley, 1933**

WATER—TOO MUCH, TOO LITTLE

In winter one does not look for water when selecting a camping place, for one can get any amount of it by melting snow. The only things to look for are shelter, wood, and evergreen boughs for a bed.
—**E. Kreps, 1910**

In selecting camping ground, look for a place where good water and wood are handy. Choose a high spot with a gentle slope if possible; guard your spring or water hole from animals, for if the day is hot your dog will run ahead of the party and jump into the middle of the spring to cool himself, and horses and cattle will befoul the water.
—**Daniel Carter Beard, 1920**

Do not depend merely on your trenching, but locate so that the nature of the soil and the "lay" of the land will care for any over-supply of water quickly and efficiently. It's no fun at all, even if you do love an adventure, to roll out at 2 A.M. in your bare feet, even in mid-summer, only to wade around in oceans of mud, trying to rescue your already drenched wardrobe. Invariably, a tackle box or two gets kicked over, or a good kodak is ruined—or something worse. "A little foresight is worth a deal of behind-sight" in forestalling such an experience.
—**Frank H. Cheley, 1933**

This matter of high ground and drainage is especially important if you are anticipating a camp on or near water, whether by a running stream or a lake—it matters little about the size. I have seen an insignificant, friendly little brook, which ordinarily ran hardly enough water to bathe in, change in a few hours of the night to a dangerous torrent, wildly reaching out for everything in its path. And I have seen a lovely camp placed too low on an inviting sand beach apparently well sheltered from all harm, completely ruined in an hour, and lives endangered, as the result of a severe on-shore storm.

Such storms invariably come when least expected, and in consequence find the camp unprepared. Avoid gullies, or dry-stream beds. Keep out in the open as far as possible, and on high, solid ground. Aside from storm danger, high, well drained ground should be sought, because such ground is always cooler, more healthful, and much freer from mosquitoes and other camp pests. In a malarial country, this is of special importance. Kephart says: "If one is obliged to camp in a malarial region, he should not leave the camp fire until the sun is up and the fog dispelled."
—**Frank H. Cheley, 1933**

Probably the second most important consideration is to locate reasonably near a sufficient supply of clear, cool drinking water. You can carry fuel some distance and enjoy the task, but when every bucket has to be toted in, the arrangement is bad, for two reasons. First, because you never have the water when you want it; and second, because if it's hard to get, you will be entirely too sparing of its use.

You cannot be too careful about your water supply. Don't take anything for granted. Investigate its source thoroughly every year before you use it.
—**Frank H. Cheley, 1933**

Go-light campers and hikers, generally speaking, will do well to carry a canteen, filling it at pumps or satisfactory springs. "When in doubt, find out," is good water wisdom.
—**Frank H. Cheley, 1933**

Major D. C. Handley, gives this bit of advice to those who camp out: "You should never drink from open streams or springs—unless it has been proved beyond a doubt that the water is pure. In case of doubt you can purify it this way in a few minutes: Take one teaspoonful of chloride of lime and dissolve it in three pints of water; this makes a stock solution. Take one teaspoonful of this stock solution and add it to every two gallons of water to be purified and allow it to stand ten minutes. It's sure death to all germs, and makes any water pure."
—**Frank H. Cheley, 1933**

WIND

A bare spot on the earth, where there are no dry leaves, is a wind-swept spot; where the dust-covered leaves lie in heaps the wind does not blow. A windy place is generally free from mosquitoes, but it is a poor place to build a fire; a small bank is a great protection from high wind and twisters. During one tornado I had a camp under the lee of a small elevation; we only lost the fly of one tent out of a camp of fifty or more, while in more exposed places nearby great trees were uprooted and houses unroofed.
—**Daniel Carter Beard, 1920**

If camping in the Western states on the shores of a shallow stream which lies along the trail, cross the stream before making camp or you may not be able to cross it for days. A chinook wind suddenly melting the snows in the distant mountains, or a cloud-burst miles and miles up stream, may suddenly send down to you a dangerous flood even in the dry season. I have known of parties being detained for days by one of these sudden roaring floods of water, which came unannounced, the great bole of mud, sticks and logs sweeping by their camp and taking with it everything in its path.
—**Daniel Carter Beard, 1920**

A belt of dense timber between camp and a pond or swamp will act as a protection from mosquitoes. As a rule, keep to windward of mosquito holes; the little insects travel with the wind, not against it.
—**Daniel Carter Beard, 1920**

SPECIAL CONSIDERATIONS

Some other desirable considerations in the choosing of a camp site that will materially add to the real joy of your outing are: Reasonable Isolation, As has been said before, you can camp anywhere with complete success, but if you can get far enough away from home to enable you to drop dull care, so much the better. New sights and sounds and smells are interesting and desirable. Get away from public roads. Steer clear, as far as is possible, of summer resorts. Get where every passing automobile cannot stop to share a meal, or sit too long by your inviting camp fire. Get away from folks. That's the half of camping. If you want to go to a picnic, go by all means, but do not call it camping.

Locate in interesting country, where there will be ample opportunity to see things worth seeing. No doubt you will be planning several all-night trips from camp, and you should be reasonably sure there is somewhere to go. It may be to famous fishing grounds for a few days' sport with the "big ones." It may be to some mountain peak, from the summit of which you can see how the world is made; or it may be to a wonderful underground cavern that sheltered some historic figure in times gone by; or to an interesting Indian village or burial ground. It may be to a sawmill, a mine, a stone quarry, a lake, a lighthouse, or some other novel place. If possible, select a camp site that can be head quarters for wide wanderings, so that you can become in a very real sense an explorer, a frontiersman, a pioneer, and thus get the very best from your outing.

—Frank H. Cheley, 1933

PREPARING

Before pitching your tent, clear out a space for it to occupy; pick up the stones, rubbish and sticks, rake-off the ground with a forked stick. But do not be rude to your brother, the ground pine; apologize for disturbing it; be gentle with the fronds of the fern; do not tear the trailing arbutus vine up by its roots, or the plant of the almond scented twin flowers; ask pardon of the thallus of the lichen which you are trampling under your feet. Why? Oh well—because they had first right to the place, and because such little civilities to the natural objects around you put your own mind in accord with nature, and make camping a much more enjoyable affair.

When you feel you are sleeping on the breast of your mother, the earth, while your father, the sky, with his millions of eyes is watching over you, and that you are surrounded by your brother, the plants, the wilderness is no longer lonesome even to the solitary traveler.

Another reason for taking this point of view is that it has a humanizing effect and tends to prevent one from becoming a wilderness Hun and vandal. It also not only makes one hesitate to hack the trees unnecessarily, but encourages the camper to take pride in leaving a clean trail. As my good friend, John Muir, said to me: "The camping trip need not be the longest and most dangerous excursion up to the highest mountain, through the deepest woods or across the wildest torrents, glaciers or deserts, in order to be a happy one; but however short or long, rough or smooth, calm or stormy, it should be one in which the able, fearless camper sees the most, learns the most, loves the most and leaves the cleanest track; whose camp grounds are never marred by anything unsightly, scarred trees or blood spots or bones of animals."
—Daniel Carter Beard, 1920

Usually old camp sites are undesirable, for health and sanitary reasons. Choose new ones wherever possible, even if it does take a bit more elbow-grease to put them into livable shape.
—Frank H. Cheley, 1933

THE TENT STOVE

Yes, sir, I'm a convert; have been for these last four years. I love a pretty, cheerful campfire, and never fail to kindle one for its light and warmth and in summer fishing camps I use one or another form of cook range campfire. But on a hunting trip in the mountains, where you get ice in the pails every night and have plenty of snow, rain and cold weather, the really practical dope is a tent stove. You can have them of any weight from 2 1/4 pounds up, collapsible and non-collapsible; the latter, as they go over your cook kit and can be used to pack things in, taking really no more actual room than the collapsible ones.
—**Warren H. Miller, 1918**

STOVE DESIGNS

BOTTOMLESS STOVES

This particular stove is simply a sheet iron oblong with cylindrical ends which slips over the two aluminum pots of the Forester cook-kit, its size being 14 inches long by 7 1/2 inches diameter by 7 inches high. The lids of the pots form the two covers of

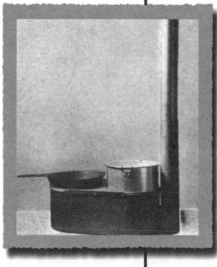

the stove, unless the pots are on duty in the stove-holes or there is a frying-pan holding down a hole on the top of the stove. Small draft-door in one side, and outtake for the stovepipe low down on the opposite side. Stovepipe is of two 20-inch lengths by 2 1/2 inches diameter. Slope of tent pyramid carries tent well away from draft. Bottom of stove is open and is to be set on a flat rock and chinked with chips of stone to keep down bottom draft. I learned this trick from an open-bottom sheet-iron stove that we used in the West.
—**Warren H. Miller, 1915**

The stove for it is of light sheet iron, in sizes 10 x 11 x 18, 10 x 11 x 25, and 10 x 12 x 32 inches. Weights run from 15 to 20 pounds. These stoves are regularly made without a bottom, being intended to be set on a

USING THE STOVE

The beauty of the camp-stove is that it runs all night. In principle it is a charcoal-making machine, with very little draft, and slow, steady combustion. You will have lots of difficulty with it on starting up for lack of sufficient draft, and the surest way to invite trouble is to fill it full of small kindlings and then touch it off, for it will at once smother itself because there is not enough air to support the flames. But go at it gradually, until you have a bed of live coals, and then you have an excellent fire for slow cooking, roasting, and baking, and you can feed it short logs ad lib., with no necessity to be forever rustling small fuel as with the open campfire. At night fill the stove up with logs. The lower ones resting on the bed of live coals burn as fast as the limited draft of air will permit, while all the rest turn to charcoal and burn slowly in their turn. As this is a process of hours, the stove gives a steady heat all night, and is in fine shape for bacon and coffee and flapjacks in the morning.
—**Warren H. Miller, 1915**

stone hearth and to fold for transportation into a flat parcel. With them is furnished a telescopic pipe of five 2-foot lengths of sheet-iron pipe, the weight of which is included in the totals given above. It is essential to have a spark-arrester with it, for the sparks from a camp-stove are tiny hot embers, and will surely burn holes in the tent when they descend.
—**Warren H. Miller, 1915**

FOLDING STOVES

There are many excellent camp stoves on the market, and if one is using a tent in winter he should have a good stove, as it will be necessary to keep a fire continually. Some of these stoves fold up into a small package and at first thought one would be inclined to select one of that style, but it is well to know that the folding stove has some faults. When new they work perfectly, but after they have been used some time they become warped by the heat, and if taken apart it will be found to be difficult and sometimes impossible to put them together again.
—**E. Kreps, 1910**

NONFOLDING STOVES

Our Montana stove was non-collapsible sheet iron, with an oven in it, which is a tremendous convenience—a real necessity, when you have four hunters to feed. . . . [T]he box stove makes a kind of trunk to hold all the kitchenware and part of your grub; it is rather an unwieldy shape, except on a canoe trip, where it would make a fine center parcel . . .
—**Warren H. Miller, 1918**

For permanent camps with board floors to the tents all the outfitting firms make a portable camp stove with legs and bottom, the whole outfit, including oven, hot water tank, pans and utensils to fit the stove, being packable inside the stove, so the whole works can be put in your big camp chest. These are a great convenience to the all summer camper.
—**Warren H. Miller, 1918**

THE BAKER

For my own use I prefer an ordinary stove with an oven unless I have a baker, in which case the oven is not needed, and there will be a larger fire box so that one can use longer wood.
—**E. Kreps, 1910**

STOVEPIPES

The stove pipe should be telescopic and of sufficient length to reach three or four feet above the roof of the tent. It will be necessary to have a cone shaped spark catcher made of wire cloth to fit on top of the pipe and prevent sparks from falling on the roof of the tent. Some campers prefer to have the stove pipe hole in the end of the tent instead of the roof, in which case the stove pipe extends diagonally through the end of the tent. This is not only as a safeguard against fire but also precludes all possibility of a leaking place about the stovepipe hole.
—**E. Kreps, 1910**

A well-managed tent stove is a delight; a poor one, a fume factory and a misery. Do not cuss the stove out; study it and see why it smokes.

The cookshack is a fixture at many permanent outpost camps.

They all draw fine if you do not attempt impossibilities. For example, to make your chimney draw requires a column of hot air in it, nothing else. The length of the pipe doesn't matter much. [M]ost of them are in three lengths averaging six to nine feet, but they all draw equally well, or poorly, depending upon whether they are hot or cold. When you first start the fire the smoke doesn't know where to go and so bursts out around the lids or pots, filling the tent with smoke. Cause, no heat in the stove-pipe. Remedy, take off the lids and let the flames rise for awhile until you have some coals in the stove and some body to your fire. As soon as you put on the lids again the flames at once hunt every opening, and so find the chimney hole right off. A few moments later the chimney is hot and a column of hot air established that will draw like a major.

FUEL ECONOMY—*Proper Harvesting*

You will be astonished at the amount of cooking that one of these stoves will do on a minimum of fuel. Compare it with the armful of good blackjack oak that you used in the open grid fire in cooking the same meal, and then note how a very few chips suffice to keep pots boiling and the frying-pan sizzling with the tent stove. As I look back over my writings on camping I feel that I have said not half enough on this subject; have not half appreciated my own stove, in fact, to say nothing of the many other good ones made by the various outfitting firms.
—**Warren H. Miller, 1918**

Like most populous states, New Jersey has had to enact very stringent fire laws. So much damage has been done to the forests from roving hunters building indiscriminate and often carelessly left campfires, that the State has been forced to protect itself against the forest fires that result.
—**Warren H. Miller, 1918**

The question of a permit to build campfires at once came up, for the fire wardens arrest any one with a campfire and no permit to build it . . . the firewarden suggested that the best way to obviate the whole permit question was to take along a collapsible stove, as confined fire does not come under the same category as the open campfire, and no permit is needed anywhere for a tent stove. We decided to follow his advice.
—**Warren H. Miller, 1918**

With an open backlog fire not only is the fuel problem serious labor and loss of hunting time, but the smoke nuisance is a matter of continuous smarting eyes and your raindrops or snowflakes are driving into the tent if a strong wind is gusting about, as it usually is in cold weather.
—**Warren H. Miller, 1918**

In a country where half the stove wood is sparky hemlock and spruce, a spark arrester is a necessity, for all pareflined tent fabrics will take a spark and make quite a hole of a small hot coal. The arrester is a nuisance, as it is continually filling up with soot and ash, but it is necessary, particularly if the stove is inside the tent and its pipe passes up through the roof.
—**Warren H. Miller, 1918**

Finally, and most importantly, the whole subject of camp stoves hangs on the use of ten-cent cooking gloves. With them you can do almost any stunt about a cook stove with impunity; without them you will be burning your fingers half the time. Be sure to take along a pair, and don't lose them. Flipping the pan baker, turning around the baking pan in the reflector baker, picking up the latter, lifting off and on stove lids, handling hot pots, adjusting fire brands and live coals—all these things you can do with impunity with a pair of cooking gloves on.
—**Warren H. Miller, 1918**

SECTION THREE

Over the Open Fire

Who does not love to watch a fire as it springs from its smoke-sheath and dances
swiftly from log to log, wrapping them about with its glowing mantle of flame?
It is a master magician who touches dull wood or coal with his wand, releasing the
bright spirits of light and heat that are imprisoned within them. In some mysterious way
it also liberates our imaginations, opens some door within us that is generally closed, so
that we dream and plan, expand into temporary poets and philosophers, sound depths
and soar to heights never explored except under the influence of fire.

Friends, lovers, comrades need no conversation when in the presence of an open fire,
for it croons and sings and dances for them, writes fiery sonnets upon the dark scroll of
the sooty back logs, and sketches charming pictures with its smoke pencil.

It is the prince of entertainers, the king of hosts! It offers bewitching divertissement,
runs the full gamut of ceremonious amusement for your benefit, then skillfully
decoys your best thoughts from their hiding-places.

Like a genial host, it removes all trace of the self-consciousness that cramps
and dwarfs expression, for, looking into its heart, we find there inspiration
unmarred by thought of self.

—Unknown

THE CAMPFIRE

The red flower that blossoms at night.
—Rudyard Kipling

THE MAGIC OF THE CAMPFIRE

What is a camp without a campfire?—no camp at all, but a chilly place in a landscape, where some people happen to have some things.

When first the brutal anthropoid stood up and walked erect—was man; the great event was symbolized and marked by the lighting of the first campfire.

For millions of years our race has seen in this blessed fire, the means and emblem of light, warmth, protection, friendly gathering, council. All the hallow of the ancient thoughts, hearth, fireside, home is centered in its glow, and the home-tie itself is weakened with the waning of the home-fire. Not in the steam radiator can we find the spell; not in the cater coil; not even in the gas log; they do not reach the heart. Only the ancient sacred fire of wood has power to touch and thrill the chords of primitive remembrance. When men sit together at the campfire they seem to shed all modern form and poise, and hark back to the primitive—to meet as man and man—to show the naked soul. Your campfire partner wins your love, or hate, mostly your love; and having camped in peace together, is a lasting bond of union—however wide your worlds may be apart.

MINIMUM-IMPACT FIRE PRACTICES

We need to keep in mind that truly fragile areas are rare; however, high use decreases the ability of even hardy places to rebound. Improper fire use is one of the most visible scars left from overuse or inappropriate use and, therefore, is generally the practice that is curtailed first. Either that or it becomes the scapegoat for arguments against traditional camping practices. Traditional campers need to learn to camp with minimal impact as a lesson to all that it is an equally practical and ethical pursuit. When it comes to fires, we need to do it better than the rest.

Minimum-impact fires can be built in almost any area with adequate fuel resources. Designated wilderness and public display areas are managed for minimal change and so fires may not be appropriate, but these areas comprise only a small percentage of available wild lands. In places like this, we should use other fuel sources, carry poles and firewood, or camp someplace else. Appropriate use may mean no use in some places.

We should take responsibility to clean up our messes and even someone else's. Chechakos have been making work for the rest of us and have even been the cause of laws being created that make it impossible for anyone to enjoy the companionship of a good campfire.

CONSERVATION PRACTICES

- Use judgement when choosing whether or not to build a fire.
- Use only small or split fuels so they burn efficiently and completely.
- Gather fuel well away from camp—disperse impact.
- If you create charcoal, pulverize it so that it will leach into the soil. White ash created by a good burn is a good soil builder. Charcoal is as much a blight as litter and should not be tolerated.
- Never bury charcoal. Crush it to ash and scatter it if possible.
- Build fires in controlled areas: new or existing fire pits, fire pans, and stoves, or learn how to manage a fire so that charcoal does not migrate or get buried. The use of a fire blanket is suggested until you can trust yourself to properly monitor the fire; otherwise, the instruction of its use is a foolish redundancy.
- Pots should be blackened with paint or soot and be void of carbon buildup. Thus, they absorb heat more efficiently, requiring less fuel.
- Pots should be suspended so that they just touch the glowing coals. The fire intensity in this configuration can actually get so hot as to melt the pot. When the tyro places the pot on the coals, it becomes an obstruction to combustion and creates inferior results. If you raise it too high, the Inverse Square Law, which states that the effect of a glowing object is 1 over the distance squared, takes affect.
- Either permanent hearth furniture or rustic field cranes may be used. If traveling, carry them with you rather than cutting new sets every night.
- The use of a woodstove not only reduces ground impact but is also a more efficient use of resources. Less fuel is needed to do the same job as an open fire.
- A camp heated with fire requires fewer food calories. When external heat sources are not available, the body must generate the needed heat. A hot-tent camper lightens his load by carrying not only less fuel but less food as well.

All my readers must remember that By Their Campfires They Will Be Known and "sized up" as the real thing or as chumps, duffers, tenderfeet and chechakos, by the first Sourdough or old-timer who cuts their trails.
　　—Daniel Carter Beard, 1920

If you should come upon a carelessly left fire in the wood, always feel duty bound to stay long enough to put it out.
　　—Frank H. Cheley, 1933

Never, under any circumstances, should you mutilate trees for dry sticks or bark. If you take dead under branches, break or cut them clean; never tear them off.
　　Don't be guilty of such poor sportsmanship. Remember, others will follow you into the woods. Conserve their interest in the important particulars of fuel and fire—as well as your own.
　　—Frank H. Cheley, 1933

The campfire, then, is the focal center of all primitive brotherhood. We shall not fail to use its magic powers.
—**Ernest Thompson Seton,** *The Nine Leading Principles of Woodcraft,* **1900**

ODES TO THE CAMPFIRE

[W]e people of the camp-fires are more interested in primitive fires just as the Neanderthal men built them, than we are in the roaring furnaces of the steel works, the volcano blast furnaces, or any of the scientific, commercialized fires of factory and commerce.

THE INVERSE SQUARE LAW

The Inverse Square Law states that the effect of a glowing object is 1 over the distance, squared.

Better stated, if a fire warms the front of a shelter from one yard away, when the camper lies down to sleep and is two yards away, he will receive only one quarter of the available heat (at three yards—one sixteenth, and so on). This is the result of the light/heat spreading out and becoming less intense as it travels from its source.

Knowledge of this law tells us that the efficiency of the popular reflector fire talked about and illustrated in many traditional texts is a myth. Most illustrations show the wall and fire so far from the camper or shelter that they provide a marginal return on the energy lost in their construction. To work at all, the wall must be as close to the fire and as close to the camper as possible. In this position, the wall creates better fire action by actuating a draught as well as spreading out and directing the glow or radiating heat from the fire.

Mors Kochanski, author of Northern Bushcraft, calls this setup a back-wall fire, noting that it's a misnomer to call it a reflector. In order for an object to be a reflector, it must have a mirror-like surface. Light waves that strike it bounce off at the same frequency. A backlog fire, on the other hand, absorbs these waves and reemits them at a lower frequency. If the fire is too far from the camper, these lower frequency waves are overcome by the Inverse Square Law and are, in most cases, rendered relatively useless.

The "Nessmuk" Night Fire

We can do without blankets, we can do without tents, and for four or five days, or even longer in a pinch, we can do without food, but we must have fire. . . . [M]atches and an axe should take first place in a camper's outfit and a thorough knowledge of their use first place in his out-of-door education.
—**Dillon Wallace, 1903**

What we love is the genial, old-fashioned camp-fire in the open, on the broad prairie, on the mountainside, or in the dark and mysterious forests, where, as our good friend Dr. Hornaday says,

We will pile on pine and spruce,
Mesquite roots and sagebrush loose,
Dead bamboo and smelly teak,
And with fagots blazing bright
Burn a hole into the night—

—**Daniel Carter Beard, 1920**

TRAINING SKILLS FOR FIRECRAFT

APPRENTICE CAMPER
- Select and prepare a fire site for heat, light, cooking, and companionship.
- Choose and learn to operate and care for a wood-fired camp stove.
- Learn how to light, utilize, and extinguish various fuels.
- Select and store a supply of natural materials for a fire.
- Discuss and observe safety and conservation practices.
- Demonstrate ability to light a fire with one paper match and wooden kitchen match.
- Identify the Fire Triad.

JOURNEYMAN CAMPER
- Demonstrate ability to:
  - Build a stove fire or open fire and cook on it.
  - Light, use, and care for several different camp stoves. Cook on one.
  - Prepare hearth furniture for an open cooking fire.
  - Reclaim a single-use fire pit so it leaves minimal trace.
  - Identify sources of fat liter, resins, and other fire-lighting aids.
  - Identify common woods of the area and know their burning qualities.
  - Light a fire using a friction and/or percussion fire set.

JOURNEYMAN WOODSMAN
- Identify the most common fire lays and discuss their uses.
- Demonstrate ability to:
  - Build a wet-weather fire.
  - Build a fire on snow.
  - Build a fire in the wind.
  - Build a safe fire in hazardous conditions.
  - Discuss the factors affecting stove design, selection, and operation in a tent.

MASTER WOODSMAN
- Build fires for a variety of camp tasks.
- Demonstrate ability to prepare a fire setup in the field and kindle a fire without matches under a variety of conditions.
- Discuss factors concerning fire use in ecologically sensitive areas.
- Reclaim fire pits and obliterate duplicate sites.
- Present a clear understanding of the arguments for and against wood- and fossil-fuel fires. Intelligently support your chosen fuel. Define a personal ethic.

An argument often urged against a night fire is that it spells hard labor. Let me imbed this in thine ear like a camp pillow—it takes just twenty logs of five inch timber to take you through an entire October night! Many's the time I've cut those logs with a 2 lb. camp axe at the witching hour of five, and never yet have I spent a chilly night, rain or shine. You put on six when you turn in at ten, six when you wake up at 1 [a.m.,] and six again at 4 o'clock. The other two are for the breakfast range. During July and August you need no night fire. Just a large flat stone propped up by two stakes and a two-hour dead wood fire from 8 to 10 [p.m.].
—Warren H. Miller, 1918

FIRE USE—
Warmth, Light, Cooking, Fellowship

I always make a little fire, if only of birch bark, and draw the frost from the blade of the axe before cutting the night's wood, for it is far more likely to break if it is cold. A broken axe, when one is far from reach of help, is a serious matter, if it is cold weather.

—E. Kreps, 1910

Even in the ordinary hunter's camp the energy spent on chopping wood for a good camp-fire at night is well worthwhile. One can get along without it, and through the long, still hours of the night a warm sleeping equipment that will defy any cold is the thing, but to miss the cheery warmth of a well-built camp-fire, substituting for it the glare of the carbide lamp and the warmth of one's mackinaws, is to lose the cream of camping out. What is really needed is the mental equipment of a knowledge of what kind of a fire to build with different forms of camps, so as to get the most comfort for the least expenditure of axemanship. For there are a whole series of camp-fires, each best adapted to its particular camp, and the veteran woodsman will build the right one for the right camp every time.

—Warren H. Miller, 1915

The open-hearth log fire is the heart of the country home. Poets, philosophers, artists—all have contributed to the world's sentiment over the sacred hearthstone. Entwined in the earliest memories of every country boy is the home fireplace, with its crackling logs, its fancy inviting flames, its good cheer of popcorn, black walnuts, and apple cider, the children's revels around the home hearthstone, the old people's comfort, the delight of the strong master of the house and his gracious life partner. Like the sound given out by the taut skin drum, there is an indefinable something about the sight of a log fire in the home fireplace that tugs at the very heart-strings of mankind. Yet if we analyze either drum or fire we find that their soul stirring appeal dates back to the remotest birth of the human race. The skin drum that calls men to war and the wood-fire that always makes every spot in which it is kindled home have been with us for untold centuries; they call to the blood of the race, and every remote ancestral strain in our being responds intuitively no matter how deep the veneer of civilization.

—**Warren H. Miller, 1915**

No one but an arrant, thoughtless, selfish Chechako will use a live growing tree against which to build a fire. A real woodcraft knows that a fire can ruin in a few minutes a mighty forest tree that God himself cannot replace inside of from forty to one hundred years.

—**Daniel Carter Beard, 1920**

HEATING THE OPEN TENT

Mankind on the trail cannot get along without external heat. The day's toil spends his energy, and his vitality grows low; the cold creeps over him and he has no strength left to drive it off with further output of toil. Cold food may yield sustenance and allow him to continue a little longer, but to really restore his vigor he needs external heat, hot food cooked over the camp-fire, warm heat-rays to penetrate his body and relax the tired muscles, drive out the cold and rheumatic aches, and put him in a state of comfort that enables mind and body to recuperate. And so we find, even in the Arctic wastes, where fuel must actually be carried along, that it is never gone without and its weight replaced by extra blanketing, but rather treasured and appreciated, for the finest part of the day, even in the snow igloo, is that hour when the day's march is done, the little spirit-lamp lighted, the frozen pemmican boiled, and the explorers, with their heavy outer furs removed, revel in the comfort and luxury of the heat from that tiny flame which soon warms the igloo far above the temperature outside and brings to an end the day-long struggle of bodily vigor against the bitter cold of the open wastes.
—**Warren H. Miller, 1915**

It is a well-known scientific fact that heat-rays travel through the air without losing appreciably of their warmth until they strike some absorbent or reflecting body. A flat, smooth surface like a tent wall will reflect a heat-ray without absorbing much of it, and the angles of the Forester were calculated with these principles in mind.
—**Warren Miller, 1915**

SMOKELESS FIRE

Modern camping practices claim that traditional axe and saw use have no place in the wilderness. Yet, the same instructions state that fires may be used in selected areas. To teach that one practice is all right without the other is irresponsible for two reasons:

1. Standing deadwood makes the most responsible fuel source, leaving the duff and cover on the ground, protecting it from compaction and erosion. Dead and down fuels are wet and/or decomposing, already starting their return to the soil. To pick up and consume all this small cover is wrong-headed. Selecting a dead tree well away from camp—dispersing impact, pushing it over—leaving no stump or mess; sawing it into short rounds that are easily split—creating solid, dry fuel; and then splitting it into wrist, finger, or smaller-sized fuel promotes better combustion and carbonization, leaving no charcoal behind.

2. Burning wood that is larger than can be broken by hand is inefficient for fire management and cannot be reduced to white ash. Smoke and inadequate burn are always a result of improper fire management. The axe and saw make it possible for the woodsman to select and prepare the best fire fuels for the least overall environmental impact and, if done right, actually creates positive benefits.

The smokeless fire is produced through a balancing of the three parts of the fire triad—heat, fuel, and oxygen. Heat is a product of good combustion created by quality fuel and draught generated by proper spacing and alignment of the fuel. Fuel must be solid, dry and split to the most desirable size for the heat wanted and for the prevailing conditions—rain, wind, snow, calm, and others. Sitting in the wood smoke is a pleasure if the fire is burning properly. Stinging eyes and choking smoke are the byproduct of improper combustion and only the Chechako would tolerate it. Leaving charcoal or fire scars in previously untouched areas or piles of charcoal and trash in existing fire rings are the habits of the tyro and need to be changed.

MANAGING THE FIRE

A good, well-constructed fire is the mark of a seasoned camper.
—**Frank H. Cheley, 1933**

> **If your fire won't burn, nine times out of ten it is you rather than the fuel or the weather.**
> —**Frank H. Cheley, 1933**
>
> **In sections where firewood is hard to find, keep your eye open at least an hour before you expect to make camp for a select piece or two of wood which can be carried with you. By cutting such into small kindling, one can do with a surprisingly small quantity for cooking purposes.**
> —**Frank H. Cheley, 1933**

T]he warmth, dryness, and healthfulness of a forest camp are mainly dependent on the way the fire is managed and kept up. . . . An experience of fifty years convinces me that a large percentage of the benefit obtained by invalids from camp life is attributable to the open camp and well-managed camp-fire. And the latter is usually handled in a way that is too sad, too wasteful; in short, badly botched.
—**Nessmuk, 1920**

The forebear of the log fire on the hearth is the camp-fire. We have it with us yet, as always, but, while the hearth has been evolved so as to yield heat with almost any huddle of logs and kindlings, the camp-fire must be built rightly for the purpose intended, or it is worse than a nuisance.
—**Warren H. Miller, 1915**

There are many, many kinds of camp-fires—probably no two seasoned campers build their fires alike or use them for exactly the same purposes, yet each is positive that his is the "best way."
—**Frank H. Cheley, 1933**

A bed of live hard wood coal, six inches deep, will cook any ordinary meal in excellent shape and not parboil the willing cook either. If cooking much, keep a green poker with a sharp crook on hand for raking over the coals.
—**Frank H. Cheley, 1933**

No matter if the sticks are but an inch to an inch and a half in diameter, split them. They burn more readily and give better heat.
—**Frank H. Cheley, 1933**

TINDER

In the North woods, in the land of the birch trees, green birch bark is universally used as kindling with which to start a fire; green birch bark burns like tar paper.
—**Daniel Carter Beard, 1920**

Remember that fine slivers of wood make a safer and more certain start for a fire than paper. All tenderfeet first try dry leaves and dry grass to start their fires. This they do because they are accustomed to the use of paper and naturally seek leaves or hay as

a substitute for paper. But experience soon teaches them that leaves and grass make a nasty smudge or a quick, unreliable flame which ofttimes fails to ignite the wood, while, when proper care is used, small slivers of dry wood never fail to give satisfactory results.
—**Daniel Carter Beard, 1920**

Small wood is all that is needed for cooking—stray sticks. For heating, larger wood that will not burn out too quickly is better, and hard wood is preferable. Even for heating I prefer the Indian method of a small fire that one can draw close to, rather than the white man's method of a roaring big blaze that drives one out into the background. The Indian way consumes less wood, too.
—**Dillon Wallace, 1933**

FAT LITER

Collecting Fat liter

Dan Beard calls them "gummy fagots of pine." As trees grow, some produce a tough inner core of heartwood. This can become impregnated with sap, and as the trees dry and decay, only the heartwood will remain because of the high amount of pitch saturating the wood fibers. When cut into short lengths and then split into twig-sized splints, they are bundled and carried as fire starters. The pitch is easily lit with a match and burns with a long, low, often smokey flame. It's a welcome addition to the pack in rainy weather, burning long enough to dry out kindling and fuel to get a much-needed fire.

Slivers of fat pine may be readily gotten from stumps and roots. These will burn readily even when wet.
—**Frank H. Cheley, 1933**

KINDLING

In wet weather, an axeman can always get dry wood by cutting into a standing dead tree, or on the under side of down timber that is not entirely on the ground.
—**Ernest Thompson Seton,** *Book of Woodcraft*, **1900**

BUILDING FIRE

[T]he seasoned camper will never be without matches, a good knife or a small ax, and with these and his intelligence he is sure to get a fire.
—**Frank H. Cheley, 1933**

Let me repeat, the first requisite of a camper's outfit is matches, and his first lesson in camping should be the art of fire-building under any and all conditions.

FUZZ STICKS

Fuzz sticks are made from a solid knot-free piece of wood. The objective is to make a shaving of at least one continuous curl. More curls show more skill. The skill is a good test piece for mastery, but also provides kindling where there is none.

If you have no birch bark, it is a good plan to shave a dry soft-wood stick, leaving all the shavings sticking on the end in a fuzz, like a Hopi prayer stick. Several of these make a sure fire kindler. Fine splinters may be made quickly by hammering a small stick with the back of the axe.
—Ernest Thompson Seton, *Book of Woodcraft*, 1900

Now, with your jackknife, whittle shavings. Don't make the shavings short and stingy. Cut them five or six inches long. Stop the knife-blade just short of the end of the stick until six or eight shavings have been cut, then, with a twist of the blade, break the bunch loose. In this way the shavings will be held together in bunches. There should be at least half a dozen of these bunches, before any attempt is made to light the fire. Patience and care is the price of success. Haste and insufficient preparation ends in failure.
—Dillon Wallace, 1933

Pine needles, pine cones, or birch bark will start a fire very quickly, are better in fact than paper or shavings. They are very light in weight, consequently some campers carry a small bag of them for starting fires on damp days.
—Frank H. Cheley, 1933

In the mountains of Pennsylvania the old backwoodsmen, of which there are very few left, invariably build their fires with dry pine, or pitch pine sticks.

With their axe they split a pine log, then cut it into sticks about a foot long and about the thickness of their own knotted thumbs, or maybe a trifle thicker; after that they proceed to whittle these sticks, cutting deep shavings, but using care to leave one end of the shavings adhering to the wood; they go round and round the stick with their knife blade making curled shavings until the piece of kindling looks like one of those toy wooden trees one used to find in his Noah's Ark on Christmas morning.

When a backwoodsman finishes three or more sticks he sets them up wigwam form. The three sticks having been cut from the center of a pine log, are dry and maybe resinous, so all that is necessary to start the flame is to touch a match to the bottom of the curled shavings.

Before they do this, however, they are careful to have a supply of small slivers of pitch pine, white pine or split pine knots handy. These they set up around the shaved sticks, maybe adding some hemlock bark, and by the time it is all ablaze they are already putting on larger sticks of ash, black birch, yellow birch, sugar maple or oak.
—Daniel Carter Beard, 1920

Making a Fuzz Stick

Fire-making in the open is an art. It must be learned by practice and experience. I might write and you might read volumes upon it, but you cannot master it in that way. You must do it yourself in wet and dry, stormy and clear weather.

Anyone can kindle a fire in dry weather with paper for tinder. That isn't the way to play the game. In the woods you must rely upon what primitive nature supplies. Before you can truly call yourself a camper you must have the lessons of fire-making so well learned that when you go into the woods you do so with the confidence that you can make a fire whenever you need one.
—Dillon Wallace, 1933

The first requisite is matches. A sufficient supply for all probable emergencies should be carried. The camper who fails to do this should be attended by a guardian.
—Dillon Wallace, 1933

We all know that a camp without a campfire would be no camp at all; its chiefest charm would be absent.

Your first care, then, is to provide for a small fire and prevent its spreading. . . .

Cracked Jimmy, in "Two Little Savages," gives very practical directions for lighting a fire anywhere in the timbered northern part of America, thus:

> First a curl of birch bark as dry as it can be,
> Then some twigs of soft wood, dead, but on the tree,
> Last of all some pine-knots to make the kittle foam,
> And there's a fire to make you think you're settin' right
> at home

—Ernest Thompson Seton, 1900

Observe the direction of the wind, and lay the sticks an inch and a half or two inches in diameter upon the ground, their ends together and at right angles to each other, the inside of the angle toward the wind. Now hold the butt end of one of the bunches of shavings in the left hand and with the right hand light a match and apply it to the thin end of the shavings. When the shavings are well ablaze, lay the butt upon the cross sticks, where they come together, and on the inside of the angle, with the small end of the shavings on the ground. This permits the flame to climb upward. Now quickly, but carefully, lay the remaining bunches of shavings upon this, the thin shavings upon the fire, the thick ends being supported by the two sticks.

The split kindling wood is now to be applied and carefully arranged, and don't monkey with it after it is once arranged. If there is any fire at all the probabilities are that it will come through and ignite the splits, though it may do so slowly. Give it time.

FUEL

One must use the axe industriously in order to procure fuel for the fire; one must plan the fire carefully with regard to the wind and the inflammable material adjacent; one must collect and select the fuel intelligently.
—Daniel Carter Beard, 1920

Standing wood is always drier than that which lays on the ground.
—E. Kreps, 1910

But whether one starts the fire with birch bark, shaved pine sticks or miscellaneous dry wood, one must remember that split wood burns much better than wood in its natural form, and that logs from twelve to fourteen inches are best for splitting for fuel; also one must not forget that in starting a fire the smaller the slivers of kindling wood are made, the easier it is to obtain a flame by the use of a single match, after which the adding of fuel is a simple matter. A fire must have air to breathe in order to live, that is a draught; consequently kindling piled in the little wigwam shape is frequently used.
—Daniel Carter Beard, 1920

Standing wood is better by far than wood that has fallen. Soft woods, such as pine and spruce, when they are to be had, light more easily than hard wood and make the best kindlings. Hard wood, after the fire is started, makes the better and steadier fire. Fell the dry stick, cut off two or three short lengths, and split them. The heart of the stick will be found to be as dry as some of the splits in fine kindling wood.
—Dillon Wallace, 1933

FLINT AND STEEL FIRE

In the good old pioneer days, when we all wore buckskin clothes and did not bother about the price of wool, when we wore coonskin caps and cared little for the price of felt hats, everybody, from Miles Standish and George Washington to Abraham Lincoln, used flint and steel. Fig. 27 shows ten different forms of steel used by our grandsires and granddames.

Flint in its natural condition may be found in many states, but, as a rule, any stone which was used by the Indians for arrowheads will answer as a substitute for flint, that is, any gritty or glassy stone, like quartz, agate, jasper or iron pyrites. Soft stones, limestones, slate or soapstones are not good for this purpose.

—Daniel Carter Beard, 1920

THE STEEL

Most of the old steels were so made that one might grasp them while thrusting one's fingers through the inside of the oval steel, Fig. 28 (left-handed). Some make their own steels of broken pieces of flat ten-cent files, but this is unnecessary because every outdoor man, and woman, too, is supposed to carry a good sized jack-knife and the back of the blade of the jackknife, or the back of the blade of one's hunting knife is good enough steel for anyone who has acquired the art of using it as a steel.

But if you must have steels manufactured at the machine shop or make them yourself, let them be an inch wide, a quarter of an inch thick, and long enough to form an ellipse like one of those shown in Fig. 27. Have the sharp edges rounded off. If you desire you may have your steel twisted in any of the shapes shown in Fig. 27 to imitate the ones used by your great granddaddies.

—Daniel Carter Beard, 1920

The "rubbing-stick" is a picturesque, sensational and interesting method of building a fire, but today it is of little practical use outside of the fact that it teaches one to overcome obstacles, to do things with the tools at hand, to think and act with the vigor, precision and self-confidence of a primitive man.

—Daniel Carter Beard, 1920

FIRE IN THE TENT

As soon as one moves the camp-fire inside of the tent, a new variety of conditions arises. All the products of combustion must be gotten out of the tent, and this applies to smokeless tent-warmers as well as fires, for a good deal of carbon monoxide is produced in all stoves, as well as the carbon dioxide which follows complete combustion. Both gases are poisonous, the former virulently so, and many a fatal termination to a night's sleep in a closed tent has been narrowly escaped by parties of explorers and hunters who trusted to one of these tent heaters without seeing to it that the tent had proper ventilation. Yet in a closed-tent camp a fire of some sort is a luxury that it is hard to make the uninitiated conceive as possible. Not only is the earth dampness and chill driven away, but the necessity of cooking a meal out-of-doors in perhaps inclement weather, often in pitch darkness, is removed, and one is cosey and at home for the night after the day's work is done—done with the stern and inhospitable wilderness for the time and at peace for once with the whole visible world. Many men, because of having to do writing, or scientific work, or having some other occupation aside from hunting and travelling, require a closed tent for the evening's work, and in wintry

FLINT AND STEEL FIRE
Continued

TO GET THE SPARK

Place the charred end of the rope on the flint, the charred portion about one thirty-second of an inch back of the edge of the flint where the latter is to be struck by the steel; hold the punk in place with the thumb of the left hand, as in the diagram (Fig. 29). Hold the knife about six inches above at an angle of about forty-five degrees from the flint, turn your knife so that the edge of the back of the blade will strike, then come down at an angle about thirty-five degrees with a sharp scraping blow. This should send the spark into the punk at the first or second blow. Now blow the punk until it is all aglow and you are ready to set your tinder afire. Push the punk into the middle of a handful of tinder and blow it until it is aflame, and the deed is done!
—Daniel Carter Beard, 1920

All these pocket contrivances for striking fire were formerly known as "striker-lights" or "chucknucks."
—Daniel Carter Beard, 1920

Flint and steel are all right if you are expert in their use, but matches are more easily kept dry than the necessary tinder for flint and steel. The day of fire sticks and flint and steel has passed, just as the day of the stage-coach has passed.
—Dillon Wallace, 1933

weather such a tent will give one more comfort with less labor than any open tent made. Wherefore the problem of how to bring the camp-fire inside the tent has been given much study by those who know.
—**Warren H. Miller, 1915**

Most fires, logs or sticks, go out and the stove is cold two hours after the party is asleep; but if care is taken to prepare a billet or two of hardwood that will just about fit inside over the coals, that billet will smolder and give out heat all night long with a pinhole draft in the stove-door, and most of these doors are provided with such a hole for that very purpose. They are all hard to start if one puts in more fuel at first than the draft can properly take care of; the thing to do is to get enough small wood burned down to coals to form a bed of them, after which large sizes of split wood can be fed in and the stove will use them up by the charcoal-making route.
—**Warren H. Miller, 1915**

For work above timber-line, the camp-fire takes the form of a spirit or kerosene lamp. Denatured alcohol, or just plain kerosene, costing a tenth as much; both have one-hole and two-hole blue-flame burners available in light, folding explorer's stoves. The kerosene-burners work on the principle of the familiar gasoline plumber's torch, a little raw kerosene first being ignited to heat the burner, after which

the affair is self-vaporizing, and the height of the flame is then controllable with a needle-valve. With these burners is supplied a sheet-iron radiating drum for tent-warming, after the cooking is done, and this drum serves as a packing-case for the lamp and its special kerosene-can when on the trail. With denatured alcohol the process is even simpler, the burner simply being lighted, when the hot blue flame of alcohol vapor is at once available, and, of course, it gives many more heat-units per pound of fuel than kerosene.
—**Warren H. Miller, 1915**

FURNISHING THE HEARTH

[E]very first-class cooking-outfit is, and should be, a complete bakery, grill, "stewry,"and frying-outfit combined, and every camper who buys one should know how to use it to the full extent of its possibilities.
—**Warren H. Miller, 1915**

THE OPEN HEARTH

No matter where the old camper may be, no matter how long a time may have elapsed since last he slept in the open, no matter how high or low a social or official position he may now occupy, it takes but one whiff of the smoke of an open fire, or one whiff of the aroma of frying bacon, to send him back again to the lone trail.

That faint hint in the air of burning firewood or the delicious odor of the bacon, for the moment, will not only wipe from his vision his desk, his papers and his office furniture, but also all the artificialities of life. Even the clicking of the typewriter will turn into the sound of clicking hoofs, the streets will become canyons, and the noise of traffic, the roar of the mountain torrent!

There is no use talking about it, there is no use arguing about it, there is witchcraft in the smell of the open fire, and all the mysteries and magic of the Arabian Nights dwell in the odor of frying bacon.
—**Daniel Carter Beard, 1920**

In the case of a small party and hasty camp, you need nothing but a pot hanger of green wood for a complete kitchen, and many hundreds of times, on prairie and in forest, I found this sufficient.

A more complete camp grate is made of four green logs (aspen preferred), placed as in the illustration. Set the top logs 3 inches apart at one end, 10 inches at the other. The top logs should be flattened in the middle of their top sides—to hold the pot which sits on the opening between the top logs. The fire of course is built on the ground, under the logs. Sometimes stones of right size and shape are used instead of the logs, but the stones do not contribute anything to the heat and are less manageable.

In addition to this log grate, more elaborate camps have a kitchen equipped with a hanger on which are pot hooks of green wood.
—*Book of Woodcraft*, **1900**

Outside of insects and bum sleeping, the rock that wrecks most camping trips is cooking. The average tyro's idea of cooking is to fry everything and fry it good and plenty. Now, a frying pan is a most necessary thing to any trip, but you also need the old stew kettle and the folding reflector baker . . . . The proper way is to cook over coals.
—**Ernest Hemingway, 1920**

HOW ANYONE MAY MAKE A RUBBING-STICK SET OF HIS OWN

First of all remember that to be able to make fire with materials you have gathered and put together yourself is quite some feat of handicraft and woodcraft. In addition, it requires considerable strength and skill.

A BOW—Get yourself a bow, say 20 to 24 inches long, of any strong wood, averaging about 3/4 of an inch thick, and, if possible, with a branch at one end so you can have a hook on which to fasten your thong. It should bow a little, but not too much.

A SOCKET—Find a hard knot like hemlock. Better still, locate a piece of stone (soapstone is good) that will fit the hand comfortably, either with a hole in it or one in which you can make a hole, say 3/8 of an inch across and 1/4 inch deep.

A THONG—Get a strip of leather. Buckskin is best, though rawhide will do if you can get the grease out without making it hard and stiff. Fasten one end on the crotch end and twist the thong so it is a tight spiral all the way down. Slip the other end through a hole in the bow and pull reasonably tight. The skin will stretch considerably at first and will have to be tightened several times after using.

A BASEBOARD—Get some dry straight grained balsam fir (white cedar, red cedar, cypress, or basswood), about an inch thick and 15 inches long and 4 or 5 inches wide. Split off a strip about an inch wide and from it whittle a stick or drill—long shoulder at top, short point at bottom, and perfectly straight.

Take your other board, which should never be less than 2 inches wide, and with the point of your jackknife make a notch. Estimate so that the point of your drill will hit a spot that will leave the outside of the drill near the edge and yet leave a little margin. Make a small hole for your drill point by twisting your knife.

SPARK BOARD— Get a piece of board, thin like a shingle or a cigar-box lid, to put under the baseboard.

TINDER—Get some dry cedar bark and shred it between your hands to make it soft, or get a mouse's nest for tinder.

HOW ANYONE MAY MAKE A RUBBING-STICK SET OF HIS OWN

FIRE PREPARATIONS

TO PREPARE THE HOLE—Place the thin board under the baseboard and, kneeling, put your left foot on the board in the position shown in the photograph. Twist the drill in the thong of the bow. Put the short point of the drill in the hole in the board and put the socket on top of the drill. Hold the socket with your left hand, holding your wrist firmly

against your shinbone. With your right hand, push the bow back and forth so as to revolve the drill. Hold it against the shinbone to steady the drill and to create greater pressure on the socket. When you have burned a hole in the board, take your knife and open the notch so that it connects with the hole.

TO MAKE A SPARK—You are now ready to make a spark. Hold your drill perpendicular and your bow parallel with the floor; keep your wrist against your shinbone. Twirl the drill until you get lots of smoke and a notch full of powder. Carefully take off the baseboard. If the pile of powder smokes, you have a spark. If it does not smoke, you have failed and must try again. Pick up the spark board and fan the spark gently until it glows.

TO GET THE FIRE—Carefully place some shredded tinder over the spark and hold it so the spark cannot blow away, being careful not to extinguish it. Blow with long breaths until you have a blaze.

If your material is right and you have followed these simple directions, shortly you will have a fire. If you do not succeed, try again until you do. When you have once learned the principle and gotten onto the knack of it, time yourself carefully, striving always to beat your own best record.

Begin work by drawing the bow slowly and horizontally back and forth until it works easily, work the bow as one does a fiddle bow when playing on a bass viol, but draw the bow its whole length each time. When it is running smoothly, speed it up.

Or when you feel that the drill is biting the wood, press harder on the thimble, not too hard, but hard enough to hold the drill firmly, so that it will not slip out of the socket but will continue to bite the wood until the "sawdust" begins to appear. At first it will show a brown color, later it will become black and begin to smoke until the thickening smoke announces that you have developed the spark. At this stage you gently fan the smoking embers with one hand. If you fan it too briskly, as often happens, the powder will be blown away.

As soon as you are satisfied that you have secured a spark, lift the powder embers on the fire-pan and place carefully on top of it a bunch of tinder, then blow till it bursts into flame. Or fold the tinder over the spark gently, take it up in your hand and swing it with a circular motion until the flame flares out.

—Daniel Carter Beard, 1920

Every real Woodcrafter likes to cook over an open fire. It appeals to the primitive and natural impulses in one. Who would not prefer a meal cooked in this way and eaten out-of-doors to the most sumptuous repast that could be offered by the finest hotels of our cities.
—**G. Clyde Fisher, 1933**

HEARTH FURNITURE

The pole from which kettles or meats are hung is usually known as a crane. This crane is made from small tough limbs of trees The pot-hooks are made from saplings or number 9 wire. The use of these hooks often prevents burning of the hands when handling kettles. If hooks of different lengths are made the desired intensity of heat can easily be secured by regulating carefully the distance of the kettle from the fire. A crane [is] especially well suited to the roasting of a bird or other meat. For such purposes the pole is much longer, and from the upper end a long wire is hung. The bird is then securely fastened to the lower end of this wire, where it is allowed to swing during the roasting process. [The parallel log lay is] a cooking fire often used in temporary camps. The large green logs are placed farther apart at one end than the other, thus giving support to kettles of different sizes as well as aiding in giving the fire a better draft. The same results may be obtained by using stones in place of green logs, thus saving time as well as reducing the danger from fire when breaking camp.
—**Frank H. Cheley, 1933**

No camp-fire should be without poker and tongs. The poker is a beech stick four feet long by two inches thick, flattened at one end, with a notch cut in it for lifting kettles, etc. To make the tongs, take a tough beech or hickory stick, one inch thick by two feet in length, shave it down nearly one-half for a foot in the center, thrust this part into hot embers until it bends freely, bring the ends together and whittle them smoothly to a fit on the inside, cross-checking them also to give them a grip; finish off by chamfering the ends neatly from the outside. They will be found exceedingly handy in rescuing a bit of tinware, a slice of steak or ham, or any small article that happens to get dropped in a hot fire.
—**Nessmuk, 1920**

[W]hen taking up the subject of cooking fire and camp kitchen, he naturally begins with the most primitive of cooking outfits consisting of two upright forked sticks and a waugan-stick to lay across from fork to fork over the fire. Or maybe a speygelia-stick thrust slantingly into the ground in front of the fire, or perhaps a saster-pole on which to suspend or from which to dangle, in front of the fire, a hunk of moose meat, venison, mountain sheep, mountain goat, whale blubber, beaver, skunk, rabbit, muskrat, woodchuck, squirrel or whatsoever fortune may send.
—**Daniel Carter Beard, 1920**

The Saster/Dingle

THE SASTER/DINGLE

According to Mr. Seton, away up in the barren lands they use the saster with a fan made of a shingle-like piece of wood, fastened with a hitch to a piece of wire and a bit of string; the wind—when it is good-natured—will cause the cord to spin round and round. But the same result is secured with a cord which has been soaked in water to prevent it from burning, and which has also been twisted by spinning the meat with one's hands. Such a cord will

unwind and wind more or less slowly for considerable time, thus causing the meat to expose all sides of its surface to the heat of the roasting fire in front of which it hangs. You will note we say in front; again let us impress upon the reader's mind that he must not hang his meat over the flame.
—**Daniel Carter Beard, 1920**

There is an old adage:
> Hasty cooking is tasty cooking.
> Fried meat is dried meat.
> Boiled meat is spoiled meat.
> Roast meat is best meat.

This reflects perhaps the castle kitchen rather than the camp, but it has its measure of truth, and the reason why roast meat is not more popular is because it takes so much time and trouble to make it a success.

During my Barren Ground trip I hit on a remarkably successful roaster that, so far as I know, was never tried before.

The usual pot-stick is set in the ground (if no tree be near), and the roast hung by a wire and a cord; where they meet is a straight or Bat piece of wood, or bark, set in a loop of the wire.

The wind strikes on this, causing the roast to turn; it goes till the cord is wound up then unwinds itself and goes on unceasingly. We used it every day. It was positively uncanny to see the way in which this thing kept on winding and unwinding itself, all day long if need be.
—**Ernest Thompson Seton,** *Book of Woodcraft,* **1900**

FIRE DOGS

The more carefully the fire is planned and built the more easily will the cooking be accomplished. The first thing to be considered in laying one of these fires is the Fire-Dogs which in camp are the same as andirons in the open fire places of our homes. . . . we use green logs, sods or stones for fire-dogs in the wilderness. Frequently we have a back-log against which the fire-dog rests. In this particular case it acts both as a back log and a fire-dog.
—**Daniel Carter Beard, 1920**

THE COOKING FIRE

[T]he biggest difference between cooking at home and cooking on camp and trail is in the fire. At home your fire is a steady, strong heat, with no flame, an oven handy for baking, and, if it is a gas stove, you can regulate the quantity of the heat. In the woods the fire will be at one time all flame, another all coals, and, in the hands of tyros, mostly out!
—**Warren H. Miller, 1918**

*L*earning to regulate a fire is matter of experience and patience. Learning to know what the fire is doing has a few tricks that anyone can master. When baking bread at home, you set the oven at 350 degrees and pop the dough in for the time you need. With a fire, you can do the same thing, but the only thermostat you have to judge the heat is your hand.

For cooking on a grill or baking with a reflector, hold your hand at the point where the food will cook and start to count: one-and-one, two-and-two, and so on. The count for a low fire may be six to eight, indicating a temperature of about 250–300 degrees. A medium fire will be four to five, with a temperature of approximately 325–400 degrees. Counting to two or three is a hot fire producing 400–500 degrees. A very hot fire will only allow a count of one, and will generate a heat of over 500 degrees.

CAMP POT HOOKS

Camp pot hooks are of various forms and designs. . . . The camp pot-hooks should be of various lengths; long ones to bring the vessels near the fire where the heat is more intense; short ones to keep the vessels further from the fire so that their contents will not cook but only keep warm; and medium ones for simmering or slow cooking.

THE GALLOW HOOK is not as the name might imply, but is a rustic and useful bit of forked stick (Figs. 60, 61, 62 and 63) made of a sapling. Fig. 60 shows how to select the sapling and where to cut it below a good sturdy fork. Fig. 61 shows the bit of sapling trimmed down to the proper length and with two forks, one at each end. Fig. 62 shows how this switch may be bent down and bound with a string or tape made of green bark, and so fastened to the main stem as to form a loop which will easily slip over the waugan-stick as in Fig. 63.

THE POT CLAW STICK is so cut that the fork may be hooked over the waugan-stick and the cooking utensils, pots or kettles may be hung over the fire by slipping their handles into the notch cut in the stick on the side opposite to the fork and near the lower end of the pot-claw (Figs. 64, 65 and 66). This is a real honest-to-goodness Buckskin or Sourdough pot-hook; it is one that requires little time to manufacture and one that is easily made wherever sticks grow.

THE HAKE is easier to make than the pot-claw. It is a forked stick like the pot-claw, but in place of the notch near the lower end, a nail is driven diagonally into the stick and the kettle hung on the nail (Figs. 67 and 68). The hake possesses the disadvantage of making it necessary for the camper to carry a supply of nails in his kit.

THE GIB is possibly a corruption of gibbet, but it is a much more humane implement. It requires a little more time and a little more skill to make a gib (Fig. 69) than it does to fashion the preceding pot-hook. It is a useful hook for stationary camps where one has time to develop more or less intricate cooking equipment. Fig. 69A shows how the two forked sticks are cut to fit together in a splice.

THE SPEYGELIA is a forked stick or a notched stick (Figs. 71, 72 and 73), which is either propped up on a forked stick (Fig. 71) and the lower end held down by a stone in such a manner that the fork at the upper end offers a place to hang things over, or in front of the fire, sometimes a notched stick is used in the same manner as Fig. 73. Where the ground is soft to permit it, the stick is driven diagonally into the earth, which may hold it in place without other support.

THE SASTER is a long pole used in the same manner as the speygelia. Meat is suspended from it in front of the fire to roast (Figs. 74 and 75), or kettles are suspended from it over the fire to boil water (Fig. 74).
   —Daniel Carter Beard

Hardly less in importance is the kind of wood the fire is made of and the arrangement of it. Trash woods, such as pine, cedar, hemlock and balsam, blaze fiercely, with little heat, and yield a white, poor coal that is ashes in ten minutes. Good cooking woods, such as blackjack oak, birch, hard maple, pignut hickory and dead white oak, burn with an intensely hot flame that gets the pots boiling in a jiffy, and yield live coals that glow for hours, the least of which will keep a large pot simmering.
—**Warren H. Miller, 1918**

The Campfire is built with an eye to two purposes: one is to reflect heat into the open tent in front, and the other is to so construct it that it may last a long time. When one builds a camp-fire one wants to be able to roll up in one's blanket and sleep with the comforting conviction that the fire will last until morning.
—**Daniel Carter Beard, 1920**

This same fire is sometimes used for a baking fire, but the real fire for this purpose is made by the Belmore Lay. (Figs. 96 and 97.) The first sketch shows the plan and the second the perspective view of the fire. The stove is made by two side logs or fire-dogs over which the fire is built and after it has fallen in, a mass of red hot embers, between the fire dogs, two logs are laid across the dogs and one log is placed atop, so that the flame then comes up in front of them (Fig. 97) and sends the heat against the bread or bannock.
—**Daniel Carter Beard, 1920**

A Frying Fire is built between two logs, two rows of stones, or sods (Figs. 98, 99 and 100); between these logs the fire is usually built, using the sides as fire-dogs, or the sticks may be placed in the turkey-lay (Fig. 100), so that the sticks themselves make a fire-dog and allow, for a time, a draught until the fire is burning briskly, after which it settles down to hot embers and is in the proper condition for frying.
—**Daniel Carter Beard, 1920**

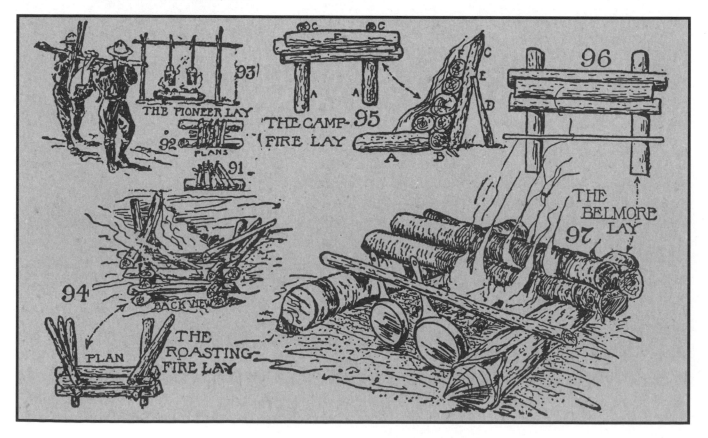

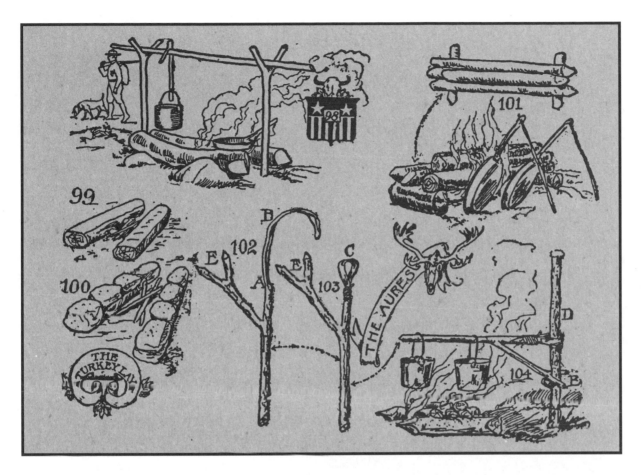

Wood is the food that the fire eats and it must be digestible; a fire with indigestion is a fire fed with punky, damp wood carelessly thrown together in place of well-selected dry split wood which the fire can consume cleanly, digest evenly, and at the same time give out the greatest amount of heat.

To produce a draught the fire must, of course, be raised from the ground, but do not build it in a careless manner like a pile of jack-straws. Such a fire may start all right, but when the supporting sticks have burned away it will fall in a heap and precipitate the cooking utensils into the flames, upsetting the coffee or teapot, and dumping the bacon "from the flying pan into the fire."

Be it man, woman, boy or girl, if he, she or it expects to be a camper, he, or she or it must learn to be orderly and tidy around camp. No matter how soiled one's clothes may be, no matter how grimy one's face may look, the ground around the camp-fire must be clean, and the cooking utensils and fire wood, pot-hooks and waugan-sticks, all orderly and as carefully arranged as if the military officer was expected the next minute to make an inspection.
—**Daniel Carter Beard, 1920**

For dinner and supper you want a good range, and the best woodland one I know of is two green logs laid side by side and staked in place, being held a few inches above the ground by two short cross-logs under their ends. Tyros always lay the logs flat on the ground and then wonder why the fire is always feeble, or else too vigorous. There is no way for the air to get at the fire from underneath. Set the two logs on two short ones and the range will steam like a major.
—**Warren H. Miller, 1915**

THE KIT

Most people take into the woods too many utensils of too heavy material. The result is a dispro-portion between the amount of food transported and the means of cooking it.
—*Camp and Trail*, **1920**

Get for a two-man outfit two tin cups with the handles riveted, not soldered. They will drop into the aluminum coffee pot. Omit the soup bowls. Buy good steel knives and forks with blackwood or horn handles. Let the forks be four-tined, if possible. Omit the teaspoons. Do not make the mistake of tin dessert spoons. Purchase a half dozen of white metal. All these things will go inside the aluminum coffee pot, which will nest in the two aluminum kettles. Over the top you invert four aluminum plates and a small tin milk pan for bread mixing and dish washing. The latter should be of a size to fit accu-rately over the top of the larger kettle. This combination will tuck away in a canvas case about nine inches in diameter and nine high. You will want a medium-size steel fry pan, with handle of the same piece of metal—not riveted. The latter comes off. The outfit as modified will weigh but a pound more than the [commercial model], and is infinitely handier.
—*Camp and Trail*, **1920**

Every camper has his opinions on what makes the best cook sets. Of course, many of the early texts spent a lot of energy telling the wonders of aluminum and its abilities at distributing heat evenly throughout the utensil. Cast iron, sheet steel, tin and other resources all have their proponents and detractors.

A few points to keep in mind:

For frying and baking, use materials that can be seasoned: that is, oil is cooked into the pores of the material, releasing foods and reducing sticking. A well-made steel or cast-iron pan or Dutch oven will fill the bill. When cooking, always control heat and move the utensil around to avoid creating hot spots and burning the pan. When cleaning up, just wipe the surface clean. Never wash with soap or water. It will ruin the character of the utensil.

Don't burn the material. Many a fine steel griddle has been ruined by cooking it dry (no grease) and burning the metal. Aluminum Dutch ovens have been known to melt down in a fire too hot for the material to withstand.

Save money by making your own gear. Simple billy pots and nesting pots can be made from tin cans. Reflector ovens can be made from old cooking-oil five-gallon cans. Gear can be made for long- or short-term use. Pots that get too dirty or charred can easily be discarded at the end of a trip without regret.

Stainless pots are light, strong, easily cleaned, and relatively expensive. They are also susceptible to scorching, and if salt is added to water and not dissolved, it will settle to the bottom and actually eat pits through the metal.

Pots should have broad flat bottoms with gently curving corners. The sides should taper slightly to allow pots to nest one within another.

Wire bail handles should have sturdy well-balanced attachment points. Wire should be heavy enough gauge to suspend the contents.

When there are six or eight in the party, all these go-light cooking-kits had best give way to the standard aluminum nesting sets manufactured for the purpose. You want at least four pails and they must hold several gallons each; you must have mixing-pans and at least two large frying-pans with detachable handles. A stout wire grate, with its own legs, replaces the cross-pole cook-range and a folding baker makes bis-cuits, a dozen at a time, or corn bread in cakes large enough for eight hungry campers.
—**Warren H. Miller, 1918**

MATERIALS AND SHAPES FOR COOK SETS

TIN

Tin is the lightest material, but breaks up too easily under rough usage. Still, it is by no means to be despised. With a little care I have made tin coffee pots and tin pails last out a season. When through, I discarded them. And my cups and plates are of tin to this day.
—*Camp and Trail*, **1920**

THE COOKING KIT

MESS KIT MAY CONSIST OF THE FOLLOWING ARTICLES—PARTY OF 6:

- ❑ pepper and salt boxes (aluminum ware)
- ❑ buckets (collapsible canvas)
- ❑ 6 cups (enameled)
- ❑ 1 bread pan (tin)
- ❑ frying pans
- ❑ 2-quart nesting stew pans (enameled ware)
- ❑ 1/2-gallon coffee-pot (enameled ware, with wire bail handle)
- ❑ 1 tin measuring cup or pint tin cup for measuring
- ❑ 4 enameled camp kettles with covers, size ranging from one to three gallons, so as to nest one within the other
- ❑ 6 bowls for soup, oatmeal, etc. (enameled)
- ❑ 1 Dutch oven
- ❑ 1 dishpan (heavy tin)
- ❑ 10 plates (enameled)
- ❑ 1 quart cup (tin)
- ❑ 2 large sharp knives
- ❑ 1 butcher knife
- ❑ 1/2-dozen steel black-handled knives and forks
- ❑ 3⁄4 dozen plated tablespoons
- ❑ 1 cooking fork (12 inches long)
- ❑ Few feet of baling wire (about 15 gauge)
- ❑ Pair of pliers (side cutting)
- ❑ 1 dozen plated teaspoons
- ❑ 1 Kerosene oil can
- ❑ White oil cloth (for table)
- ❑ Towels
- ❑ 1 wash basin (enameled ware)

> Further, if the cook-kit is of the right shape to stow on top of the pack-sack it will be handiest there, as easier to get at for noon lunches, first out of the way when making camp at night, and last to be packed on hitting the trail again next morning.
> —Warren H. Miller, 1918

ACCESSORIES

Wall pockets, one-gallon pickle jars, flour sacks, and calico sacks are all common camp accessories. Any inexpensive, collapsible, or reusable resource was pressed into service in camp.

The most practical towels to carry are those made from house-lining muslin. They have the advantage of absorbing water readily even when new.
—*Camp Cookery,* 1933

[Making use of] mess boxes, one for cooking utensils, the other for tableware and light provisions, made of pine or cedar, screwed together, with hinged tops and compartments; also an inside cover, the full width of the top, which may be used as a bread board. When the lids are opened out and the two mess chests placed together they form a table of the width of the mess chests placed together and a length four times their thickness. These chests should be 2 feet deep, 20 inches wide, and 24 to 30 inches long. . . .

Even the kitchen sink comes to camp.

The above chests, although desirable, are by no means indispensable, for the resourceful camper can improvise similar conveniences with the available materials and tools at hand.
—Frank H. Cheley, 1933

Comfortable eating is the feature most often neglected by the tyro. To grab a plateful of food and squat down somewhere not out of range of the acrid smoke of the campfire seems to him all right and part of the fun. So it is, for the first day or so maybe, but it soon palls. The necessity of an eating table of some sort has been given much study by veteran outfitters, so important is it in the long run. For the permanent camp the log and plank tables solve the problem amply and, with a log bench on each side, make for comfortable, happy meals. The right height for a table with benches is 30 inches (the length of your gun barrels), and the height of the bench is 18 inches, from soles of feet to just below the kneecap. If the meal is eaten standing, 40 inches is a better height for the table. A mere plank, or two logs side by side and packed in with pebbles to form a level surface, will make a very comfortable table for four men and will not take over an hour's time with the belt-axe for some ambitious member of the party. A four-log table, also gravel-filled, will take a setting for eight, the logs being 4 inches in diameter by 6 feet long, and a light fly over it makes eating in rainy weather possible without bringing the food into the tents.
—Warren H. Miller, 1915

My entire outfit for cooking and eating dishes comprises five pieces of tinware. This is when stopping in a permanent camp. When cruising and tramping, I take just two pieces in the knapsack.
—**Nessmuk, 1920**

ENAMEL
Agate- or enamelware is pleasing to the eye and easily kept clean. But a hard blow means a crack or chip in the enameled surface, and hard blows are frequent. An enamelware kettle, or even cup or plate, soon opens seams and chasms. Then it may as well be thrown away, for you can never keep it clean.
—*Camp and Trail*, **1920**

The "modern" aluminum cook kit.

[I]f one is fitting a permanent camp, the white enameled plates will be found to be excellent, also enameled cooking ware.
—*Camp and Trail Methods*, **1910**

IRON
A very light iron pot is durable and cooks well. Two of these of a size to nest together, with the coffee pot inside, make not a bad combination for a pack trip. Most people are satisfied with them; but for a perfect and balanced equipment even light-gauge iron is still too heavy.
—*Camp and Trail*, **1920**

In the old-fashioned open fire-places where our grandparents did their cooking, a Dutch oven was considered essential. The Dutch oven is still used by the guides and cowboys and is of practically the same form as that used by Abraham Lincoln's folks; it consists of a more or less shallow dish of metal, copper, brass or iron, with four metal legs that may be set in the hot cinders. Over that is a metal top which is made so as to cover the bottom dish, and the edges of the cover are turned up all around like a hat with its brim turned up. This is so made to hold the hot cinders which are dumped on top of it.
—**Daniel Carter Beard, 1920**

ALUMINUM
For a long time I had no use for aluminum. It was too soft, went to pieces, and got out of shape too easily. Then by good fortune I chanced to buy a pail or kettle of an aluminum alloy. That one pail I have used constantly for five years on all sorts of trips. It shows not a single dent or bend, and inside is as bright as a dollar. The ideal material was found.

Short experience taught me, however, that even this aluminum alloy was not best for every item of the culinary outfit.

The coffee pot, kettles, and plates may be of the alloy, for it has the property of holding heat, but by that very same token an aluminum cup is an abomination. The coffee or tea cools before you can get your lips next to the metal. For the same reason spoons and forks are better of steel; and of course it stands to reason that the cutting edge of a knife must be of that material. The aluminum frying pans I have found unsatisfactory for several reasons. The metal is not porous enough to take grease, as does the steel pan, so that unless watched very closely flapjacks, mush, and the like are too apt to stick and burn. In the second place they get too hot, unless favored with more than their share of attention. In

Boiling and baking all in one sit.

the third place, in the case of the two I have owned, I have been unable to keep the patent handle on for more than three weeks after purchase.
—*Camp and Trail*, **1920**

Aluminum is much used for camp kits, but is not generally liked by practical woodsmen.
—*Camp and Trail Methods*, **1910**

Aluminum, however, makes the best camp cooking utensil, not only because it is light but because, as aluminum has four times the conductivity of steel, it will scorch things much less easily, since the superfluous heat flows through the metal to cooler parts of the utensil instead of being concentrated in one spot where it must inevitably scorch what is inside unless constantly stirred. This is an important point for campers, as you are always getting some flame played on one spot by a single over-ambitious brand, and steel-ware or agate generally scorches with such a flame, while aluminum will distribute its heat and save the dish.
—**Warren H. Miller, 1918**

OUTDOOR COOKING

Most people seem to think they are missing something in their camping unless everybody squats down to burn a piece of meat on a forked stick over a camp-fire.
—**Warren H. Miller, 1918**

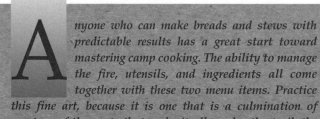

*A*nyone who can make breads and stews with predictable results has a great start toward mastering camp cooking. The ability to manage the fire, utensils, and ingredients all come together with these two menu items. Practice this fine art, because it is one that is a culmination of mastery of the parts that make it all work—the trail, the camp, the tools, the woods.

Cooking over an open fire or on a wood stove, is unlike any other kind of food preparation. The task goes beyond the simple function of just getting food ready to eat. Cooking is a skill that is never quite mastered, and a process that always has something new to teach you. It is a process loaded with the virtues inherent in the traditions of the old style. Learn to savor the process as well as the product.

I will tell only of the foods and the style of cooking that I have found good. There are many better ways, and I will not feel in the least offended if you do not like my style, for really my own cooking has given me indigestion more than once.
—*Camp and Trail Methods*, **1910**

Cooks are the bane of American existence—I may say, proudly enough, that we cooks are the élite of society, the most recherché and sought after of all human beings! And so it comes to pass that, of all my twelve monthly camps during all the years, I have not had one when I was not the cook and dishwasher for a crowd, which crowd usually did all the

fishing or hunting and came back to dub me a "good fellow" when it came to the eats.
—**Warren H. Miller, 1918**

We may live without friends, we may live without books,
But civilized man cannot live without cooks.
—**Nessmuk, 1920**

It is probably true that nothing connected with out-door life in camp is so badly botched as the cooking. It is not through any lack of the raw material, which may be had of excellent quality in any country village. It is not from lack of intelligence or education, for the men you meet in the woods, as outers or sportsmen, are rather over than under the average in these respects. Perhaps it is because it has been dinned into our ears from early childhood, that an appetite, a healthy longing for something good to eat, a tickling of the palate with wholesome, appetizing food, is beneath the attention of an aesthetic, intellectual man. Forgetting that the entire man, mental and physical, depends on proper aliment and the healthy assimilation thereof; and that a thin, dyspeptic man can no more keep up in the struggle of life, than the lightning express can make connections, drawn by a worn out locomotive.
—**Nessmuk, 1920**

THE COOK

Partner busied himself with this and then with pegging down the floor tarp and rolling out his sleeping-bag, while I mixed my cornbread batter and poured enough for two into an aluminum baking-pan which I always carry for small parties. Raking out some coals through the draught-door I put them on top of the pan-cover with the cooking-gloves, took off the forward pot, raked back some more coals and covered them with fresh sticks. On the rear hole of the stove went the pan, with its cargo of hot coals on top and the front hole covered with a fry-pan doing duty as a stove-lid. Into this pan went a nice steak for two and, with it covered with a tin plate, I cleaned out the batter-mixing pan and poured the fruit stew off into it. Two cups of water next went into the former stewpot, and it was high time to go digging for my cake pan, for one must watch it to see that it doesn't burn. A peek inside showed the cake fully risen, so the pan was capsized and put on top of the stove, where it could get plenty of baking heat, but would not likely burn. Some undivided attention to the

Learning to cook the Brigand steak of the old-time camps.

precious cake for five minutes more ended with a perfect golden specimen, ready to be set leaning against the stove to keep warm—still in its pan.

Back went the steak for a finishing; a sniff of the mulligan, and in a few minutes more the steak was set aside, while a pot went on in its place to boil up for tea. Last ceremony: Already the mulligan is being poured out into two waiting tins, the steak is finishing on the rear hole; butter, cow-can and sugar-bag are produced, and the cake is tipped out of its pan smoking hot and divided between partner and me. Good with butter and mulligan. Now the tea is set off and steeped; a potful of water for washing up goes on in its place, and we divide the steak, more cornbread, and two big cups of bully old tea are poured, "cowed" and sugared to taste. Then the stewed fruit; the pipes are lit; the stove fed some more hardwood, and we wash up and put away the kitchen in the rear of the teepee.

It was snowing again outside, and dark, pitch dark, by this time, and the wind was howling over the mountain, but we were warm, light and comfortable inside the tent.
—**Warren H, Miller, 1918**

THE SYSTEM

A certain amount of system is, then, advisable in getting up a woods meal to fit the campfire conditions, and an experience of some thirty years of camp life, when I have generally been the cook of the expedition, leads me to set down here what I have found practical in getting results quickly. I lay my fire—dry duff and twigs for a starter if the woods are dry; peeled birch bark, cedar bark and white pine shavings if they are wet—and set alongside everything necessary to build it up complete; and, further than this, have my water in pots, mulligan stew essentials such as potatoes and onions, peeled, rice in its pot, salted; stewed dried fruits in theirs, sugared; everything ready before the match is applied. As soon as the blaze is assured, these are hung on the dingle stick or set on the wire grate, and they then get the full benefit of the high flames while the wood is burning down to coals. Meanwhile I am at my breadstuffs—corn bread batter, dough gods, squaw bread, etc.—and, when the batter or dough for these is ready, the fire is generally less fierce and more tractable for baking, the pots are all boiling like fiends, and a few blazing brands are available for high fires for the reflector baker or Dutch oven as the case may be. While the bread is baking I get at my fried work—elk steaks, fish, birds—and set these over all the coals I can spare from the main fire. The frying takes fifteen minutes, by which time the baking is done, and the boiled foods, which generally take at least 35 minutes, are ready and grub is served hot and all finished at the same time. . . .

[C]onsider a meal in the woods strung along any old way by an amateur. He generally starts off with his frying,

The cook himself should never be required to rustle firewood and water; that job devolves upon some one else in the party, for he cannot leave his work of preparing and watching the meal, tending fire, and the like, to provide wood and water also.
—Warren H. Miller, 1918

The assistant cook's first duty is that of fire and water commissioner. While he is getting the canvas camp-bucket filled with fresh water from the brook he should see to it that the larger pots are filled also, to give the chef something to start on. If there is a wire grate in the outfit, it is set up, and the assistant cook splits a grid of 2-inch logs of blackjack oak, red-maple, pignut hickory, or birch for it.
—Warren H. Miller, 1915

In general, for trail cookery, one should know how to make fresh breadstuffs, to cook good, palatable soups, stews, vegetables, and desserts, to make such beverages as tea, coffee, and chocolate, to broil wild meats of all kinds, and to fry fish, flapjacks, and fritters without getting them greasy. Further than this, he should know how to serve these things without letting them get cold and indigestible. Even poor cooking will taste well at first in camp, as one's appetite is ravenous and the open air brings our bodily efficiency up to the 100-per-cent mark; but inside of a week I warrant you that such cooking will result in headaches and indigestional upsets and take half the pleasure out of your outing in the woods. But any good cook-kit can do all the above mentioned cooking operations if you only know how to use it.
—Warren H. Miller, 1915

when the flames are so high that everything gets scorched including his own fingers; his pots are set in the back part of the fire where they get little heat and are forever in coming to a boil, and fifteen good minutes are gone before he can take his attention off the fry pans for an instant. Then a long wait while the bread is got ready, and another fifteen minutes baking it; meanwhile the fried food is getting cold and indigestible. Finally he looks at the pots and notes that they have only just begun to boil, the rice is hard, the potatoes like rocks—another long wait while everything else gets cold. The meal is generally eaten on the installment plan, as the rest of the party is too hungry to wait any longer, and, when through, there is an empty feeling, as most of the boiled stuff was half done, the fried work tasteless, and the bread scorched. No, sir; system is the one thing to nail fast to in the woods!

—Warren H. Miller, 1918

Outside of insects and bum sleeping, the rock that wrecks most camping trips is cooking. The average tyro's idea of cooking is to fry everything and fry it good and plenty. Now, a frying pan is a most necessary thing to any trip, but you also need the old stew kettle and the folding reflector baker.

A pan of fried trout can't be bettered and they don't cost any more than ever. But there is a good and bad way of frying them.

The beginner puts his trout and his bacon in and over a brightly burning fire; the bacon curls up and dries into a dry tasteless cinder and the trout is burned outside while it is still raw inside. He eats them and it is all right if he is only out for the day and going home to a good meal at night. But if he is going to face more trout and bacon the next morning and other equally well-cooked dishes for the remainder of two weeks, he is on the pathway to nervous dyspepsia.

The proper way is to cook over coals. Have several cans of Crisco or Cotosuet or one of the vegetable shortenings along that are as good as lard and excellent for all kinds of shortening. Put the bacon in and when it is about half cooked lay the trout in the hot grease, dipping them in cornmeal first. Then put the bacon on top of the trout and it will baste them as it slowly cooks.

The coffee can be boiling at the same time and in a smaller skillet pancakes being made that are satisfying the other campers while they are waiting for the trout.

With the prepared pancake flours you take a cupful of pancake flour and

Horace Kephardt savors solitude by the glow of the fire in his rustic shanty.

add a cup of water. Mix the water and flour and as soon as the lumps are out it is ready for cooking. Have the skillet hot and keep it well greased. Drop the batter in and as soon as it is done on one side loosen it in the skillet and flip it over. Apple butter, syrup or cinnamon and sugar go well with the cakes.

While the crowd have taken the edge from their appetites with flapjacks, the trout have been cooked and they and the bacon are ready to serve. The trout are crisp outside and firm and pink inside and the bacon is well done—but not too done. If there is anything better than that combination the writer has yet to taste it in a lifetime devoted largely and studiously to eating.

The stew kettle will cook you dried apricots when they have resumed their predried plumpness after a night of soaking, it will serve to concoct a mulligan in, and it will cook macaroni. When you are not using it, it should be boiling water for the dishes.

Nothing like trail life to bring on a healthy appetite

In the baker, mere man comes into his own, for he can make a pie that to his bush appetite will have it all over the product that mother used to make, like a tent. Men have always believed that there was something mysterious and difficult about making a pie. Here is a great secret. There is nothing to it. We've been kidded for years. Any man of average office intelligence can make at least as good a pie as his wife.

All there is to a pie is a cup and a half of flour, one-half teaspoonful of salt, one-half cup of lard and cold water. That will make piecrust that will bring tears of joy into your camping partner's eyes.

Mix the salt with the flour, work the lard into the flour, make it up into a good workmanlike dough with cold water. Spread some flour on the back of a box or something flat, and pat the dough around a while. Then roll it out with whatever kind of round bottle you prefer. Put a little more lard on the surface of the sheet of dough and then slosh a little flour on and roll it up and then roll it out again with the bottle.

Cut out a piece of the rolled-out dough big enough to line a pie tin. I like the kind with holes in the bottom. Then put in your dried apples that have soaked all night and been sweetened, or your apricots, or your blueberries, and then take another sheet of the dough and drape it gracefully over the top, soldering it down at the edges with your fingers. Cut a couple of slits in the top dough sheet and prick it a few times with a fork in an artistic manner.

Put it in the baker with a good slow fire for forty-five minutes and then take it out, and if your pals are Frenchmen they will kiss you. The penalty for knowing how to cook is that the others will make you do all the cooking.

—From Ernest Hemingway
Dateline: Toronto, The Complete Toronto Star Dispatches, 1920–1924

BREADMAKING

Unleavened bread properly made is better as a steady diet than any of the baking powder products. The amateur cook is usually disgusted with it because it turns out either soggy or leathery. The right method, however, results in crisp, cracker-like bread, both satisfying and nourishing.

—*Camp and Trail*, 1920

It is in making bread that the amateur is most likely to fall down. . . . I make bread by winding the dough around sticks and standing them up by the side of the fire.

—E. Kreps, 1910

I advise making baking powder bread. To a pint of flour add one teaspoonful of good baking powder and half of that amount of salt. Mix it well and then add a lump of lard or bacon grease the size of a walnut. Work this well through the flour and then pour in enough cold water to make a thick but rather smeary dough. Mix it as quickly as possible but do not knead it. . . .

The one thing to remember is that the baking powder commences to act as soon as the water is added. It will be seen then that it should not be worked with more than necessary and should be put to bake as quickly as possible, for the baking powder will only act once. . . .

When camping out I seldom carry bread with me but carry the flour, already prepared, and make bread when I camp for the night. In such cases I frequently omit lard from the dough and simply turn the dough into the greasy pan after frying the bacon. I have bacon almost every meal when camping out on the trail.

—*Camp and Trail Methods*, 1910

MAKING DOUGH

Roll the top of your flour bag back, then build a cone of flour in the middle of the bag and make a crater in the top of the flour mountain.

In the crater put in baking powder [and] salt; mix these together with the dry flour, and when this is thoroughly done begin to pour water into the crater, a little at a time, mixing the dough as you work by stirring it around inside your miniature volcano. Gradually the flour will slide from the sides into the lava of the center, as the water is poured in and care taken to avoid lumps.

—Daniel Carter Beard, 1920

TWISTERS

Jack-Knife recipe for bread on a stick, our so-called Twister.

Ingredients:
1. One heaping fistful of flour.
2. One five-finger pinch of Baking Powder
3. One four-finger pinch of sugar.
4. One three-finger pinch of salt.
5. One two-finger gob of grease (fat, butter, lard, etc)
6. One or two fistfuls of water.

NOTE: (1) Fistful: 1/2 cupful. (2) Five-finger pinch: 2/3 teaspoonful. (3) Teaspoonful. (4) 1/8 teaspoonful. (5) Size of one wad of chewing gum, or 1/2 teaspoonful.

Now, with a wooden paddle, which you will carve, on the spot, out of a piece of soft wood, make a small imitation of the Plug-Hat Hole in your bag of flour. Into this little pit put your ingredients in the order named above. When you come to grease (No. 5) mix all up, using your hands to do this rather messy job thoroughly. Add water slowly which will, when stirred by your wooden paddle, absorb your fistful of flour and the other ingredients. The trick is to avoid lumps. Knead it well and quickly. Mix these, all dry, together at home before you start on your trip, carried in a small bank-bag or canvas bag, if you want to lose half the fun. If not, do it on the spot.

Now roll out your dough in a longish string, the size of a banana, and roll it on a sweet, green wood twig the size of your third finger, and sharpened at both ends. Sweet wood is determined by tasting it. Willow, for example, makes Kabobs and Twisters taste like quinine. Pine wood makes them reek of turpentine. Sometimes one can roast out this bitterness in the fire. Green wood stands the heat without burning. Jab one end in the ground so that the "twister" is about two inches from the coals. Watch it! Twist the stick round and round, until the flour puffs up and acquires a bit of crust. Then four or five inches from the fire is enough (maybe) until your twister turns a lovely dark brown. Now, screw out the stick. Split your twister, toast the inside, if it needs it, and there's your bread to eat with your kabob, which has cooked at the same fire along with your "Twister."

TWISTERS

The twist is made of dough and rolled between the palms of the hands until it becomes a long thick rope (Fig. 138), then it is wrapped spirally around a dry stick (Fig. 139), or one with bark on it (Fig. 137). The coils should be close together but without touching each other. The stick is now rested in the forks of two uprights, or on two stones in front of the roasting fire (Figs. 140 and 141), or over the hot coals of a pitfire. The long end of the stick on which the twist is coiled is used for a handle to turn the twist so that it may be nicely browned on all sides, or it may be set upright in front of the flames (Fig. 142).

—Daniel Carter Beard, 1920

The white man calls bread the staff of life. In a tight pinch he will abandon everything but his wheat. Not the sickly, faded, white flour that the dudes eat, but the whole wheat—man's natural and best food. Man has been eating wheat for about 50,000 years and human bodies have grown used to it. One can swim a river with a bag of flour and only lose a little by wetting a thin skin of dough! Mile for mile (weight-mileage— pounds per mile) wheat is acknowledged the food to travel on. So every boy should know how to cook it quickly and well.

—*Jack-knife Cookery*, 1929

BANNOCK

Create a smooth place on dry hard earth and brush it clean. On this make a fire and keep it going for at least two hours. Have a bed of coals ready, broken up fairly small by punching it down with a stone. Make a dough cake, "So big" . . . big boy, big bannock or Chupatty, as the Hindus call them. Use the Twister recipe and pat your cake to about half an inch thick. Place it gently on the hot ground, rake the coals over it and in about ten or fifteen minutes turn it over. Then test it with a smooth sharp splinter. When no dough sticks to the splinter . . . done. Eat it cold, split and toasted.

Raisins, nuts, berries—(not too many) worked into chupatties with more sugar! Try chocolate, milk, jam—grated fresh coconut meat. Any odds and ends—mashed potato, mashed sweets, cooked peas, etc.

—*Jack-knife Cookery* , 1929

DAMPERS

The Chupatty on a larger scale. Here your fire must be on hard flat ground and must burn all night . . . three hours anyhow. Ten pounds of flour makes a small cart wheel and will feed twenty people or more. Measured out by Double Fistfuls, you must count up how many pinches of Baking Powder, butter, Crisco, etc., you need, which should be easy, for you had best not try a big Damper until you are very proficient with Chupatties and Twisters. Mix this on a tent flap, dust it with plenty of flour, to keep it clean, roll it up like a huge jelly roll. Carry this on your extended arm to your hot space of ground, swept clean with a long stick and a broom of leaves—sweet ones, no pine!—and as gently as you can manage it, for shocking the dough tends to make it slump, unroll it. Then comes the hard part . . . raking the coals on top of the dough without a spade. Scrape the coals all over the top ashes and all, using a long flattened stick, for you will find it hot work, and do it as quickly as you can. The coals must be hot and close together. In about twenty minutes the puffing up process will have ceased. Now turn it over to brown the bottom. Now test it with a long sharp pointed "splinter" and if done, roll it against a tree to become cold. This is real bread and to be perfect should show no burned places. If these appear shave off the harmless carbon with your Jack-knife.

—*Jack-knife Cookery*, 1929

PAN BREAD

Usually the menu consists of baking powder bread, butter sometimes, bacon, and black tea. I try the bacon first by raking a few coals out before the fire and placing, the frying pan over them, supported by two chunks of green wood. While the bacon is frying I mix the bread. This I do in the top of the flour bag. Opening, it up as wide as possible I gouge a hole down into the center of the flour and pour in the proper amount of water, the flour having been prepared before starting, out, and then with a flattened stick I stir the flour into the water until I have a ball of dough, which I turn into the hot bacon grease in the frying pan, the bacon having been removed. I then flatten it out as much as possible and put fresh coals under the pan. The dough absorbs the grease, and when it has baked to a nice brown on the under side I turn it over and bake the other side. While the bread is baking I also prepare the tea, and in a half hour or less after I have commenced the cooking I have a meal.

—E. Kreps 1910

ORDINARY CAMP STAPLES

In most camps the staples are. Coffee (or tea), bacon, game, fish and hardtack, bannocks or biscuit usually and most appropriate!! called "sinkers" and "damper." To make these necessary evils, take:

1 pint flour,
1 teaspoonful of baking-powder,
Half as much salt,
Twice as much grease or lard,
With water enough to make into paste, say one half a pint.

When worked into smooth dough, shape it into wafers, half an inch thick, and three inches across. Set in a greased tin, which is tilted up near a steady fire. Watch and turn the tin till all are browned evenly.

—Ernest Thompson Seton, *Book of Woodcraft*, 1900

BISCUITS

For bread stuffs, biscuit, or corn bread. The former are easy to make in camp. Mix a cup of flour, a teaspoonful of baking powder, a little salt, and a tablespoonful of pork-fat suet. This latter is to be mixed in thoroughly with the hands, working it over and over in the mixing pan until thoroughly incorporated into the flour. Add one cupful of diluted cream to make a stiff dough. Roll out on the back of a large plate, handling gently, and having plenty of flour on your hands, on the roller, and on the plate.

Cut out biscuits with the top of the baking-powder can and put them in your baking-pans, first sprinkling a little flour on the bottom of the pan. Bake as with corn bread. The things to guard against are getting too much suet, or shortening, and handling or beating your dough too much; also putting the biscuits too close together. They want room to rise and swell up.

— Warren H. Miller, 1915

CORN BREAD

Corn bread will stick under your ribs in a hard day's work longer than any of the others and is easily made in twenty minutes' time. My own recipe is:

1 cup flour to 3/4 cup of corn-meal,
2 heaping teaspoonfuls of baking-powder,
1 level teaspoonful of salt,
1 tablespoonful of sugar

Mix these dry, add a beaten egg and enough milk-water to make a batter that will just pour, add a tablespoonful of melted butter, and stir vigorously. Grease your baking pans, pour half an inch of the batter in each, and into the oven with them. This last sentence means more in camp than it does at home. If you have a reflector baker of tile 12 x I5 x 8-inch size, the above recipe will just fill one pan nicely for a thick cake, or, better, divided into two pans, making two cakes about an inch thick when baked. Without a reflector baker the batter can be baked in the frying pans of the nesting set, with one of the mixing-pans inverted over the frying-pan and hot coals on top. Set in a bright, clear heat, but not on live coals, or the bottom of the cake will surely be burned. — Warren H. Miller, 1915

JOHNNY CAKES

Johnny Cake is mixed in the same way as the pone or ash cake, but it is not cooked the same, nor is it the same shape; it is more in the form of a very thick pancake. Pat the Johnny-cake into the form of a disk an inch thick and four inches in diameter. Have the frying pan plentifully supplied with hot grease and drop the Johnny-cake carefully in the sizzling grease. When the cake is well browned on one side turn it and brown it on the other side. If cooked properly it should be a rich dark brown color and with a crisp crust.

Before it is eaten it may be cut open and buttered like a biscuit, or eaten with maple syrup like a hot buckwheat cake. This is the Johnny cake of my youth, the famous Johnny-cake of Kentucky fifty years ago. Up North I find that any old thing made of corn meal is called a Johnny-cake and that they also call ashcakes "hoe-cakes," and corn bread "bannocks," at least they call camp corn bread, a bannock.

— Daniel Carter Beard, 1920

ASH CAKES

This ancient American food dates back to the fable times which existed before history, when the sun came out of a hole in the eastern sky, climbed up overhead and then dove through a hole in the western sky and disappeared. The sun no more plays such tricks, and although the humming-bird, who once stole the sun, still carries the mark under his chin, he is no longer a humming-birdman but only a little buzzing bird; the ash cake, however, is still an ash cake and is made in almost as primitive a manner now as it was then.

Mix half a teaspoonful of salt with a cup of corn meal, and add to it boiling hot water until the swollen meal may be worked by one's hand into a ball, bury the ball in a nice bed of hot ashes (glowing embers) and leave it there to bake like a potato. Equaling the ash cake in fame and simplicity is Pone. Pone is made by mixing the meal as described for the ash cake, but molding the mixture in the form of a cone and baking it in an oven.

SOUPS AND STEWS

Good soups and stews may be made occasionally if one likes them; for my part there are few to which I am partial.
—E. Kreps, 1910

[T]he mulligan—This is the camper's generic name for the big stew of the evening meal. Experienced men do not leave it out, for it is a great internal cleanser and regulator, besides being most easily digested. It is made of most everything shot during the day: grouse, fish, elk chunks, moose ditto, pieces of deer, a handful of rice, an onion sliced in for each man, a spud for each and a handful of dried soup greens. This invention is the first thing over the fire and the last to leave it, for the longer it cooks the better it gets. About six quarts for four men is about right, if the men are up to normal capacity (the mulligan always is). I usually tip in a cube of beef capsule for each man just before serving. After the mulligan and hot bread are well stowed, the party attacks the meat, rice, more hot bread, and tea, and when that is gone you lift off the fruit stew and set it in the snow to cool, and when that is down they are about ready for their pipes. Then the sleeping bags are unrolled, and soon the animals are snoring like majors and the mulligan is getting in its fine work. With that and the mountain air to see you through the night you will wake up next day with a fighting edge on and be ready to labor like a horse and so store up bodily health against the ravages of the mind when you get back to the worries of business.
—Warren H. Miller, 1918

BRUNSWICK STEW

Take two large squirrels, one quart of tomatoes, peeled and sliced, if fresh; one pint of lima beans or butter beans, two teaspoonfuls of white sugar, one minced onion, six potatoes, six ears of corn scraped from the cob, or a can of sweet corn, half a pound of butter, half a pound of salt pork, one teaspoonful of salt, three level teaspoonfuls of pepper and a gallon of water. Cut the squirrels up as for fricassee, add salt and water and boil five minutes. Then put in the onion, beans, corn, pork, potatoes and pepper, and when boiling again add the squirrel.

Cover closely and stew two hours, then add the tomato mixed with the sugar, and stew an hour longer. Ten minutes before removing from the fire cut the butter into pieces the size of English walnuts, roll in flour and add to the stew. Boil up again, adding more salt and pepper if required. —Daniel Carter Beard, 1920

HOT DRINKS

One thing which I would like to know, is how to make good tea from melted snow. I have tried it hundreds of times when there was no water to be had and could never make good tea in that way; it always has a rotten taste. I have tried everything I could hear of or think of but it was just the same. I have drank good tea made by others from melted snow but could not make it myself. I have watched the Indians make it and tried the same way without success.

One of my friends advises the following method which to date, I have not had the opportunity to try out.

"Have the pail clean, then fill it with snow. Rake a pile of live coals to one side of the fire and place the pail over them. When the snow is melted fill it up again and when this melts you have that much more pure water with which to make the tea. Tea so made will have no bad taste. I think your trouble is caused by the fact (supposed) that you are always in a hurry and melt the snow too fast."
—*Camp and Trail Methods*, 1910

This is the way to make tea. I bring the water to a boil then drop in the tea, remove the pail from the fire and cover it. The tea is well drawn in about five minutes.
—*Camp and Trail Methods*, 1910

ONE MONTH'S SUPPLY FOR ONE MAN ON A FOREST TRIP.

- ❑ 15 lbs. flour (includes flour, pancake mix, cornmeal in proportion to suit)
- ❑ 15 lbs. meat (bacon or boned ham)
- ❑ 8 lbs. rice
- ❑ 1/2 lb. baking powder
- ❑ 1 lb. tea
- ❑ 2 lbs. sugar
- ❑ 150 saccharine tablets
- ❑ 8 lbs. cereal
- ❑ 1 lb. raisins
- ❑ Salt and pepper
- ❑ 6 lbs. beans
- ❑ 3 lbs. or 1/2 doz. Erbswurst
- ❑ 2 lbs. or 1/2 doz. dried vegetables
- ❑ 2 lbs. dried potatoes
- ❑ 1 can Bakers' eggs.

—*Camp and Trail*, 1920

ONE MONTH'S SUPPLY FOR ONE MAN ON A PACK HORSE TRIP.

- ❑ 15 lbs. flour supplies (flour, flapjack flour, cornmeal)
- ❑ 16 lbs. ham and bacon
- ❑ 2 lbs. hominy
- ❑ 4 lbs. rice
- ❑ 1/2 lb. baking powder
- ❑ 1 lb. coffee
- ❑ 1/2 lb. tea
- ❑ 20 lbs. potatoes
- ❑ A few onions
- ❑ 2 lbs. sugar
- ❑ 150 saccharine tablets
- ❑ 3 lb. pail cottolene, or can olive oil
- ❑ 3 lbs. Cream of Wheat
- ❑ 6 lbs. mixed dried fruit
- ❑ Salt, pepper, cinnamon
- ❑ 3 cans evaporated cream
- ❑ 1/2 gal. syrup or honey
- ❑ 5 lbs. beans
- ❑ Chilis
- ❑ Pilot bread (in flour sack)
- ❑ 6 cans corn
- ❑ 6 cans salmon
- ❑ 2 cans corned beef
- ❑ 1 can Bakers' eggs
- ❑ 1/2 doz. Maggi's soups
- ❑ 1/2 doz. dried vegetables—beans and Julienne.

—*Camp and Trail*, 1920

CAMP PROVISIONS

PLANNING A MENU

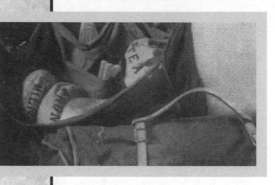

We get three sorts and periods of enjoyment out of a hunting trip. The first is when the plans are being discussed and the outfit assembled; this is the pleasure of anticipation. The second is the enjoyment of the actual trip itself; and the third is the pleasure of retrospection when we sit round a blazing wood-fire and talk over the incidents and adventures of the trip. There is no general rule to know which of the three gives the keenest joy. I can think of a different expedition in which each sort stands out in pre-eminence.
—**Kermit Roosevelt**

In no department of outdoor life does the mistaken notion of "roughing it" work more harm. I have never been able to determine why a man should be content with soggy, heavy, coarse and indigestible food when, with the same amount of trouble, the same utensils, and the same materials he can enjoy variety and palatability. To eat a well-cooked dinner it is not necessary to carry an elaborate commissary.
—*Camp and Trail*, 1920

Most veterans in the art of living out-of-doors and hitting the trail daily are agreed that the Indian and guide's way of two meals a day, with a light pocket lunch at noon, is the only way to get time enough to make progress. Wherefore, count on cooking a breakfast about eight times as substantial as the coffee, rolls, and fruit affair of civilization, putting away part of it for a warmed-up lunch at noon; and then when camp-making time comes, usually 3:30 to 4 P.M. in the spring and fall, or 6 in the summer, another tremendous feed will be assembled.
—**Warren H. Miller, 1915**

However closely you confine yourself to the bare necessities, be sure to include one luxury. This is not so much to eat as for the purpose of moral support.

[O]n a trip with an Englishman who, when we outfitted, insisted on marmalade. In vain we pointed out the fact that glass always broke. Finally we compromised on one jar, which we wrapped in the dish towel and packed in the coffee pot. For five weeks that unopened jar of marmalade traveled with us, and the Englishman was content. Then it got broken—as they always do. From that time on our friend uttered his daily growl or lament over the lack of marmalade. And, mind you, he had already gone five weeks without tasting a spoonful! So include in the list your pet luxury. Tell yourself that you will eat it just at the psychological moment. It is a great comfort.
—*Camp and Trail*, **1920**

INGREDIENTS

[Food] lists are not supposed to be "eaten down to the bone." A man cannot figure that closely. If you buy just what is included in them you will be well fed, but will probably have a little left at the end of the month. If you did not, you would probably begin to worry about the twenty-fifth day. And this does not pay. Of course if you get game and fish, you can stay out over the month.
—*Camp and Trail*, **1920**

The secret of successful camp cookery is experimentation and boldness. If you have not an ingredient, substitute the nearest thing to it; or something in the same general class of foods. After you get the logic of what constitutes pudding, or bread, or cake, or anything else, cut loose from cook-books and invent with what is contained in your grub bags. Do not be content until, by shifting trims, you get your proportions just right for the best results
—*Camp and Trail*, **1920**

WEIGHT

If the camp is a nomadic one instead of a permanent location, it is imperative to select only such foodstuffs as are light in themselves and to which many times their weight of water is added when cooking. There is no sense in packing a lot of water in the form of potatoes, green vegetables, meat, and eggs when every brook you meet is full of it, and you have a rifle or rod to accumulate fresh meat as you go. Your provisions should have an average capacity of making 6 pounds of cooked food for every pound of provisions carried.
—**Warren H. Miller, 1915**

TRAINING SKILLS FOR FOOD AND MENUS

APPRENTICE CAMPER
- Plan, prepare, and pack balanced trail meals requiring no cooking.
- Prepare a well-balanced meal demonstrating three kinds of simple outdoor cooking.
- Share in setting up a trail kitchen for overnight or longer.
- Share in planning menu and food list for a two-day trip, including dehydrated and easily packed foods. Consider the quantity of water needed and its sources.

JOURNEYMAN CAMPER
- Dry a variety of foods for use and long-term trail storage.
- Share in:
  - Planning a trail food menu for eight persons for four days.
  - Preparing at least eight kinds of trail foods.
  - Baking bread.
- Listing the trail-food items found on the shelves of a supermarket.
- Assisting in purchase of food items for the trip, packing, and storage.

JOURNEYMAN WOODSMAN
- Demonstrate skills for providing food from the outdoors—in season:
  - Fishing.
  - Hunting/Trapping.
  - Gathering.
- Discuss factors regarding avoidance of bear confrontations.

MASTER WOODSMAN
- Discuss factors concerning fasting when food is unavailable.
- Demonstrate ability to make and use tools and techniques for obtaining food:
  - Nets and snares.
  - Fishing rigs.
  - Bow and arrows.
  - Digging stick.
- Demonstrate ability to:
  - Cook without utensils.
  - Fashion cooking vessels.

FOOD TO LAST SIX FELLOWS ONE WEEK:

Oatmeal	6	lbs.
Rice	2	lbs.
Crackers	10	lbs.
Cocoa	3	lbs.
Tea	1/2	lbs.
Coffee	3	lbs.
Lard	5	lbs.
Sugar	6	lbs.
Condensed milk	12	tins
Butter	7	lbs.
Eggs	3	doz.
Bacon	15	lbs.
Preserves	5	lbs.
Prunes	3	lbs.
Maple syrup	3	qts.
Cheese	1	lbs.
Raisins	3	lbs.
Potatoes	1/2	bushel
White beans	3	qts.
Canned corn	3	tins
Flour	25	lbs.
Baking-powder	1	lbs.
Concentrated soups	1/2	lbs.
Salt	2 l	bs.
Pepper	1	oz.

Fresh fish and game are pleasant variations, but seem to make little difference in the grocery bill.

For cooking fish and game the old, simple standbys are the frying-pan and the stew-pan.

As a general rule, mix all batters, mush, etc., with cold water, and always cook with a slow fire.

— Ernest Thompson Seton, *Book of Woodcraft*, 1900

The choosing of proper food for a lengthy trip into the woods is an important matter worthy of some study. . . . One should choose such foods as give the maximum amount of nourishment and the minimum of weight and bulk. It should also be something which may be cooked very simply and be easily digested.
—**E. Kreps, 1910**

Necessarily bulk and weight are such important considerations that they will at once cut out much you would enjoy. Also condensed and desiccated foods are, in a few cases, toothsome enough to earn inclusion—and many are not.
—*Camp and Trail*, **1920**

PACKAGING

Food is best transported in bags. Cotton drill, or even empty flour sacks are pretty good on a pack horse; but in canoe and forest traveling you will want something waterproof. Even horseback a waterproof bag is better, for it keeps out the dust. Again I must refer you to Abercrombie & Fitch. Their food bags are of light, waterproof, and durable material, and cost only from a dollar to a dollar and a half a dozen, according to size.
—*Camp and Trail*, **1920**

The principal trouble with provisions in a packsack is that they may get wet, and they are not particularly available, especially the small parcels. If you put them all in one water-proof bag inside the pack, said bag is likely to be lumpy and knobby and not in the least accommodating to artistic stowing. My cogitations on these matters led me to the principle that all small provisions are better stowed in the cook-kit, where they cannot get wet or lost, than anywhere else, leaving but a few large bags of bulk provisions to go in the top of the pack.
—**Warren H. Miller, 1918**

For a party of four or five men for two or three weeks' grub, the best scheme I have yet encountered is the paraffined muslin food-bags, 8 inches diameter and 6 to 10 inches height. These collapse to flat packages like thick, round pancakes when packed and piled one atop the other in the food bags. To get the one you want without pawing over all the others, a side-opening tump-bag is the thing, and when rolled up tight and strapped this bag is as rain and water proof as the standard 10-inch end opening tump-bag.
—**Warren H. Miller, 1915**

SECTION FOUR
Life in Camp

Go forth a greenhorn camper if you must, but return a thoroughbred,
having learned the art of living with nature by actual experience.
On such the Red Gods smile.

—Frank H. Cheley, 1933

CAMPING: THE SPORT

And do not camp just for the sake of camping. There must be an objective—bass, trout, a canoe trip, feathered game, or general hunting. Camping is hard work if you do it right. It is the most healthful occupation in the world and your bodily efficiency rises to 100 per cent; but there must be some object to it all—some keen, good sport that repays for all your labor.
—Warren H. Miller, 1915

Camp life may take place on the trail while roughing it, on the road with a camp trailer, or at a lakeside resort with platform tents and dining lodge. The common trait is rustic design and a healthy dose of self-reliance. Even though a manicured camp with gravel trails, screened porches, and furnished tent cabins lacks Spartan living conditions, the plan of such places was to relieve the hardship of the trail so the sport could spend time relaxing and enjoying the full benefits of the outdoor setting. Guides and instructors took campers on nature walks and guided canoe outings. Many of the crafts and pleasures held over from Victorian times were still taught as well: pressing plants, clipping silhouettes, making twig frames and knot boards, and doing taxidermy were common program offerings.

The heading "Camping The Sport" can be read two ways: one is "camping, the sport"—identifying camping as the object; the other is "camping the sport"—with the focus on providing structured activities for the camper, making the camp experience more fulfilling. For many, the call is to "let the mountains speak for themselves"; the simple act of going to wild places will affect people. This may or may not happen. However, when a guide or teacher is present to help the camper interact with his or her surroundings and call attention to the beauty and simple gifts that might otherwise go unnoticed, the experience can be enriched.

Driving four days to pull a mobile aluminum cabin into a paved lot, then spending the evening eating microwaved popcorn while watching movies and planning the next day's checklist of high points and views so they can be visited with efficiency and speed allows moving on quickly to the next point of interest tomorrow. That's not camping, that's tourism—the instant-gratification scheme of a society with a huge appetite for quantity over quality.

To those we say, SLOW DOWN . . . SPEND TIME; enjoyment requires investment, and time is the currency.

Many people are so accustomed to have other people wait upon them that they are absolutely funny when you meet them in the woods; when their canoe runs its prow up upon the sandy beach and there is a portage to make, such people stand helplessly around waiting for some red-capped porter to come and take their baggage, but the only red caps in the woods are the red-headed woodpeckers, and they will see you in Germany before they will help tote your duffel across the portage.

When one gets into the real woods, even if it is only in Maine, Wisconsin, the Adirondacks, or the Southern pine forests, one soon discovers that there are no drug stores around the corner, the doctor is a long way off, the butcher, the baker, the candle-stick maker, trolley cars, telephone and taxi cabs are not within reach, sight or hearing; then a fellow begins to realize that it is "up to" himself to tote his own luggage, to build his own fires, to make his own shelters, and even to help put up the other fellows' tents, or to cook the meals. Yes, and to wash the dishes, too!

One reason we outdoor people love the woods is that it develops self-reliance and increases our self-respect by increasing our ability to do things; we love the work, we love the hardship, we like to get out of sight of the becapped maids, the butler and the smirking waiters waiting for a tip, and for the same reason the real honest-to-goodness American boys love a camp. Why bless your soul! Every one of them in his inmost heart regrets that he did not live away back in the time when the long-haired Wetzel, Daniel Boone and Simon Kenton roved the woods, or at least back when Colonel Bill Cody, Buffalo Jones and Yellowstone Kelly were dashing over the plains with General Miles, General Bell and the picturesque blond, long-haired General Custer.

Sometimes the author is himself guilty of such wishes, and he used to dream of those days when he was a barefooted boy. But, honest now, is it not really too bad that there are no longer any hostile Indians? And what a pity that improved firearms have made the big game so very shy that it is afraid of a man with a gun.

Because of the stampede for the open, in which people of all ages have joined, there are so many kinds of camps nowadays: scout camps, soldier camps, training camps, recreation camps, girls' camps and boys' camps, that it is somewhat difficult for a writer to tell what to do in order to "Be Prepared." There are freight car side-track camps, gypsy wagon

TRAINING SKILLS FOR NATURE AND CONSERVATION

APPRENTICE CAMPER

- Consider the effects of your outdoor-living practices upon the environment.
- Indicate good conservation practices in your immediate camp or trip area.
- Indicate violations of good conservation.
- Make a daily observation journal of signs pertaining to:
  - Weather
  - Geology
  - Flora and fauna
  - Natural systems

JOURNEYMAN CAMPER

- Identify several types of useful native material for:
  - Fuel and Shelter
  - Fiber
  - Medication
  - Tools and weapons
- Demonstrate interest in and awareness of the common natural resources of the area.
- Indicate knowledge of weather signs significant to good camping in the area.
- Compile and learn from a collection of insects, plants, or rocks.

JOURNEYMAN WOODSMAN

- Demonstrate an in-depth appreciation for the environment when:
  - Wildcrafting
  - Traveling
  - Camping
- Complete projects that will benefit the campsites and trails in your area.

MASTER WOODSMAN

- Demonstrate skill in creating wild-craft projects from natural materials:
  - Baskets, sheaths, and containers
  - Toys, games, and dolls
  - Musical instruments
  - Tools and more

camps, houseboat camps, old-fashioned camp-meeting camps and picnic camps; the latter dot the shores of New Jersey, the lake sides at Seattle, and their tents are mingled with big black boulders around Spokane; you will find them on the shores of Devil's Lake, North Dakota, and in the few groves that are back of Winnipeg, Manitoba.

But such camps have little attraction for the real hardboiled camper, and have no better claim to being the real thing than the more or less grand palaces built in the woods, camouflaged outside with logs or bark, and called "camps" by their untruthful owners; such people belittle the name of camp and if they want to be honest they should stick to the bungling bungalow—but wait a minute—even that is far-fetched; the bungalow belongs in East India and looks as much like one of these American houses as a corn-crib does like a church.

When we talk of camping we mean living under bark, brush or canvas in the "howling wilderness," or as near a howling wilderness as our money and time will permit us to reach; in other words, we want a camp in the wildest place we can find, except when we go to our own scout camp, and even then we like it better if it is located in a wild, romantic spot.

—Daniel Carter Beard, 1920

illing a plant press with natural wonders, collecting insects at night off a lit sheet, or gathering leaves, nuts, dried seed heads, and stalks for simple arrangements are all part of our outdoor tradition. Although collecting and wildcrafting should never be done in public-display areas or areas with limited or fragile resources, there are still plenty of places or less-intrusive ways to collect. Photo and sound records and sketching in a journal—an almost lost art—are all ways to record enjoyments.

The modern alternative is called "Click it—Don't pick it," encouraging photography as a better alternative to collecting. The interesting thing about this concept is that every week hundreds of acres of Canadian forest are logged because the pulp is the best product for photographic paper. Balance and judgement are the key.

Seton encourages us to carry what he calls a "talley book." In it we keep a record of our accomplishments, observations, and experiences. Records may include trailblazing, weather, stars and moon phases, bird sightings, animal signs—skulls, tracks, and scat.

Camp sports like archery, swimming, and fishing are all disciplines that when mastered take on Zen-like powers within the practitioner. Learning from a mentor moves the novice through a rapid learning curve, but also exposes the learner to the insights and life lessons from one who has perhaps dedicated a lifetime to the craft.

CRAFTING, COLLECTING, AND SPORT

I have a sudden passion for the wild wood
We should be free as air in the wild wood
What say you? Shall we go? Your hands, your hands
—*Robin Hood*, **by St. Nicholas**

THE SETON CHALLENGES

- ❏ List of Skulls and Tracks
- ❏ Make a Target
- ❏ Learn to Snowshoe and Ski
- ❏ Make Primitive Furniture
- ❏ Learn Semiphore and Morse Code
- ❏ Whittle
- ❏ Practice Distance Judging and Personal Measurements
- ❏ Make a Hunter's Lamp

- ❏ Tin-Can Craft
- ❏ Taxidermy
- ❏ Make Nesting Boxes, Tool Boxes, Storage Boxes
- ❏ Rock Collecting
- ❏ Flower Press
- ❏ Butterflies
- ❏ Loom Weaving
- ❏ Spore Prints
- ❏ Knot Boards
- ❏ Beading

COLLECTING

Most outdoor boys are great naturalists and collectors, and if the thing is not overdone it should be encouraged. As the curator of a great museum once said to me, "[T]he self-reliance, woodcraft, and love of Nature that your boyhood collecting trips taught you, far more than repaid any slight drain that you may have made on wild-life resources."
—Warren H. Miller, 1915

If you have a flair for nature study—trees, botany, birds, outdoor photography—or, if you want to indulge in the sterner sports of angling for gamy fish, wing shooting for wildfowl and the game birds of the wilderness, or hunting the big game that abounds; to camp right on the ground and live the life of the woodsman for a while is by far a better solution than to attempt some fisherman's boarding house, hunter's "camp" or other form of quasi-hotel life, in which your companions are not of your own choosing.
—Warren H. Miller, 1918

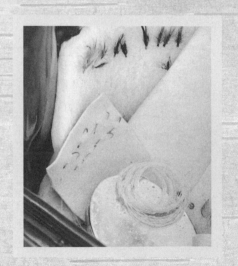

Old-style hooks, flies, horsehair line, and a cane pole, circa 1820.

FISHING

It is well known that no person who regards his reputation will ever kill a trout with anything but a fly.
—Nessmuk, 1920

In the ditty bag, without which I never take any trip, were little primer-boxes filled with butter, salt, tea, and sugar, and there was also a variety of hooks and lines, a steel 'possum hook, and a pickerel hook for froging.
—Warren H. Miller, 1915

By that time the sun and wind are going down and conditions are right for fishing again. You put out in the boat and cast the lily pads over the placid waters, glowing like burnished gold in the setting sun. Then comes the sunset, the wonderful June afterglow, with rose and purple reflections on the waters and splashes of rising bass and pickerel along the dark cattails—oh, boy! but that's the cream of bass fishing! Then home, and to bed by candle light. This is the schedule I prefer, and as I had no one but myself to cook for and there was no three-meal-a-day man to cater to, life was sweet and easeful.
—Warren H. Miller, 1918

COMMON SENSE PRECAUTIONS IN FISHING

The Outdoor Handy Book:
for Playground, Field and Forest,
by Daniel Carter Beard, 1900

WHY AND HOW FISH ARE EASILY FRIGHTENED—
The Lessons of Nature and of Experience

If you will sit perfectly quiet on the bank of a clear stream or lake, it will not be long before the inhabitants of the water will venture out of their hiding-places and swim around in plain view of the observer. What does this mean? If you shoot a pistol over your head, and make no quick motion with your arms or hands, even then the creatures under the water will not flee. What does this mean?

Of course, my reader can answer for himself that all this means that sound has not much, if any, effect upon the fish, but that their eyes are quick to detect the slightest suspicious movement overhead or on shore. If you are in boat and make a noise with your feet or anchor, the case is different, because you jar the water and that frightens the fish, but if you sit still, you may talk with no danger of alarming the game.

Some may doubt this; nevertheless, I have fired a pistol over the water and killed a frog with the bullet without alarming the other frogs or the fish in plain sight. But as soon as I made a movement to gain possession of the dead frog, not only all the other frogs plumped into the water, all the turtles slipped off the logs where they had been peacefully baking their backs in the sun, but every fish in sight darted away to be out of reach of the dangerous two-legged animal they saw approaching.

NATURE AS A TEACHER

The inference is that we must keep as motionless as possible when fishing, and when compelled to move, do so with great deliberation. If any one of my readers has ever watched a black-crested night-heron or any kindred bird as it fished in the shallow water, the motionless poise or the slow, deliberate movement of the bird could not have escaped notice. When you want to learn nature's secrets go to nature to find them out. Watch how the hunters with four legs and fishers with feathers act, and the nearer you conform your methods to theirs the greater will be your success.

It is understood, of course, that in fly fishing, casting and skittering, motion is constant and unremitting, even then the better you are concealed, the better will be your luck.

COMMON SENSE
PRECAUTIONS IN FISHING (*Continued*)

OUT OF SIGHT OF THE POOL

Fishing down [a] stream a few summers ago, I came suddenly upon [a] pasture, but in place of climbing the fence, I cautiously poked my rod through the bushes until my fly hung directly over the spot where I supposed the pool to be. Then I gently allowed the fly to settle down, and I only knew when it struck the water by the sudden pull on the line.

Without once seeing the pool, I landed fourteen fine trout; there were no very large ones. But I had enough fish for breakfast and returned home.

The next time I visited the brook I fished up the stream, and when I struck the pasture I climbed the fence and cast my fly from the bank; but I had been seen, and not one trout came near my hook.

TROLLING WITH A SPOON

In trolling, the longer the line the better, for the very palpable reason that the boat frightens the fish, but with a long line the fish has time to recover from his fright before the spoon comes glinting by him. Of course, a spoon does not look like any sort of a live creature when it is stationary, but a darting silver sheen is all that can be seen in the water, and that does look like a very brilliant and very lively young fish disporting himself with youthful impudence under the very noses of his cannibalistic grandsires; and it is no wonder they snap at it, if only to teach the young rascal a lesson. But, alas! They find that they are the pupils in the severe school of experience, and seldom do they live to relate their adventure to their companions.

A WORD ABOUT FLY-FISHING

Now, in regard to fly-fishing, fly-rods, reels, lines, hooks, fly-hooks, and all the numerous accessories of the modern fisherman, there are books and books written upon such subjects, and there is not room here for a hundredth part of what might be and has been well said upon these topics; but bait-fishing and bottom- or still-fishing are the choice methods for boys, and could not be well left out of the spring sports.

THE CRAFTING TRADITION

My first insight into the popularity of natural crafting came early in my career as a survival and wilderness living skills instructor. In the evenings, when the course was over for the day, an individual would begin to carve something and in a short time everyone was doing the same. I instituted carving as an evening pastime mainly to have the students learn how to use a knife more effectively. When students were provided with an appropriate material such as the easily carved black poplar bark, and offered direction on how to carve a face . . . they were ecstatic with the results.

Crafts and skills are practiced in the shelter of the canvas ramada.

Eventually, I incorporated many other crafts and all elicited a similar response. Once, in gathering sedge for making snare cord and lashing material, as a frivolous aside I demonstrated how quickly a doll could be made with handfuls of grass, something I had read about a few days before. The enthusiasm with which participants immediately made their own dolls led me to teach this craft at every opportunity.

It is hard to describe adequately the usual reaction of a person making his or her first cattail doll or carving a first face. You can make instant friendships by simply giving people . . . crafts. You will create an even stronger impression by constructing the objects in front of them, and a better one yet if you show them how to make their own. . . . Natural crafting is, above all, meant to be enjoyed.
—Mors Kochanski, 1989

WHITTLING

*"TRADITIONS PASS
WITH THE JACKKNIFE."*

Pick out some particular thing you want to make. Try your hand at a whistle of basswood or willow, in the Spring, or a water squirter of elder, or just take a stick and see how evenly and straight you can cut it.

Make a Fuzz Stick. Take a dry piece of soft wood like white pine, say twelve or eighteen inches long and about an inch thick. Take your knife and shave a little sliver as long as you can make it comfortably, taking care not to cut it off the stick. Then cut another, and another, making them all very thin and feathery. After you have shaved several you will not have to exercise such great care. Keep on cutting until you have the whole stick cut away. If you can do it without losing one sliver, you are a good whittler. Then turn the fuzz stick upside down out on some vacant lot, light it with a match, and see how easy it would be to make a fire even on a wet day if you had two or three fuzz sticks like the ones you have just made.

- Don't carry an open knife.
- Don't cut nails.
- Don't cut hemlock, balsam, or other knots. They are likely to chip your blade.
- Don't put your knife in the fire—it will ruin its temper.
- Don't use your knife as a screw-driver, a crowbar, or a hammer, but take as good care of it as you would of your best watch.
- Remember, a good, sharp jackknife is the most useful tool a boy can own.

There seems to have been two classes of the old-fashioned American whittlers—those who whittled to aid their thought and those who thought to aid their whittling. While it is true that the second class turned out some excellent wood engravers and artistic decorators of furniture, the first class seems to have been the product which left the more lasting effect upon life. The man who whittled while he thought left nothing of his shingle save a clutter of shavings, but he usually had a well-rounded idea in his head when he had finished. The closing of his jackknife usually meant that the argument was ended, to his satisfaction at least.
—**Phillip D. Fagans, 1933**

It is safe to say that when the old-timers were boys themselves, there was not a lad among them who could not whittle with considerable skill and many a twelve year old boy was an adept at the art. I remember with the keenest pleasure the rings, charms and knickknacks which I carved with a pocket knife before I had reached the scout age of twelve. Today, however, the boys handle their knives so awkwardly as to make the chills run down the back of an onlooker.

In order to properly open a knife, hold it in your left hand, and with the thumbnail of your right hand grasp the blade at the nail notch in such a manner that the line of the nail makes a very slight angle; that is, it is as near perpendicular as may be, otherwise you will bend back your thumbnail until it hurts or breaks. Pull the blade away from your body, at the same time drawing the handle of the knife towards the body. Continue this movement until the blade is fully open and points directly from your body.

Practice this and make it a habit; you will then never be in danger of stabbing yourself during the process of opening your knife; you will open a knife properly and quickly by what is generally termed intuition, but what is really the result of training and habit.
—**Daniel Carter Beard, 1920**

HOW TO WHITTLE

The age of whittling began with the invention of the pocket knife and reached its climax about 1840 or '50, dying out some time after the Civil War, probably about 1870. All the old whittlers of the whittling age whittled away from the body. If you practice whittling that way it will become a habit.

Indians use a crooked knife and whittle towards the body, but the queer shape of their knife does away with the danger of an accidental stab or slash.

When you whittle do not whittle with a stick between your legs, and always whittle away from you. . . . Do not try to pry the stick apart with a knife or you will sooner or later break the blade, a serious thing for a wilderness man to do, for it leaves him without one of the most useful tools.
—**Daniel Carter Beard, 1920**

THE PERMANENT CAMP

It is all right to talk about roughing it in the woods. But the real woodsman is the man who can be really comfortable in the bush.
—Ernest Hemingway, 1920

Camping out is a fine art; one of those things that are worth doing well if done at all. It is quite easy to bungle it, and so sentence yourself to a variety of nuisances from which you are normally shielded by the bulwarks of civilization. It is also very easy to do it right; the formulas are few and simple, and camping with modern equipment involves really so little deviation from civilized standards of existence that it is well worth learning. Living for a while in some wild beauty spot under canvas, close to the busy life of nature, steeped in the ozone of the forest air, is an aesthetic enjoyment, relished the more keenly the more intellectually inclined is the normal bent of the camper-out.
—Warren H. Miller, 1918

Every boy looks forward to camping out . . . camping out is the only complete outdoor life.
When a boy, I was of course eager for a chance to camp out, but I had a very wrong idea about it. I believed that one must undergo all sorts of hardships, in order to be really "doing it"; such as, sleep on the ground with one blanket, go without proper food, etc.
—*The Book of Woodcraft*, 1900

That eminent satirist, Mr. George Jean Nathan, regards camping out as the most terrible of modern diversions. While this simply proves that the critic's judgment is pronounced from a mere playgoer's viewpoint—material on camping gathered, most likely, from some movie screen—the fact is that most people, while fascinated with the idea, regard it as something which only the elect can do with any degree of comfort.
—Warren H. Miller, 1918

Of course, if you intend to have a permanent camp, and can reach it by boat or wagon, lightness is not so important, though even in that case it is well to guard against taking a lot of stuff that is likely to prove of more weight than worth.
—Nessmuk, 1920

We have come to assume that camping has to be mobile and that any gear worth the investment must be lightweight so that everything can be carried on the back. Lightweight camping is only a small segment of the camping experience. It has a long tradition, but is still just part of the traditional camping spectrum. The most common form of camping is by car, rail, or other form of transport to a destination where a camp is pitched and left in place until it is struck at the time the camper decides to return home.

The permanent camp still requires mobile equipment so that it can be packed or shipped with minimum space. But the variety of gear and the number of luxuries that can be included make the camping life a comfortable life with the most splendid surroundings. The view from the tent door is what we seek, but to relax in a comfortable camp chair with friends and family—unhurried, hassled, or stressed—requires gear that is brought along or added to the camp from local materials.

PLATFORM TENTS AND CAMPS

Fig. 309 shows some of the ordinary forms of tents, the wall tent, the Baker tent and the canoe tent. Fig. 310 shows a tent with a fly extending out in front, thus giving the piazza or front porch. In the background is a tipi tent. Fig. 311 shows two small Baker tents in the background, and the Dan Beard tent in the foreground. These comprise the principal forms, but the open-front tents to-day are much in vogue with the campers. A mosquito netting in front will keep out the insects and allow the air to come in freely, whereas the old-fashioned way of closing the tent flap stops circulation of air and makes conditions as bad as that of a closed room in a big house, and the air becomes as foul as it did in the little red school houses and does now in the Courts of Justice, jails and other places of entertainment.
—Daniel Carter Beard, 1920

THE DEMOCRACY OF CAMPING

The subject of camping . . . strikes at the very roots of life. At its best it holds up a mirror to us all, showing how far civilization and overpopulation have combined to separate us from the easy formula of life which the Creator intended; how they have driven thousands to starvation within a stone's throw of the fabulously rich, whereas Nature gave every man the equal strength of his own two hands, which were once ample to win him livelihood and happiness.
—Warren H. Miller, 1915

[T]he goal of camp-life is to arrange to spend the whole summer out-of-doors, beside some favorite lake or river. To most of us this must be somewhere within commuting distance of some large city. To a few it is given to be able to live thus in a good game country, leaving the business cares for the winter months. It is this kind of camp of which I wish particularly to speak, for it is an ideal life. Every morning the sun streaks through the trees, vivifying all the delicious night scents with a warmth and radiance that is pure joy to one who can spend his waking hours breathing the rich forest air; every night the moon makes pictures of lake and woods that live and live in one's memory long after more noted sights are forgotten; and every day that can be stolen from the city is one more store of golden hours for this, the most delightful of all plays.
—Warren H. Miller, 1915

No camp that is at all worthy of the name can be far from some open sheet of water, and water usually means plenty of bathing and bathing-suits, canoes, sunburn, fishing-tackle, and absolute cleanliness—blazing with health and wide-open pores. Even in the hunting season there is still the bath, and then the rub-down and the invigorating change into a clean flannel hunting-shirt, corduroys, and canvas. Keep in close touch with the water your camp is located beside, brothers, and you will never fly to the city for relief.
—Warren H. Miller, 1915

There is another brand of water, not so welcome or healthful as that which one bathes in, canoes in, and sails over, and whips for pickerel. I refer to the variety that comes a-rearin' and a-tearin' out of black, rolling clouds, along with enough wind to last twenty summers; ripping up tent-pegs, sinking boats, and wetting down everything not under tarpaulins. This also numbers itself among the petty annoyances that drive the

long-stay camper to the city, and the only way to beat him out in the long run is to make the camp just as near permanent as possible. If you can get a board floor, so much the better; but be very sure that none of the boards reach out from under the walls of the tent so that the water can follow them inside.
—Warren H. Miller, 1915

If you have the homing instinct you will get to love that little shack as you do your boyhood town, and will put in all sorts of spare hours and rainy days in improving it and making it more comfortable.
—Warren H. Miller, 1915

The easiest way to make a floor in the woods is to choose some lazy afternoon when every one is tired of fishing and floor the whole of the shack with flat stones taken from the natural rock of the forest. Wash this over with an inch of thin, watery grout, of eight parts sand to one of cement, smoothing it with a straight-edge and trowel while the other fellow pours it from the pail. It will make a more durable, snakeproof, and vermin-proof floor than split logs or dirt.

The whole floor space is, by this arrangement of sleeping accommodations, available for living-room; canvas camp-chairs, log tables, etc., can be put in and one has a comfortable lounging and eating room (in bad weather).
—Warren H. Miller, 1915

The principle use of such a woodland shack is in the promotion of what Dr. Van Dyke has aptly named "Days Off." Without it, many a holiday, especially the combination ones occurring on Thursday or Friday, when Saturday and Sunday are thrown in for good measure, are wasted because one feels more or less unprepared and undisciplined to break a new trail for so short a time. But if it is merely a matter of packing some provisions and the sleeping-kit, whistling up the "pups," and taking a train to the nearest jumping-off place in the vicinity of "Loafers Glory," or whatever you have named the shack, you will get out of it many a pleasant little outing, each one a diamond point in your memories.
—Warren H. Miller, 1915

ROUGH IT

This advice is not for the tenderfoot, for he should never attempt to "rough it . . ."
—*Camp and Trail Methods*, 1910

amping bits, wits, and skill require mastery of the woodcraft traditions. To walk out with only the tackle in one's pack, sled, canoe, or panniers and those simple essentials always accompanying the body—knife and matches—is the traditional camper's skills refined to a keen edge. It is also seen by some as the masochist's search for the ultimate torture. Why go without, when comfort can come at such little expense?

The camper who chooses to use skill in place of technology gains insights that the comfort camper will never attain. Contrary to popular belief, he or she doesn't go out to hack out a life in the bush. Instead, the traditional camper camps in harmony with the surroundings. He or she replaces technology with practiced skill and knowledge. The rewards are intrinsic, and if done with style, may also benefit the natural world. The real camper is a steward and child of his special place. His goal is to make sure that minimizing the buffers he places between himself and his hearth will increase an appreciation for the natural world and require him or her to work hard for its betterment by keeping it clean, reducing his or her visible impact, and conserving the natural beauties and resources for others to enjoy.

When one is hunting big game, or on a canoe trip, or such nomadic camp-life, the less of everything taken along the better. A good sleeping-bag is often preferable to a tent; a single skillet will provide the utensil to cook with; and rifle, axe, and knife are really all the necessities that can be mentioned. I even once went on a trip where I took nothing along except a note-book and two sheets of blank music-paper. A bully tramp over the mountains it was, too, and I slept in piles of leaves raked up in dry ravines that were already filled a solid foot deep with dry leaves.
—**Warren H. Miller, 1915**

Warren Miller in one of his many sleeping-bag inventions.

With a large majority of prospective tourists and outers, "camping out" is a leading factor in the summer vacation. And during the long winter months they are prone to collect in little knots and talk much of camps, fishing, hunting, and "roughing it." The last phrase is very popular and always cropping out in the talks on matters pertaining to a vacation in the woods. I dislike the phrase. We do not go to the green woods and crystal waters to rough it; we go to smooth it. We get it rough enough at home; in towns and cities; in shops, offices, stores, banks—anywhere that we may be placed—with the necessity always present of being on time and up to our work; of providing for the dependent ones; of keeping up, catching up, or getting left. "Alas for the life-long battle, whose bravest slogan is bread."
—Nessmuk, 1920

CUTTING DOWN ON DUFFEL

[T]wo more bits of camp philosophy which you formulate to yourself about [are] as follows: An article must pay in convenience or comfort for the trouble of its transportation; and Substitution, even imperfect, is better than the carrying of special conveniences.
—Warren Miller, 1910

Since we have worn coats all our lives, we include a coat in our list of personal apparel just as unquestionably—even as unthinkingly—as we should include in our calculations air to breathe and water to drink. The coat is an institution so absolutely one of man's invariable garments that it never even occurs to him to examine its use or uselessness.

In like manner no city dweller brought up in proximity to laundries and on the firm belief that washing should be done all at once and at stated intervals can be convinced that he can keep clean and happy with but one shirt; or that more than one handkerchief is a superfluity.

Yet in time, if he is a woodsman, and really thinks about such affairs instead of taking them for granted, he will inevitably gravitate toward the correct view of these things. Some day he will wake up to the fact that he never wears a coat when working or traveling; that about camp his sweater is more comfortable; and that in sober fact he uses that rather bulky garment as little as any article in his outfit. So he leaves it home, and is by so much disencumbered. In a similar manner he will realize that with the aid of cold-water soap the shirt he wears may be washed in one half hour and dried in the next. Meanwhile he dons his sweater. A handkerchief is laundered complete in a quarter of an hour. Why carry extras, then, merely from a recollection of full bureau drawers?
—**Warren Miller, 1910**

CAMP CHORES

If there is a spot on earth where trifles make up the sum of human enjoyment, it is to be found in a woodland camp
—**Nessmuk, 1920**

CAMPING IN STYLE

The way in which an average party of summer outers will contrive to manage—or mismanage—the camp and camp-fire so as to get the greatest amount of smoke and discontent at the least outlay of time and force, is something past all understanding, and somewhat aggravating to an old woodsman who knows some better.
—**Nessmuk, 1920**

SETTING A SCHEDULE

[W]e soon settled down to a fine regime as follows: Sunrise, bath in the lake; grub, painting and writing music, more bath in the lake, dinner at four, bass fishing around the islands until eight P.M.; bed. Nobody did a stroke of honest work. It was delicious.
—**Warren H. Miller, 1918**

And so the golden days slipped by; an ideal existence—I could have kept it up all summer—freedom to loaf and invite your soul, charming and entertaining companions, all the time in the world to work at that which you liked to do best, and—no worries!
—**Warren H. Miller, 1918**

CAMP ROLES

Essentially a camp consists of a group of tents, a fire, and a fat man for chef. The rest do not count—as essentials. But, even with the above, and of extra-fine quality, the camp may be a sorrowful memory unless a certain amount of organization, of routine, is agreed upon and lived up to. I have known camps where the star hunter blandly laid him down on the browse that others had picked, and informed all and sundry that, as he knew nothing whatever of fires or cooking, his job forthwith would be to keep the camp in game! Whereupon the fisherman, taking his cue, declared that he would attend to the fish market, and the naturalist, following suit, arose to remark that cooking and dish-washing was no gentleman's job, and that he would attend strictly to the fruit supply. Just at this juncture the cook appeared in the doorway with the camp-bench poised above his head, vociferating that, by the devil's caldron, if all three of them didn't dig out and rustle fire-wood, slick up the camp, and clean all the pots and pans in less than two minutes, he would beat them all as flat as so many Shrovetide-pancakes
—**Warren H. Miller, 1915**

Each of the four men went at his appointed task. One man looked after the horses, another got timber for the tent, a third went for the tent stove and grub supplies, while I started after browse. Three of us first cleared a space ten by fifteen feet with our snow shoes, down-to the hard ice-pan, scraping the last of it off with the back of the axe. Then I set out into the darkness with belt axe, armed with a carbide lamp. A clump of feathery balsams was my object, and a few blows with the axe brought down the snow from them in showers, which, as they fell on my broad-rimmed cowboy Stetson hat, were no bother at all. A man in a toque would have had his neck filled with snow avalanches, then and there! The balsams were cut down and the boughs cut off and hung wheel-wise around a forked stick about four feet high, until I had a sort of fat, furry caterpillar of browse shoots, each about two feet long. It is the best way to carry browse in quantities. Meanwhile the others had got up the ridge-pole and I went around the walls and tied each peg rope to a short stick, burying it deep in the snow and finally shoveling snow up all around the sides with my snowshoe, burying the sod cloth and holding it down tight and firm. By the time this was done and I was back with a second caterpillar of browse, the tent stove was up and the evening meal simmering. . . . I spread the browse thick on the ice, and topped it with a tarp. The bed rolls were dusted of their snow and brought inside, and presently all four men sat down to a steaming meal. At about the second quart of mulligan, two of us gave up, leaving the Indian and the cow man still prodding into the camp kettle, at which business they remained long after we had unrolled our beds and retired to pipe-dream and watch our socks drying over the stove. The blizzard howled outside, but within all was warm and comfortable. A large acetylene lamp and a candle lantern supplied plentiful illumination, and the talk ran mostly on art and literature, with the cowman and the Indian drinking in hungrily this discussion from a world so foreign to their daily lives and therefore so attractive to listen to.
—**Warren H. Miller, 1918**

As soon as all are on the ground, with their baggage, let the Leader allot the places of each band or clan. Try to have each and every dwelling-tent about 25 feet from the next, in a place dry and easy to drain in case of rain and so placed as to have sun in the morning and shade in the afternoon.

Each group is responsible for order up to the halfway line between them and the next group.

Loose straw, tins, papers, bottles, glass, filth, etc., out of place are criminal disorder.

Pitch at a reasonable distance from the latrine, as well as from the water supply.

As much as possible, have each band or clan by itself.

As soon as convenient, appoint fellows to dig and prepare a latrine or toilet, with screen.

All will be busied settling down, so that usually there is no methodic work the first day.

But the second day it should begin.
—Ernest Thompson Seton, *Book of Woodcraft*, 1912

The naturalist just naturally takes over the care of water-supply from the spring, berries from the patch over on the shoulder of the mountain, watercress out of the brook, mushrooms from the fields. And all three of them take the dish-pan job in rotation.
—Warren H. Miller, 1915

Every woodsman should know how to prepare everything that his rod and gun get him and how to use the simplest herbs and plants of the forest. But the man in whom the study of food preparation is a yearning and an art, a consuming interest, is the one who naturally steps forward to be cook.
—Warren H. Miller, 1915

To perform the chemical operation aforesaid requires the application of just the right heat for just the right time. Therefore, it is impossible for the cook to get results in the open if he has to leave his job continually to rustle fire-wood or water. These must be right at his elbow, and the other members of the party must put them there, as getting the meals takes a lot of the cook's time, and no man in the party should have to take any more time than any one else away from the pursuits of the sports that all came into the woods to enjoy. Neither should he wash dishes or set the table. Once the meal is cooked and served, the chef's work is done, and he should be allowed to return to his pipe in peace.
—Warren H. Miller, 1915

SETON'S IDEAL

When two or three young people camp out, they can live as a sort of family, especially if a grown up be with them, but when a dozen or more are of the party, it is necessary to organize.

What manner of organization will be practical, and also give full recognition to the nine principles of scouting? What form of government lends itself best to Recreation; Outdoor Life; Self-rule; The Campfire; Woodcraft Traditions; Honors by Standards; Personal Decoration for Personal Achievement; A Heroic Ideal; in my opinion, the Tribal or Indian form of organization.

Fundamentally, this is a republic or limited monarchy, and many experiments have proved it best for our purpose. It makes its members self-governing; it offers appropriate things to do outdoors; it is so plastic that it can be adopted in whole or in part, at once or gradually; its picturesqueness takes immediate hold of all; and it lends itself so well to our object that, soon or late, other forms of organization are forced into its essentials.

No large band of boys ever yet camped out for a month without finding it necessary to recognize a leader, a senior form (or ruling set whose position rests on merit), some wise grown person to guide them in difficulties, and a place to display the emblems of the camp; that is, they have adopted the system of the Chief, Council, Medicine man, and Totem-pole.

Moreover, the Ideal Indian stands for the highest type of primitive life. He was a master of woodcraft, and unsordid, clean, manly, heroic, self-controlled, reverent, truthful, and picturesque always.

America owes much to the Redman. When the struggle for freedom came on, it was between men of the same blood and bone, equal in brains and in strength. The British had the better equipment perhaps. The great advantage of the American was that he was trained in Woodcraft, and this training which gave him the victory, he got from the Redman.

But the Redman can do a greater service now and in the future. He can teach us the ways of outdoor life, the nobility of courage, the joy of beauty, the blessedness of enough, the glory of service, the power of kindness, the super-excellence of peace of mind and the scorn of death. For these were the things that the Redman stood for; these were the sum of his faith.
—*The Nine Leading Principles of Woodcraft*

A WORD ABOUT CLOSING CAMP

Repair all canvas before putting away for the winter. Put on new guy ropes where necessary. Be sure your canvas is thoroughly dry, well folded, and protected in either old canvas, burlap bags, or grain sacks, each sack tagged with a good tag, giving size, condition, and general memoranda concerning the bundle.

Pull all nails, hooks, etc., from each pole (if you have any) and tie poles in bundles with a tag.

Give all tin kitchen equipment a coat of grease to keep it from rusting. Empty all salt, pepper and the like. Invoice the contents of each chest, and tack invoice on the outside, making copy for your loose-leaf camp book. Clean the ashes thoroughly out of your stove and pipes, and tighten up loose bolts, nuts, and screws.

Give your toilet seat a good coat of linseed oil or paint.

Repair and paint your boats or canoes.

Make a list now, while things are fresh in your mind, of articles that need replacing; also add to your list items of equipment that should be gotten before another season. Discard worn out and useless equipment.

Clean the camp grounds up thoroughly. Gypsies and tramps leave a trail of tin cans, litter, old browse beds and the like behind them, but good campers never do. Burn everything that will burn—bury the rest. You may wish to return yourself; if not, some other party may choose to use your site. Pay your bills and thank all those who have contributed to make your outing a success. Incidentally, government rangers, as well as settlers, appreciate this last point. Earn for yourself and comrades the reputation of being thoughtful, reliable, and courteous.

When you reach home, carefully overhaul your own duffel, putting it in shape as far as possible. Also give your camp note-book the "once over" with an eye to checking up and improving it for future use.

Then, and not until then, can you consider your camp another completed chapter in your life.

—Frank H. Cheley, 1933

TRAINING SKILLS FOR HEALTH AND SANITATION

APPRENTICE CAMPER
- Discuss simple health and safety practices in relation to outdoor living.
- Demonstrate use of:
  - Health and safety practices
  - Basic signaling techniques
  - Survival preparation and priorities
- Outline preventive measures and first-aid procedures for common emergencies in outdoor living.
- Outline principles to consider for human needs—food and water.
- Describe benefits and health factors in personal cleanliness.
- Identify harmful plants and animals and know proper precautions.

JOURNEYMAN CAMPER
- Develop pre-trip list of potential precautions and hazards.
- Demonstrate a method of purifying water supply for drinking and for cooking.
- List common emergencies possible in outdoor living in your locality.
- Construct a first-aid kit to take care of such emergencies on a trip.
- Possess first-aid training for emergencies ranging from cuts to amputations.
- Demonstrate ground-to-air signals.

JOURNEYMAN WOODSMAN
- Possess first-aid training to deal with long-term concerns and medical emergencies.
- Demonstrate ability to:
  - Use emergency procedures.
  - Maintain personal cleanliness.
  - Assess and avoid hazards of traveling on ice, snow, and water.
  - Evacuate sick or injured campers.
  - Make do without toilet paper and flush toilets.
  - Explain trail sanitation and acclimatization.
  - Identify harmful plants and animals and know protection and treatment.
- Display knowledge of seasonal food and water concerns.

MASTER WOODSMAN
- Construct a field sauna or steam bath.
- Demonstrate skill in dealing with issues concerning long-term:
  - Human waste
  - Waste and refuse
  - Animal and pest invasions
  - Food storage
  - Water quality
- Discuss the use of herbs and remedies in dealing with field illness and injury.

> There are many kinds of mosquitoes; all of them are Bolsheviks, and with the black flies and other vermin they argue that since nature made them with blood suckers and provided you with the sort of blood that they like, they have an inherent right to suck your blood—and they do it!
> —Daniel Carter Beard, 1920

> Mosquitoes are not the only vampires which infest our woods. The "punkeys" (black flies) and "midgets" can outstrip them for ferocity and the painful character of the wound which they inflict.
> —W. H. Gibson, *Camp Life in the Woods*

A camping party should have their work so divided that each one can immediately start at his own particular job the moment a halt is made. One chops up the firewood and sees that a plentiful supply of firewood is always on hand; usually he carries the water. One makes camp, puts up the tents, clears away the rubbish, fixes the beds, etc., while a third attends strictly to kitchen work, preparing the meals, and washing up the dishes.

With the labor divided in this manner, things run like clock work and camp is always neat and tidy.
—**Daniel Carter Beard, 1920**

BUGS, HEALTH, AND SANITATION

There are all sorts of camps, from the hasty voyageur bivouac of the big-game hunter to the serene summer retreat when one invites his soul to ease in Nature's lotus-land— that "place where it seemed always afternoon." Indeed, I think that the quintessence of camping is reached when one knows the game thoroughly enough to be able to draw from Nature alone all the comforts that civilization affords, in addition to the thousand joys which no civilization can give. It is far easier to do this than one would suppose, for the reason that most of the drawbacks of camp-life come from neglect of simple cleanliness and ordinary bodily comforts, such as homo sapiens have become accustomed to from his cradle.
—**Warren H. Miller, 1915**

We go to the woods for health and refreshment. If we violate those basic needs, we come back determined never to go again. Even on the harsh trails with those who rough it, comfort and relaxation can be achieved. But we are constantly taught to remain apart from nature, because it seems that nature is out to get us. Cancer from the sun, deadly parasites, and bugs in the water are the modern version of the bears, wolves, and panthers that threatened the dudes of yesterday. Big guns and crowds managed to defend the tyro back then. Now it's a whole arsenal of gadgets, gizmos, chemicals, and hardware that are needed to do the job.

Technology is no match for goods wits—what we used to call common sense. Knowledge may cost you something to regain, but once you have it, it doesn't require spare parts, replacements, or batteries. And it's lighter than anything the market can dream up to try to take its place.

Bad water can be boiled in a tin can found on the ground. Putting on a hat or making a pair of woodcraft goggles can alleviate sun sensitivity. There are simple solutions to most of what ails us on the trail, and they don't have to cost money or add weight to the duffel.

BUGS

The enthusiastic camper, as he starts for his outing in the wilderness, should not be unmindful of the swarms of bloodthirsty flies, gnats, mosquitoes, chiggers, and numerous other common camp pests which infest the woods and hills in the summer and early autumn months, for they are always there in countless millions and lying in wait for the unprepared. These camp pests often become a source of great annoyance, to say nothing of the health-danger they occasion.
—**Frank H. Cheley, 1933**

"When the bugs begin to huddle, the world will soon become a puddle." — Old weather adage.

WHAT'S IN A NAME

Once inside for the night you close and tightly lace the front, and then with electric flasher, calmly murder each and every mosquito, black fly, punkey, squeazlegeaques, and midge that has accumulated inside, after which you will have a night of peace.
—Warren H. Miller, 1918

Mosquito

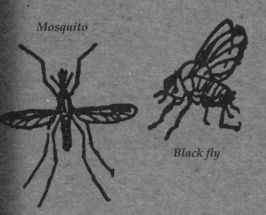

Black fly

Certain times of year, when one goes camping in the neighborhood of the trout brooks, one needs to BE PREPARED, for one can catch more trout and enjoy fishing better if protected against the attacks of the black flies, mosquitoes, midges and "no-see-ums."
—Daniel Carter Beard, 1920

The black fly is a very small hump-backed pest; the young (larvae) live in cold, clear running water.
—Daniel Carter Beard, 1920

In the first place he overlooked the insects. Black flies, no-see-ums, deer flies, gnats and mosquitoes were instituted by the devil to force people to live in cities where he could get at them better. If it weren't for them everybody would live in the bush and he would be out of work. It was a rather successful invention.

But there are lots of dopes that will counteract the pests. The simplest perhaps is oil of citronella. Two bits' worth of this purchased at any pharmacist's will be enough to last for two weeks in the worst fly- and mosquito-ridden country.

Rub a little on the back of your neck, your forehead and your wrists before you start fishing, and the blacks and skeeters will shun you. The odor of citronella is not offensive to people. It smells like gun oil. But the bugs do hate it.

Oil of pennyroyal and eucalyptol are also much hated by mosquitoes, and with citronella they form the basis for many proprietary preparations. But it is cheaper and better to buy the straight citronella. Put a little on the mosquito netting that covers the front of your pup tent or canoe tent at night, and you won't be bothered.
—Ernest Hemingway, 1920

BLACK-FLY DOPE
Three ounces pine tar
Two ounces castor oil
One ounce pennyroyal oil
Rub it in thoroughly and liberally
    —*Forest and Stream, 1883*
Nessmuk, 1920

FLY DOPE
Pure pine tar	1 OZ.
Oil pennyroyal	1 OZ.
Vaseline	3 OZS.

Mix cold in a mortar. If you wish, you can add 3 percent carbolic acid to the above. Some make it 1-1/2 OZS. tar.
    —Ernest Thompson Seton, *Book of Woodcraft, 1912*

SOME GENERAL SUGGESTIONS ON CAMP PESTS

Eat your breakfast and get to going before the insect swarm comes to life. They are usually not very active until a warm sun is shining.

Camp, whenever possible, on a wind-swept knoll or point. This helps materially.

Keep your head and bed net mended: one tiny hole is enough to bring you misery. If the smaller of insects insist on crawling through the meshes, dope your nets.

Do not scratch insect bites. Very often such sores become infected with poison ivy or the like.

Keep them clean, sterile, and doped, and they will soon get better.

Don't wash any oftener than absolutely necessary, if once well "dopped." The older the dope the better the gloss, and in consequence the more sure the protection.

Don't forget your fly dope. A small reserve is often a good thing.
—Frank H. Cheley, 1933

However that may be, the meal was eaten with all haste, as the punkies were upon us; also the black flies, and they soon drove us to bed. The Doc retired to his tent, Joan was ushered into her cot and I slid blissfully into my stretcher bed and sleeping bag. I pulled the mosquito blind down and laughed at the buzzing demons outside. Just as I was dozing off a fiery itch on my face called for a hand-slap out of the bag. Horrors! Punkies! Also midges ! Also black flies! They went through that mosquito blind like a tennis net, nor did I get a wink of sleep that night. Joan hardly fared better, as the punkies and midges found the cheese-cloth a simple matter of perseverance to penetrate; and the Doc, having put his tent up, leaving sundry holes under the sod cloth, soon had his abode full of the pests.

Fly dopes only served as a mire to grind the myriads of demons.
—*Warren H. Miller, 1918*

FLY-DOPE RECIPES

In the black fly belt it is wise to add a bottle of fly dope (Fig. 251) to one's personal equipment. If you make your own fly dope, have a slow fire and allow to simmer over it
3 oz. pine tar
2 oz. castor oil
1 oz. pennyroyal
or heat 3 oz. of pine tar with two oz. of olive oil and then stir in 1 oz. of pennyroyal, 1 oz. of citronella, 1 oz. of creosote and 1 oz. of camphor.
—Daniel Carter Beard, 1920

The most satisfactory remedy for mosquito bites is moist soap. Wet the soap and rub generously on the puncture. The irritation will soon pass away. Others recommend household ammonia, alcohol or glycerine, iodine, or the juice of a crushed onion.
—L. O. Howard, *Department of Entomology, Farmer's Bulletin No. 44.* 1933

SMUDGES

But, while all these flies were at us, they were not overly bad, as yet, for the punkie does not come out in force until dusk, when the spruce smudge is your only sure protection. I gathered a handful of dead balsam twigs and started a sassy little fire.
—**Warren H. Miller, 1918**

The smoke of smoldering birch bark will effectively drive mosquitoes from tents at night, but the smoke is offensive to many.
—**Frank H. Cheley, 1933**

*B*lack flies, mosquitoes, punkies, midges, no-see-ums, or even squeazlegeaques—or whatever they're called—cause no end of concern over how to rid the camp of them. Each sourdough has his dopes, smudges, and other bug rituals for keeping them at bay. Our modern concoctions have been responsible for heart attacks, chemical poisoning, elevated blood pressure, and more, when lighting several cow pies that will provide a smokey smudge for hours is all that's really needed.

If the tent becomes filled with hordes of houseflies, it's time to keep an eye on the weather. The low pressure associated with rain makes insects fly low to the ground or seek shelter. Campers can kill them, trap them, or herd them outside by swinging a towel, then they should prepare for the weather.

BUG GEAR

If you propose traveling where there are black flies and mosquitoes, let your mother sew onto a pair of old kid gloves some chintz or calico sleeves that will reach from your wrists to above your elbow (Fig. 246), cut the tips of the fingers off the gloves so that you may be able to use your hands handily, and have an elastic in the top of the sleeve to hold them onto your arm. Rigged thus, the black flies and mosquitoes can only bite the ends of your fingers, and, sad to say, they will soon find where the ends of the fingers are located.
—**Daniel Carter Beard, 1920**

A piece of cheese cloth, fitted over the hat to hang down over the face, will protect that part of your anatomy from insects, but if they are not very bad use fly dope, and add a bottle of it to your pocket outfit. One doesn't look pretty when daubed up with fly dope, but we are in the woods for sport and adventure and not to look pretty. Our vanity case has no lip stick, rouge or face powder; it only possesses a toothbrush and a bottle of fly dope.
—**Daniel Carter Beard, 1920**

He showed us his bathing suit, sewed up at the arms, which he pulled over his head at night so as to sleep free of flies, while a pair of socks protected either hand and an extra shirt kept them from biting into his back. . . . Joan and I solved the punkie problem by putting our two tarps up as a wedge tent and sewing in ends of thin lawn, which the tiniest of squeazlegeaques cannot get through. Nicky slept on a rock in his awe-inspiring costume.
—**Warren H. Miller, 1918**

Anything swung by a strap across one's shoulder will in time "cut" the shoulders painfully unless they are protected by a pad. A few yards of mosquito netting or cheese cloth occupies little space and is of little weight, but is very useful as a protection at night. Bend a wand into a hoop and bind the ends together, with safety pins; pin this in the netting and suspend the net from its center by a stick.
—**Daniel Carter Beard, 1920**

LATRINES

Each small camp or group of tents in a large camp must have a latrine, that is a sanitary ditch or hole. For a small camp or short use, this is a narrow trench a foot wide, surrounded by a screen of bushes or canvas. It is made narrow enough to straddle. Each time after use, a shovel full of dry earth is thrown in.

But a large camp needs the regulation army latrine. This is a row of seats with lids over a long trench which has a layer of quicklime in the bottom. The wooden structure is banked up so no flies can get in. The lids are down tight when the seat is not in use. A shovel full of quicklime is then thrown in after each occasion. A running trough is arranged along side so it is tributary to the main trench; this also is kept coated with quicklime. The place should be thoroughly screened, but is as well without a roof except over the seats.

All camps should be left as clear of filth, scraps, papers, tins, bottles, etc., as though a human being had never been there.

—**Ernest Thompson Seton,** *Book of Woodcraft*, **1912**

The camp latrine is often a very big problem. If you want to know just what sort of folk any party are, investigate the latrine. Too long we have had the idea that anything would do, when, as a matter of fact, it of all things should be a clean, sanitary place. Many times they are allowed to become so offensive that campers use the open to avoid them, and of course, when there are more than two hikers, that is contrary to every law of good camping. Some merely use a rail and a pit, always having a shovel handy with which to keep fresh dirt in the pit. For a very small party on a very brief camp, this may be made to serve, but at best it is only a makeshift. A far better way is to

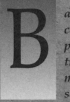

SANITATION

Backcountry living and hygiene has some new considerations we need to address. Whatever refuse produced must be packed out. One problem the traditional camper avoids with a passion is the modern trend of over packaging. Cooking from scratch or simple components reduces waste at both the checkout counter and in the field. If less is bought, there is less to pack out. The traditional camper recognizes his place in the big picture. Many campers seem to forget that all actions have a ripple effect that need to be considered in place of the quick fix and convenience of modern gadgets.

Burnable garbage should be incinerated in the stove and the ashes sifted for nonbiodegradable trash. Leftover charcoal should be crushed to ash and spread, only when cool, near shrubs and plants that can benefit from it.

We should camp well away from trails and points of congestion, such as springs and trail junctions, and camping too close to water sources; 200 to 300 feet is not too far away. Carrying a collapsible bucket makes water retrieval a breeze.

Toilet paper or paper products must never be left at a campsite. A fire or stove makes quick work of contaminated refuse. Burying such items only insures that frost or animal action will create toilet paper flowers for the next visitors to encounter. Feces decomposes in a matter of days if dealt with properly—toilet paper can last for months or years.

A wash basin provided with a hot-water bucket suspended over the fire is an attractive addition to any camp. It's easy to keep water warm, a much nicer comfort than the rough trail practice of the cold-water dunk.

include in your equipment a well-made set of holes, the number of holes in the set to be determined entirely by how many campers there are in the party. Each seat should then have hinged, just back of the opening, a convenient top lid, well cleated to keep it from splitting. Such an affair can easily be shipped along with the other equipment; and with it and a few boards, a rough yet fly-tight box can be quickly constructed. Set the box on stout poles placed across the ends of the pit, and then bank in well with brush and dirt. If no boards are available, make a frame of poles upon which to place the seat-board, then close it in with building paper, old canvas, or the like.

A field privy.

Pitch the latrine tent about your seat, arrange a sapling back of each separate lid so that it can never be left open, and you have a simple, inexpensive, sanitary latrine. When the camp is over, burn your boxing, and cover the pit well with earth.
—**Frank H. Cheley, 1933**

HYGIENE

Roughing it is making the best of it; only a slob and a chump goes dirty and has a sloppy-looking camp. The real old time veteran and sourdough is a model of neatness and order. But a clean, orderly camp is much more important than a clean-faced camper. Some men think so much of themselves and their own personal cleanliness that they forget their duty to the others. One's duty is about in this proportion: first to the animals if any, secondly to the men, and lastly to oneself.
—**Daniel Carter Beard, 1920**

A toilet can be made from a 50-gallon barrel.

Most folks have a very mistaken idea about what roughing it really means. Contrary to the popular idea, it does not mean that even a boy, under the guise of camping-out should hie himself into the woods and there quite completely forget every principle of personal health and sanitation. The question of keeping healthy in camp merits more consideration than it usually receives. Practically all sickness in camp is due to neglect which the observation of a few simple rules of hygiene would have prevented; and if campers would exercise a little more care, nearly all of the ills of camp life could be avoided.
—**Frank H. Cheley, 1933**

A final word—on cleanliness. When the tyro camper comes out of the woods his first dash is for the tub, where he soaks out three or four weeks of grime; his next is for the barber's, where a fuzzy stubble is hoed off; and the last is to the haberdasher's, where he gets on him all the stiff chokers, pink socks, and nobby ties that his purse will permit, "to forget the backwoods."

He hasn't really camped, you know. He just slid gracefully back to savagery because the well dressed city crowd was not present to shame him.

Now, in camp one should be cleaner and nattier than anywhere else. There is plenty of exercise to keep the pores open, and one can bathe all day long and get a fine, healthy coat of tan all over one's hide without half trying. If there is a better or more healthful summer-camp apparel than a good jersey bathing-suit without any sleeves, I have yet to hear of it. For strenuous work there is the gray flannel shirt and the forestry suit and hunters' shoes. Set one day a week for washing, have plenty of hot water, and take along a small sack of washing-powder—and mind that you do not try to make corn mush with it!

In a word, cut out all dirt and petty annoyances and live as nearly as you're accustomed to in your own home as your brains and ingenuity will permit.

—Warren H. Miller, 1915

GENERAL HEALTH TIPS

A small cake of soap in an oiled silk bag or a rubber tobacco pouch is convenient for light marching: compact and does not rattle around. "Grandpa's" tar soap makes good lather in any kind of water, hard or soft, warm or cold.

—Horace Kephart, 1917

Perhaps as good a receptacle as comes for the purpose is the kit roll, about 16 inches long by 8 inches wide when opened out flat, and which is provided with rows of pockets to hold soap, shaving tackle, comb, and brush, night-cap, night socks and slippers.

Collapsible-canvas water buckets are a good addition.

Looking-glass, tooth-brush, mending-kit, etc. This is hung up on two stakes alongside your sleeping bag, and then each article is handy and there is a place for every one of them when you get up in the morning. As you divest yourself of knife, watch, compass, pipe, bandanna, belt, tobacco-pouch, electric flasher, and the like, on retiring,

A wooden washbasin.

these go into the pockets lately occupied by the night outfit, and atop of one of the stakes is just the place to swing the carbide lamp by its pointed hook. When packing the kit up in the morning the pillow is folded flat and laid lengthwise across the roll; an inspection shows that all the articles are in their accustomed pockets, and the kit is then rolled up around the pillow and tied with its tapes.
—**Warren H. Miller, 1915**

A similar but smaller bag is useful to be reserved entirely as a toilet bag. Tar soap in a square knot round—celluloid case is the most cleansing. A heavy rubber band will hold the square case together. The tooth brush should also have its case. Tooth wash comes in glass, which is taboo; tooth powder is sure sooner or later to leak out. I like best any tooth soap which is sold in handy flat tin boxes, and cannot spill.
—*Camp and Trail*, **1920**

If you are sensible you will not be tenderfoot enough to go in for the discomfort of a new beard. Razors can be kept from rusting by wrapping them in a square of surgeon's oiled silk. Have your towel of brown crash—never of any white material. The latter is so closely woven that dirt gets into the very fiber of it, and cannot be washed out. Crash, however is of looser texture, softens quickly, and does not show every speck of dust. If you have the room for it, a rough towel, while not absolutely necessary, is nevertheless a great luxury.
—*Camp and Trail*, **1920**

On dressing in the morning, after one's hunting boots have been softened up and put on, the first thing wanted is a good wash; and the thing to do it with is hot water, poets and amateur campers to the contrary notwithstanding. A very little out of the cook's big boiling water-pail will make an astonishing quantity of water as hot as your face can bear, and so you sidle up to him with your folding canvas wash-basin already part full of cold water and get a dipperful. Somewhere at the bottom of your tump-pack, or flat in your knapsack should be a small, 12-inch canvas basin of this type. It folds down flat as the proverbial pancake, and opens up to about 3 inches high, and it's one of those little comforts weighing an ounce or so that will repay its weight by keeping you looking fresh and well and feeling so, too.
—**Warren H. Miller, 1915**

A variety of water containers

A wash basin built on the same principle is often a veritable godsend, and a man can even carry a similar contrivance big enough for a washtub without adding appreciably to the bulk or weight of his animal's pack. Crushed flat all three take up in thickness about the space of one layer of blanket, and the weight of the lot is just a pound and a half.
—*Camp and Trail*, 1920

There are some little personal things to which one should give one's attention before starting on a long trip. If it is going to be a real wild camping trip it is best to go to the barber shop and get a good hair cut just before one starts. Also one should trim one's nails down as close as comfort will allow. Long nails, if they are well manicured, will do for the drawing room and for the office, but in camp they have a habit of turning back—and gee willikens, how they hurt! Or they will split down into the quick and that hurts some, too! So trim them down snug and close; do it before you start packing up your things, or you may hurt your fingers while packing. But even before trimming your nails, go to your dentist.

Well, never mind the details, they are too painful to talk about, but remember the lesson that they teach—go to the dentist and get a clean bill of health on the tooth question before you start for a lengthy camp.
—**Daniel Carter Beard, 1920**

Nature has provided no comforts at all, and she launches her armies of insect life or her legions of chilly particles of air and water against the poor body without respite and without pity. The veteran woodsman automatically puts up screens against any and all these annoyances with the same skill with which he follows the faint game track. Comfortable sleeping, comfortable eating, comfortable cooking, and comfortable washing are his without fail, for he knows the necessity of guarding the body against the fret and wear of minor hardships.
—**Warren H. Miller, 1915**

Remember, Lad or Lass, that you take your "regular" stomach camping with you, and therefore you must treat it much as you do at home, only better. It will no more stand abuse in camp than in school; yet many a summer outing is a sad failure because folks somehow get the notion that the fact that they are in the woods makes it possible for them to "eat like hogs."
—**Frank H. Cheley, 1933**

Every meal must be well cooked and eaten with a relish, or else you pay for it later on. That is the reason why everybody should learn simple cooking before he starts camping. Eat sparingly the first few days in camp—not all you want, but all you ought to have. Look out sharply for headaches, biliousness, cramps, and diarrhea. Study the sections of this book covering food and camp menus until you have mastered the principles—every one. Be certain there is at least one good cook among you, not by hearsay, but by demonstration; then you are ready to camp.
—**Frank H. Cheley, 1933**

SECTION FIVE

Life on the Trail

Oh. for the life of the open camp
On horseback, ski or sail.
To travel as gypsy, gent or tramp,
Oh, for the life of the trail
—Unknown

THE AUTO GYPSIES

For real adventures, crowding one upon another, just go camping with an auto!
—Author Unknown, 1933

Beginning about 1910, the affluent urban dwellers felt harassed and compromised by schedules, obligations, and the altogether too-formal life of the twentieth century. Fleeing their homes and jobs, they packed the touring cars with family, gear, and pets and hit the road, hoping to rediscover freedom, if only for the weekend. The urban auto gypsy was a common sight on the road, in campgrounds, and at the end of the trail.

As the automobile became more available to the masses and roads improved to accommodate them, the summer travelers began to expand their destination base. Early camps were found in school yards, at local beaches, or simply along the roadside. The travelers' transportation was simple but effective. Auto camps were built adjacent to and within many of the nation's great parks and tourist attractions. By 1925, pressures produced overcrowding and unsanitary conditions to the point that many of the auto camps had to be abandoned.

About this same time the new auto campers sought the pleasures of the outdoor life, but they also wanted the privacy and comforts to which they were accustomed. Around 1925, the era of the roadside cabin came into its own. Many local farmers provided unfurnished cabins that could be rented by the week or the month. Their produce was available for purchase, making camping a great financial boon for the rural resident. Later, affluent travelers were lured to the open road, but preferred roughing it by trailering a camper or purchasing one of the new house cars. By the late 1920s, campers and trailers were so widely available that the "tin-can tourist" was a common sight. The TCT club was founded and grew to 100,000 members in ten years. But it all came to an end in 1930 when the Great Depression drove people to the road life, not by choice but for survival.

THE MOTORING SONG
by C. Wiles Hallock

Who's for a hike to the hills?
Who's for the wind in the wood?
Autumn is sighing—Summer is dying
Russet and scarlet and gold!
Morn is a murmur of thrills
'Wakening echoes afar!
Gay leaves are falling—wild winds are calling—
Who's for the Road and the Car?

Who's for the chill of the dawn
Steeped in a shimmering haze?
Skimming the highway, straight for the skyway,
Who's for a camp and a blaze?
Night's misty curtains withdrawn,
Greeting the pale morning star,
Daybreak is glowing—scud-drifts are blowing—
Who's for the Road and the Car?

Who's for the dusk in the pines?
Night and the hush creeping down,
Firelight dancing—Oh, how entrancing
Twinkle the lights of the town!
Ho! for the hill-gusts a-whine,
Chill in the still of the dark!
Autumn is calling—singing—enthralling!
Ho! for the Road and a lark!

THE MOTOR CAMPER

Camping with a motor is a comparatively new development of the camping-out idea, but promises soon to head the list of popular choice, for it has many advantages that, combined, make such camping by all odds the sort for a family outing. With the tremendous improvement in roads, and the increased popularity, as well as splendid performance, of the moderate-cost car, automobile camping has suddenly become a practical possibility for numberless families, east, west, south, and north; for almost any section of the country affords attractive and altogether satisfactory camp country easily accessible with a motor.
—**Frank H. Cheley, 1933**

In addition to being able to get the whole family there and back again with convenience, it offers opportunity for short trips or long trips; to permanent camps or for "gypsying" through the land. You may go spring, summer, autumn, or all three, if you desire. The cost is reasonable; necessary equipment is not large; and oh, what a series of adventures, all the way from patching an inner tube by the light of a camp fire in some lonely wilderness . . .
—**Frank H. Cheley, 1933**

ON THE ROAD
Touring with a motor, however, is not even distantly related to camping with an auto. One party goes dressed up to the best wayside hotels, or from resort to resort, buying everything that is done for them, even to applying the pressure gauge to their tires; while the other carries the "best hotel" with them, pitching it where and when fancy strikes them, and glorying in the comfort of khaki, high boots, and a favorite old hat. Then with the aid of a few choice bits of "squaw wood," a side of fragrant bacon, and a can of good coffee, along with all the "et ceteras" that belong to a camp commissary, they proceed to smooth it in delightful fashion in rough places. For as Nessmuk says: "We do not go to the woods to rough it; we go to smooth it. We get it rough enough in town. But let us live the simple, natural life in the woods, and leave all frills behind."

Do not be ambitious to cover ground. Take it easy and enjoy every mile. You will be entirely independent of everybody and everything. . . . If you are a speed demon, seek out nice paved boulevards and "go to it," but don't fool yourself into believing that you are camping. Camping is the quiet, easy, simple life, with strain and tension left at home.

The medium-weight touring car is best—five to seven passenger. Runabouts are too light, and space too limited. If the party is large, two medium cars are far better than one large one. The car should, of course, be in first-class repair. Tires should be such as will stand hard and unexpected usage, with, of course, two good "spares" and an extra tube or so.

Auto-camping, like all true sport, has a delightful degree of uncertainty.

Remember that invariably when auto-campers become cross, crabbed, and unsociable, they are very likely "road weary." Stop, camp, and rest until "cheer" and "good will" again take up their abode with you. A worn-out disposition is much more serious than a "blow-out" or a "burned brake band." By all means, stop and "fix it." Only by so doing will you all reach home enthusiastic about each other and your modern adventure.
—Frank H. Cheley, 1933

CHOOSING GEAR

The fact that any well-built car can penetrate into all good game country, outside of the big game localities reached only by canoe or mountain and forest trail, has led to a continuous development of its use as transportation to good hunting and fishing grounds. As many of the best of the latter are located where there is no inn, and so far away that a return home leaves but little time for sport, some sort of camping adjunct to the automobile has been very desirable. It was soon realized that the car itself made an excellent framework to secure at least one wall of the tent to, and so especial designs were made to fit an automobile frame, with a jointed pole carried in the car along with the other duffel . . .
—Warren H. Miller, 1918

The interesting thing about auto-camping is that no two parties go in just the same fashion. There is even a wider diversification of equipment possible than in any other type of camping. The absolutely essential thing that needs attention by all, however, is to think through thoroughly and in detail all the phases of the proposed trip . . .

Many an auto-camping party make themselves ridiculous by the looks of the poor car on such a trip. You may see them with everything attached, from iron bedsteads to washtubs and packing boxes. Limit the actual weight of each member's duffel. Think

through ways to reduce the weight and bulk of your equipment, in addition to placing it to best advantage on the car. Consult auto equipment catalogues for ideas; watch how others do it. . . . If you find, because of the length of the proposed trip, or the size of the party, more equipment is necessary than can be nicely packed on the running boards and bumper, use a trailer. Make one, or buy one that fits your pocketbook. Canoe campers and pack campers have reduced equipment to a science. The auto camper can do likewise if he will. Don't look like a moving second-hand store just because you have been too lazy and unresourceful to reduce weight and bulk.
—Frank H. Cheley, 1933

CAMP TRAILERS

As the car cannot get far in from a road, and good level tent sites, near spring water and yet near an accessible lumber road, are hard to find, the automobile camping idea developed still further in the automobile trailer, in which the entire camp—tent, cots, kitchen and ice box—is carried on a two-wheeled trailer so as to be immediately available as a comfortable forest home. One of the troubles of camping with an automobile is that the party is limited below the seating capacity of the car because there is no room for all the duffel. I suppose I have been on two dozen automobile camping

trips where we had to pack in any old way, perched on our duffel, with part of it lashed on behind, some of it on the running boards and some tucked in on each side of the radiator—but still the back tonneau was crowded with duffel bags, and a car that could have taken six was limited to four. And, when you add in a couple of husky setters and pointers, none on particularly good terms with each other—good night!
—Warren H. Miller, 1918

The trailer has been developed from such simple ideas to a complete house, with four cots, two on a side, or double tiered, a galley and ice bog and a tent pulled over all, and the whole works can be unlimbered in some fifteen minutes and limbered up in about the same time. At first the builders did not realize that everything about such an outfit will shake loose on the road unless every bolt and nut is secured by cotter-pin, or else upset, and the troubles from falling apart due to road vibration were so aggravating as to cause many dealers to abandon the trailer altogether as a nuisance.... As the trailer industry is a new one and has grown to considerable dimensions, we will have a look at some of the leading designs....

[B]eds are of woven wire springs, with a regular mattress such as you would have at home. They are double, 42 inches wide, sleeping two each. A folding table is set up on the trailer floor with the beds as seats, and the ice box is pulled out sideways from under the trailer, always accessible, the denatured alcohol stove lit up, and soon you have a feed ready to serve in the trailer. Even in bad weather, with all the flaps pulled down front and rear, you still have plenty of light, for the tent roof has a celluloid skylight of large size on both sides....

Another way of getting at the same thing is exemplified in a design which is not a trailer, but a compact camp home to be carried on the running board. When packed, this is a stout lacquered box, 11 x 18 x 48 inches. Inside it are

a full sized double-decked bed, with two wire springs, two mattresses for the beds, two camp stools, and a wall tent, 7 x 8 x 7 feet to the ridge, while the box itself is a table 3 x 4 feet when opened out flat and its interior legs let down and locked. When unpacked this outfit sets up to give you a wall tent and a double-decked bed for four, the frame of the latter being also the frame of the tent. It weighs altogether about 160 pounds, and leaves you plenty of room in the car for personal duffel bags and food bags, cook kit and the like.
—Warren H. Miller, 1918

AUTO TENTS

By no means has the original automobile tent been lost sight of during the development of the trailer idea. A good many autoists do not want a trailer astern, preferring to make camp with a tent every night, and this has been met with several designs. . . .

Another design provides two lean-to tents, one on each side of the car, utilizing the interior of the car itself as part of the storage room, while still another utilizes the running board of the car as the front end of a double cot bed with the tent attached to the under edge of the car top coming out in a lean-to over the cot. What was needed was some sort of flexible spring mesh that would go in a collapsible pressed steel frame on which a mattress can be laid, for, in a bed of this width, a canvas bottom would simply bag in the middle. This bed is 48 x 78 inches, and weighs 60 pounds with mattress, and the shelter top is of 12-ounce duck canvas. . . .

Another idea in touring-car tents consists in having a tent large enough to close the entire car, using the car top as the tent roof support and pegging out the slant of the roof on each side of the car to make a double tent extending out about 7 feet each side of the car. This is made to fit the 11-foot Ford touring car . . . gives plenty of headroom, and the double tent permits the eating-table on one side of the car and sleeping quarters on the other.
—**Warren H. Miller, 1918**

If you have chosen a tent that pitches independent of the car, place it first and unpack your duffel into it, if there are signs of bad weather. If you use a lean-to as a part of the car, place your car, not the tent, into the wind. Keep your beds and bedding always dry. The pneumatic beds are best for both bulk and comfort, if you can afford them; if not, use a serviceable folding cot, unless you are where browse is plentiful. (Such places are becoming fewer and fewer—better not count too much upon them.) If you have room, a small fly to cook under, lounge under and so forth, will be appreciated, and can be used as a ground cloth for the tent, if you wish it. Probably you will rig some sort of a folding table, using one running board for seats, and supplying simple folding camp chairs for the balance. A hammock is a luxury that takes little room and gives one a good place to rest. Keep a sharp three-quarters ax handy, encased in a leather sheath, and strap an auto shovel securely to your running gear.
—**Frank H. Cheley, 1933**

The first United States bicycles were manufactured in about 1878. They were far from an instant sensation as the horse was still the primary method of conveyance and the adoption of such trifle was the domain of the senseless and irresponsible. But as the age of the machine took hold, the bicycle became a workman's tool, and eventually became a popular leisure pursuit. Of course, anyone committed to his or her sport will find new ways to apply it, and it wasn't long before a vehicle used for neighborhood chores and fun became the mode of travel for adventurers on both road and trail.

Their kit was light and Spartan, with food usually being purchased from local farmers and heavier goods shipped to rendezvous points along the way. Rigid panniers carried over the front and rear wheels on simple frames, handlebar bags, and complex canvas and cardboard packs suspended under the top tube and between the pedals were handmade or purchased from outfitters. Leather traps, roller buckles, and packs of canvas were common. Heavy-gauge pasteboard was used to make stiff trunk-like boxes lined with brightly colored cloth. Cardboard dividers and shelves kept all of the necessaries in their given place.

I f ever there was an icon for all that it means to camp in the old style, the wood-and-canvas canoe is probably the most commonly envisioned. The classic lines, varnished decks and ribs, painted and brass details, and all the accessories of travel by canoe, pay homage to those who have passed down this great legacy of camping tradition. Forms that evolved from decades of continuous use have been refined and perfected. No craft made from chemicals has ever matched the grace and performance of one of these handmade classics.

The great thing about canoe camping is that because of the ability to haul loads, a comfortable camp can be taken into the backcountry. On the other hand, those who camp with a canoe know its limitations, and have developed their gear and style to match. Canoeing allows a wide variety of people to enjoy the comforts it provides but still requires discipline and commitment to do it well. It's not a sport for everyone, even though it has the capacity to be so. Perhaps this is another reason why canoe campers hold fast to tradition. It holds no patience for the Chechako.

Graceful motions, quiet calm, and trappings that have marked time—canoe camping is the epitome of traditional style.

CAMPING WITH CANOE

The canoe is coming to the front, and canoeing is gaining rapidly in popular favor, in spite of the disparaging remark that "a canoe is a poor man's yacht."
—Nessmuk, 1920

Ten pounds of well made cedar ought to carry one hundred pounds of man.
—*Forest and Stream*, 1920

There is something about canoe cruising that is different from any other kind of camping. In the first place, there is the zest of uncertainty, not knowing just where your next camp will be, or what will appear around the next bend of the river. Then there is the problem of navigating, picking difficult channels, or running rapids, or studying the wind conditions on a lake to find the easiest going. Then there is the choosing of the camp site at night, selecting a spot which is high and dry, with lots of wood and with shelter from the wind or weather. But best of all is the intimate contact the canoe cruiser gets with Mother Nature. The canoe is the Indian's boat, and somehow it almost makes a fellow feel like an Indian when he grasps his paddle and shoves off. A boy in a canoe sees things that he cannot see in any other way. The canoe glides so quietly that one can creep up close to the wild creatures and study them at close range, or he can lie concealed in overhanging bushes like a bit of the landscape, while the birds and animals live their lives around him. And after all, it is the making friends with the little outdoor people that is the best part of camping.
—**Frederick K. Vreeland, 1933**

CANOE GEAR

Outfitting for a canoe cruise is different in many ways from preparation for ordinary camping. In a fixed camp you do not have to consider weight, and can bring along all the junk you like. For a back-packing trip, on the other hand, the outfit has to be cut down to the last ounce, or life becomes a burden. The canoe hiking outfit lies between these extremes. The chief point is to have everything portable, to provide a tent that is quickly pitched and taken down, and to have the outfit conveniently packed so it can be easily handled and not littered all over the boat like a rat's nest.
—Frederick K. Vreeland, 1933

During a canoe cruise across the Northern Wilderness in the late summer, I met many parties at different points in the woods, and the amount of unnecessary duffel with which they encumbered themselves was simply appalling. Why a shrewd business man, who goes through with a guide and makes a forest hotel his camping ground nearly every night, should handicap himself—well, it is one of the things I shall never understand. My own load, including canoe, extra clothing, blanket-bag, two days' rations, pocket-axe, rod and knapsack, never exceeded 26 pounds; and I went prepared to camp out any and every night.
—Nessmuk, 1920

There are a number of light canoe tents made, all with the idea of having something that can be quickly put up with a few short poles. You should not have to allow more than fifteen minutes to getting the tent up and three to striking it.
—Warren H. Miller, 1918

The wanigan rests comfortably in the bottom of the canoe.

Of all forms of outdoor travel the most pleasurable and the easiest to tackle for the tyro is canoe voyageuring. Back-packing requires a high degree of organization, of making the wilderness supply one's comforts, of carrying the essentials and them only. Horse packing requires a considerable knowledge of horsemanship, even for the beginner, and a good deal of fatiguing training of special muscles. Dog and sledges require even more experience and specialization. But for the outdoorsman who has passed the first novitiate of learning plain camping and camp cookery, who has practiced with rod and gun until he can depend on himself to bring home the meat in a gamey country, the first spreading of his wings, so to speak, will be in a canoe.
—**Warren H. Miller, 1918**

I think by this time every boy who did not know it already will realize that canoe cruising is the greatest thing he ever tried for developing all his faculties of woodcraft, efficiency, and resourcefulness. The best part of it is that there are no two camps alike, and each day brings new problems to try your wits and to test your preparedness. Do not hesitate, but choose your bunkie, get out your maps, and plan the cruise now.
—**Frederick K. Vreeland, 1933**

CANOE GEAR

The chief point in selecting a tent is to get one that is quickly pitched and taken down, for when you are traveling and making a new camp every night there's no time to be wasted in fussing. A pyramid tent has advantages for all you have to do is to peg down the four corners, tie the peak rope to a pair of sheer poles and raise the poles, one on each side of the tent, until it is drawn taut. An "A" tent is almost as easy to pitch, especially if it is hung on a ridge rope tied between two trees.
—Frederick K. Vreeland, 1933

The cooking outfit should be carefully chosen for convenience in packing. A miscellaneous lot of kettles and pans littered about the canoe is a nuisance. The different kettles (and there should be at least three or four) should be of different sizes so that they will nest one inside of the other. . . . A cover of canvas or fiber is made to fit the largest kettle, with room enough on top to put in the plates and the frying pan (with a detachable handle), and the knives, forks, and spoons are stuck in around the edges.
—Frederick K. Vreeland, 1933

For cooking outfit there is no need to go beyond aluminum in any of the well-known kits. While tin will do all right for eating plates and mixing pans, for the fire you want aluminum because of its great conductivity of heat, which prevents a hot spot localising and scorching the edibles. That and its lightness and durability. For drinking cups, enamel is the thing, as it will not burn your lip as tin and aluminum will surely do. Your mouth can stand (and craves) more heat than your lips can bear when pressed on raw metal.
—Warren H. Miller, 1918

For carrying the grub the side-opening grub bags which roll up the lips around maple rods are good, and will float and keep things dry in spray, upset, etc. Inside them go the paraffined muslin food bags, 9 by 8 inches diameter and 12 by 8 inches diameter.
—Warren H. Miller, 1918

The harness for packs is varied enough, but the principle remains simple. A light pack will hang well enough from the shoulders, but when any weight is to be negotiated you must call into play the powerful muscles lying along the neck. Therefore, in general, an ordinary knapsack will answer very well for packs up to say thirty pounds. Get the straps broad and soft; see that they are both sewed and riveted.
—*Camp and Trail*, 1920

When, however, your pack mounts to above thirty pounds you will need some sort of strap to pass across the top of your head. This is known as a tumpline.
—*Camp and Trail*, 1920

By far the best and most comfortable pack outfit I have used is a combination of the shoulder and the head methods. It consists of shoulder harness like that used on knapsacks, with two long straps and buckles to pass around and secure any load. A tumpline is attached to the top of the knapsack straps. I have carried in this contrivance over a hundred pounds without discomfort. Suitable adjustment of the head strap will permit you to relieve alternately your neck and shoulders. Heavy or rather compact articles can be included in the straps, while the bulkier affairs will rest very well on top of the pack. It is made by Abercrombie & Fitch, and costs two dollars and seventy-five cents.
—*Camp and Trail*, 1920

CANOES

[T]he choice of a canoe . . . depends entirely upon the nature of the water, the length of the trip, and whether or not the outfit has to be carried over portages.

For hard service in the wilderness there is nothing equal to the canvas-covered canoe, made over a light but strong white cedar frame. These can be bought from a number of standard makers, and will stand an amazing amount of punishment. This type is almost a necessity where the water is shallow and the canoe is likely to bump frequently on rocks. If the canvas is cut the leak is easily mended, and it takes a very hard blow to break the wooden sheathing under the canvas.

The size of the canoe should be carefully considered. The standard canoe for grown men in wilderness cruising is 18 feet long, and about 34 inches beam, and 12 inches depth amidships. Such a canoe will carry three months' provisions for two men besides all the camp outfit. But this is too heavy for boys of average size to carry easily. The 16-foot size is much better for older boys on long trips.
—**Frederick K. Vreeland, 1933**

Be careful in selecting paddles. The stern paddle should reach your chin as you stand on the ground, and should have a good broad blade, which takes a firm hold on the water without wasting energy in eddies and splashing. The bow paddle should be about 3 inches shorter.
—**Frederick K. Vreeland, 1933**

Nothing speaks of outdoor traditions more than the open canoe.

In selecting paddles, I prefer a heavy maple paddle for the stern man and a light spruce one for the bow. The maple one should be of 28-inch blade, 6-1/2 inches wide and copper shod, and of length for the average man of five feet. The bow paddle should be of the same length, 26-inch blade, 5-1/2 inches wide. The choice of length depends upon your individual height. A six-foot man would do best with a 5-1/2-foot paddle.
—**Warren H. Miller, 1918**

The Indian paddle is a very long and very narrow blade, just as long as the height of its wielder. For use in swift and somewhat shallow water, where often the paddle must be thrust violently against the bottom or a rock, this form is undoubtedly the best in more open, or smoother water, however, the broader and shorter blade is better, though even in the latter case it is well to select one of medium

length. Otherwise you will find yourself, in a heavy sea, sometimes reaching rather frantically down toward the water. Whatever its length, attach it to the thwart nearest you by a light strong line. Then if you should go overboard you will retain control of your craft.
—*Camp and Trail*, 1920

On any trip wherein you may have to work your way back against the current, you must carry an iron "shoe" to fit on a setting pole. Any blacksmith can make you one. Have it constructed with nail holes. Then when you want a setting pole, you can cut one in the woods, and nail to it your iron shoe.
—*Camp and Trail*, 1920

Some prefer the 16- or 17-foot because of its greater ease of turning and handling in tight places; others swear by the 18-foot because of its lesser draught for the same load and its greater speed on the same paddle power. Some like the inch keel, owing to the greater staunchness that it gives to the canoe frame and the protection to the bottom that it affords from scraping rocks and sunken tree trunks; others prefer the keelless, because of its lesser draught and the ease of turning and handling such a canoe; while still others compromise on a flat maple strip for a keel, protecting the bottom against scraping and at the same time adding staunchness.
—**Warren H. Miller, 1918**

The reason why many canoes are so tipply that one has to part one's hair in the middle when paddling them is because they have not the flat bottom so essential for stability. They lack what sailors call bilge; they are too like a barrel in cross section and turn and roll as easily as a barrel in consequence. . . . The flat bottom, on the contrary, gives her stability so that she stands up staunchly

Icons of the wild-wood way include the crooked knife carried on the guide's hip.

under sail and it takes more than a good deal of leaning by both bow and stern man together to make her go over. . . . [S]ee that she has at least 20 inches of comparatively net bottom before the round turn of the bilge begins.
—**Warren H. Miller, 1918**

You can buy these canvas canoes at all prices from $20 for a fairly well built one up to $60 for extra staunch models with reinforced gunwales and superior construction throughout. The popular Guide's Models run around $30 for both and 18-foot sizes. The wooden Peterborough canoes, essential in the rough rocky streams of the Hudson's Bay country, weigh more and cost $60 to $80, but will stand much harder usage. The canvas canoes weigh from 40 to 70 pounds. Of the decked wooden sailing canoes for open waters the cheapest-cost about $100 with centerboard and rudder. The rig is extra, or you can sew up a set of sails yourself. If you expect to canoe much on big lakes or the big salt water bays of the Atlantic Coast, they are the best canoe.
—**Warren H. Miller, 1918**

A wooden canoe, of some sort, is perhaps better for all smooth and open-water sailing, and all short trips nearer home. It will stand a great deal of jamming about, but is very difficult to mend if ever you do punch a hole in it. You will need to buy a longer craft than when getting a birch. Seventeen or eighteen feet is small enough for two men, although I have cruised in smaller. Cedar is the lighter material—and the more expensive—but splits too readily. Basswood is heavier, but is cheaper and tougher.

—*Camp and Trail*, **1920**

PACKING

Properly stowing the outfit in the canoe is a high art; and you can always judge the experience of a cruiser by the way his duffel is packed.

The first thing is to distribute the load so that the canoe will run properly. The heavy things, provisions, etc., should be flat on the bottom with the weight just far enough aft of the middle to make the bow ride an inch or so higher than the stern. The lighter things, bedding, etc., can be placed on top. The cooking kit should be placed so that you can get at it for lunch without disturbing the rest of the outfit. The whole should be covered with a waterproof tarpaulin, which is lashed on with ropes stretched across the thwarts. Be sure that your ax is wedged in with the duffel so that it will not cut anything, and will not fall out if you upset.

Loading the outfit loosely and carelessly into the canoe is a sure sign of a duffer. I remember reading an article by a well known writer on exploration, telling how he lost his ax, his gun, and the greater part of his provisions in an upset in the wilderness, and describing the hardships that resulted as if he had done something heroic, instead of feeling foolish for not seeing that his outfit was properly packed. . . .

The packing of the provisions is the most important thing of all; for while a boy never expects to be upset he is always prepared for emergencies, and rain will fall on the best regulated outfits. All the provisions therefore should be packed in waterproof canvas bags. My favorite method is to put each article in a separate bag securely tied at the mouth, and pack these bags in larger bags of waterproof canvas, 9 inches in diameter by 24 inches long, arranged with a neck that can be tied tightly so that water will not leak in. The small bags are made of just the right diameter to fit inside the larger bags, one on top of the other, and can be made by the boy, of ordinary strong muslin, dipped in melted paraffin, which makes them waterproof.

—Frederick K. Vreeland, **1933**

The folding canvas boat is an abomination. It is useful only as a craft from which to fish in an inaccessible spot. Sooner or later it sags and gives, and so becomes logy.

—*Camp and Trail*, **1920**

A canoe is made, however, and much used by the Hudson's Bay Company, exactly on the frame of a birch bark, but covered with tightly stretched and painted canvas. It is a first-rate craft, combining an approach to the lightness of the birch bark with the sweeter lines of the wooden canoe. All ordinary small tears in its bottom are easily patched by the gum method. Its only inferiority to the birch rests in the facts that it is more easily torn; that a major accident, such as the smashing of an entire bow, cannot be as readily mended; and that it will not carry quite so great a weight. All in all, however, it is a good and serviceable canoe.

—*Camp and Trail*, **1920**

PORTAGING

Another test of a canoe cruiser's experience lies in the way he handles a portage. On nearly every stream there are places where the canoe has to be taken out and carried. You can always tell a duffer by the way he goes over the portage with kettles and frying pans and all sorts of junk dangling around his knees.

If your outfit is properly packed it is a very simple matter to strap one or more bundles together with a pack strap or tump-line, sling it over your back, take an ax or a fishing rod in your hands and walk over the trail. Do not try to carry a load in your hands or arms. That is a sign of the rankest amateur.

To carry a canoe is a good deal of an art. A wilderness voyageur almost always carries the canoe alone, sometimes using a wooden yoke made for the purpose to fit his shoulders, but more often making a yoke by lashing the two paddles to the thwarts, side by side, just far enough apart to let his head between and in just the right position to balance the canoe properly upside down with the nose in the air. For boys, however, a canoe is usually too heavy to carry alone. In that case the two boys should take it together, one going ahead with the paddles, lashed to the front thwart, resting on his shoulders, the other following behind with his head in the peak between the gunwales. In this way a long portage can be made very easily.
—Frederick K. Vreeland, 1933

Between lakes and around bad rapids you will have to portage. Look for a blaze, or tin can or other signs of a landing place marking the end of the portage trail. If it seems much used, it is a sign that better men than you have preferred portaging to shooting the rapids and you are in for a portage. Here is where light loading counts.
—Warren H. Miller, 1918

All of which brings us to the important question of weight of outfit. Where there is little or no portaging to be done outside of hauling over down trees and around dams it is not necessary to pare down fine, but on a regular trip with lots of portages the brother who insists on taking more for his personal comfort than the whole load of his partner including his share of the grub—well, he is one of those one-time campers, the kind you do not go with again.
—Warren H. Miller, 1918

In portaging, I have always had pretty good luck with the primitive Indian fashion—the two paddles lengthwise across the thwarts and resting on the shoulders, with perhaps a sweater or other padding to relieve the pressure. It is possible, however, to buy cushions which just fit, and on which you can kneel while paddling, and also a regular harness to distribute the weight. I should think they might be very good, and would certainly be no trouble to carry. Only that makes one more thing to look after, and the job can perfectly well be done without.
—*Camp and Trail*, 1920

CANOE CAMP LIFE

When you are traveling you and your partner should plan a strict division of labor, so that each knows exactly what he is expected to do and does it promptly and efficiently.

Choose a camp site on a bank high enough to be dry, where the tent can be pitched without spending too much time in clearing. On landing the bowman is responsible for tying the canoe so that it will be sure not to get away. Then both together unload that part of the outfit that is needed at once. One boy takes his ax and starts to cut wood. The second takes the hatchet and the tent; clears the ground, cuts the tent poles and pegs and pitches camp. When he has done this he finishes unloading the canoe, carrying up the bedding and provisions, and turning the canoe upside down on the shore where it will dry until morning. Meanwhile the first boy has cut enough wood to start the fire and got the kettle boiling. If he understands his job he will have supper ready by the time his partner has got things snugged up for the night. Then there should be enough daylight left to cut the wood needed for the evening camp fire.

In the morning the routine is reversed. While the cook is getting breakfast his partner is knocking down the tent and stowing the duffel so that they are ready to push off as soon as the dishes are washed and the cooking kit packed.
—Frederick K. Vreeland, 1933

CAMPING ON THE BEACH

For shelter, a very light one-man tent should be carried, light but very strong and waterproof. Many such tents may be found in the sporting-goods houses, but their cost, in these times of high prices, is prohibitive to most of us. However, a very good tent may be made of unbleached muslin dyed green. . . . Sew in a mosquito net front, as the "skeets" descend in swarms at nightfall.

A tent that can be set up with short poles must be selected, as very few stakes of any great length are to be found on the beach; in the woods it is different; cut all you need.

A light three-pound blanket will do for summer; but to keep out the frosty air of autumn, a five-pound army blanket or light all-wool sleeping bag will be none too warm. Pull on an extra pair of warm wool socks if cold; however, if the feet are warm and comfortable the rest of the body usually will be.

A head net will add greatly to one's comfort and may be made easily by constructing a cylinder of netting or scrim about 2-1/2 feet long and large enough to slip over head and shoulders. Draw the top together with a draw or pucker string, slip over the head and tuck the bottom into your jacket. The visor of your cap or hat will keep it from the face, and you may laugh at the mosquitoes and at your less fortunate companions. Also provide yourself with a pair of 10-cent cotton gloves, which may be used, also, at the fire when handling hot pans or sticks.

Blowing sand is another hardship on the beach; driven by a heavy wind it cuts like sleet, covers up everything not taken care of and sifts into every conceivable nook and cranny. The tent, therefore, must be put up strongly and staked down with care, the sod cloth carefully packed down with sand; if the wind shifts to the front, drive a couple of stakes into the sand to support a wide board on edge to keep out the flying particles.

To avoid sanding everything in the tent, it is better not to lie on the sand, soft as it may seem the first night. It is far

CAMPING ON THE BEACH
Continued

better to make a bed of dry sea-grass that you will find rolled up by the sea at high-water mark. Spread this out in the sun, and at bedtime you will have a mattress not to be beaten by the best on the market. Not only will this be more comfortable, but the sand that drips from shoes and out of them on entering will sift down through the grass and not get into and all over your blanket. Lay a few boards in front of the tent for the same reason and knock your shoes off on them before retiring.

Never lay a thing down on the sand if you expect to see it again; moreover, it is dangerous. I nearly cut my fingers off on a sharp ax that had become sanded over.

On arriving at the camp site, put all the duffel on a log or box and immediately build a table, rack, or something to keep the outfit up out of the sand.

You will find trouble, too, at the cook fire with blowing sand—but build a wind-break or board fence on the windward side of the fire and that will help a lot, although at times sand simply will find its way into things. Lids on every cooking thing on the beach is another rule to be observed.

As to fuel for the fire, one has little choice of woods—all is sun-dried or water-logged. Avoid very punky stuff, however, or wood with too much resin in it.

Have all hands at odd times bring up wood of any kind for the big heap that will be fired at night to illuminate the beach for the night fishing, which, by the way, is the best.

Use any old clothes that are wool; plenty of wettings in the surf will occur, but if wool is next to the skin no chilling will result. Take a sweater for cool evenings, a poncho or light raincoat, extra underclothes and wool socks, bathing suit if needed and extra sneaks or slippers.

A little wall pocket, made of brown denim, is a handy trick to have along; support it by two stakes in the tent and put in all your small stuff, toilet articles, etc.

To carry all this, some kind of a pack must be provided or else a duffel bag; as a duffel bag to my mind is unwieldy, a pack is used in all my trips.

Possibly the most important part of the trip is "the eats"—but let me emphasize one point—do not eat too much fried stuff; if you do, sooner or later headaches and indigestion will surely show up. Try fish-chowder, steamed clams, planked fish, boiled rice and raisins, corn meal mush, creamed potatoes, boiled onions, prunes, and apricots.

The best way of all [to go] is with a light sail-dory, with cockpit tent in which you can camp at night, and an alcohol galley so as to cook your meals on board out of the blowing wind and drifting sand.

Another way . . . is by small batteau, taking along a beach camping outfit. This is mere labor in mild weather, but it is a sure misery when heavy head winds force you to go overboard and push the boat bodily against the wind every step of the way. A third way is to hike along the beach . . . you choose a low or mid-tide so that you can walk on the hard, firm sand of the surf wash; this method is one of the nicest and most independent of all, for head winds cause you no concern and you can stop and fish every likely hole all the way, making a sort of progress, as it were, arriving not at all if the fishing above proves good enough.
—A. F. Westevelt, 1933

TRAINING SKILLS FOR THE TRAIL

APPRENTICE CAMPER
- Demonstrate ability to:
  - Read a compass by giving bearings to designated objects.
  - Find direction by the sun and stars.
  - Give and follow simple directions using sketch map, trail signs, etc.
  - Use compass in a field project.

JOURNEYMAN CAMPER
- Make a simple topographic map of your campsite.
- Lay out and follow a compass course of several points.
- Demonstrate ability to:
  - Orient and read a topographic map and four other kinds of maps.
  - Measure heights and distances by personal measurements.
  - Interpret all basic map symbols, margin details, and terrain features.

JOURNEYMAN WOODSMAN
- Be able to interpret and follow navigation and trail markers.
- Demonstrate ability to:
  - Use charts, maps, and compass under trip conditions.
  - Travel at least four miles over trail-less terrain.
  - Identify your location along the trail at any time.
  - Travel at night.

MASTER WOODSMAN
- Demonstrate ability to travel under a variety of conditions with varied modes of transportation.
- Display mastery of trail-time planning techniques and leadership.
- Plan and conduct a trip using traditional travel methods:
  - Snowshoes/skis and toboggan
  - Canoe / kayak
  - Horse pack
  - Foot trekking
- Travel cross-country using only natural direction indicators.

s much as canoe camping demands discipline, winter camping demands precision. The ease with which one moves on the snow-packed trail tells a lot about the skills he or she possesses, just as it does about one who guides his canoe without a ripple or splash from the paddle's blade. Motion—moving on snow without wasted energy, setting up camp in harmony with trail-tested comrades, hoisting a pack into place for another day's march, resting tired muscles and thawing chilly parts next to a well-tended stove—is evidence of mastery.

Winter is a welcome season. Clothes that have become old friends are retrieved from storage: hats, mittens, shoe packs, wool knickers and sweaters, and silk scarves and gaiters. Dressing for winter camping becomes almost ritual, and the clothes the woodsman wears are a lesson in history, both from the standpoint of time-honored designs and fabrics to the odors that hang close to them like last season's ghosts. Woodsmoke, pine pitch, and a host of other aromas tell a story. One whiff brings memories flooding back in waves of excitement while getting ready and waiting for the first flakes to fall.

Traditional hot-tent camping methods bring winter camping into the reach of anyone willing to take the risk to sleep in the snow with style. However, sofas are ripe with never-agains—people who tried winter camping with a duffer as a teacher and swore that if they survived the night, they would never again make the mistake of venturing out into weather that wasn't intended for mankind to endure. In some ways that's good for the rest of us. A mantle of white is a renewing mechanism. Those not up to enjoying it, stay home—bears hibernate, bugs die, fresh water is always at your fingertips, and all lands take on an aura of wilderness. Snow is a sound deadener, so everything is alarmingly silent. The woods in winter are never crowded.

WINTER CAMPING

It must not be supposed that the camping season is past because the summer vacation is over. The real camping season begins in the Wild Rice Moon, that is, September. Even if school or business takes all our time during the week, we still have week-ends in which to camp.
—Daniel Carter Beard, 1920

I will say, though, that some of my most unpleasant camping trips were summer ones.
—E. Kreps, 1910

"Dress warmly, sleep dryly, and eat plenty," is an old woodsman's recipe for a successful winter camp, declaring that under such circumstances the cold stimulates the entire being, often even developing an undreamed of amount of vitality and vigor.
—Frank H. Cheley, 1933

ODE TO WINTER CAMPING

Aside from the joy of visiting or exploring new country and seeing wild life in abundance, practically all that makes the winter camp and trail fascinating can be experienced in any of our northern forests, within easy reach of rail or trapper's cabin in case of misfortune. There is a zest and an invigoration about midwinter camping that puts it far ahead of the summer equivalent to many hardy souls well provided with the proper equipment, for all insect troubles vanish, no rainy spells intervene to stop all outdoor enjoyment, the going is pleasant and easy, particularly over the frozen and snow-clad surface of some waterway, and there is a sparkle in the winter air and a coseyness about a well-managed snow camp that no other season can give.

We hear much of the long-closed season, when the outdoorsman is cooped up in his office, but even if it be but for a few days, every outdoorsman should make it a point to spend some of his time under canvas during every month of the year—spring, summer, fall, and winter.
—Warren H. Miller, 1928

Many of the finest recollections of my boyhood are centered about a crude little shanty well back in the hills, with the snow-hung roof and long frozen trails. I can hear the merry ring of the sharp ax in pitch pine. I can smell the slowly-curling fragrant smoke. I can see the bowl of steaming soup, and my mouth waters in spite of me. The old black kettle hanging on the crane, the little circle of firelight faces and the stories. Those were wonderful days, full of the purest of joys, and not to be compared with even the summer camp days.

Comparatively few folks ever really experience the wonders of the winter woods, because they have never investigated. Go once; and forever afterward, if your circumstances will permit you, winter as well as summer will find you camping out, at least for a few days.
—Frank H. Cheley, 1933

Yet there is no more reason why any average boy should not camp in winter as well as in summer, if he will prepare in the same thorough manner, and use a bit of ingenuity and common sense. As a real matter of fact, if I have to choose between black flies, midges, mosquitoes, and all the pests of the summer, and the apparent problem of warmth and comfort in winter, I would most times choose the winter. To be sure, comfortable camping in winter, no less than in summer, is dependent upon a few simple fundamentals.
—Frank H. Cheley, 1933

Camping out in winter looks like a brave thing to do, but really there is nothing to it. Your usual fall hunting outfit, plus an extra blanket and a good axe, are the principal ingredients for success. The best time to go is the latter part of February and the early part of March, when you will have warm sunny winter days, with a thaw under way and the snow packing well. With no insects and snakes, with the woods a wonder of sunlit whiteness, it will prove a most enjoyable experience!
—Warren H. Miller, 1918

I can conceive that an outing in the dead of winter, with inadequate clothing and bedding, would prove anything but pleasurable, and even dangerous.

But let me hasten to show the woodsman's side of the picture, so that you can see how different the affair becomes with a real outfit.
—Warren H. Miller, 1918

"But camping is for summertime," I hear you object. "You cannot swim, or fish, or hike in winter; besides, all the wild things have disappeared, and—"

Never was there a greater mistake. One of the most attractive places in all the world is a snug little shanty in the deep woods in real winter.
—Frank H. Cheley, 1933

If you are an outdoorsman, do not den up all winter because of the weather. There is plenty to do in the winter woods; ice fishing, trapping, shooting foxes and hawks—lots of red-blooded sport.
—Warren H. Miller, 1918

WINTER CLOTHING

Beyond a doubt clothing is a matter of prime importance. Here again you need to remind yourself that "no matter how warm and dry you are, cotton is always cold and wet, and no matter how cold and wet you are, woolen is always warm and dry." The only real difference between clothing yourself properly for summer camping and clothing yourself properly for winter camping is that you need twice or three times as much of the same thing—woolen underwear, woolen shirts, pajamas, socks, woolen trousers, sweater, and knitted cap. Put on as many separate layers as the actual cold demands; watching out carefully for the danger of too much pressure from tight-fitting clothes that may impede the normal circulation and lay you open to freezing. In this connection, one needs specially to watch the feet. Preferably, wear light, fine, all-wool hose next the skin, then a pair, and if necessary two pairs, of heavy wool hose over these. This demands roomy shoes or oil packs, but insures warm, dry feet, which often are the real secret of being comfortable in winter woods. If you are to snowshoe considerable, the wool, felt-lined arctics, worn by the north woods lumberjack, are light, durable, and warm, and preferred by some winter campers to the regular moccasin.
—**Frank H. Cheley, 1933**

For general clothing, probably mackinaw cloth is the best in the long run, for it is soft and warm, and will turn a considerable amount of water. (Some prefer the light, windproof leather jacket, with mackinaw sleeves.) A knitted woolen toque makes the best headgear, as it may be easily pulled over the ears and worn at night to advantage. Select neutral colors. If much tramping or snowshoeing is to be done over the snow, a serviceable pair of amber glasses will give the eyes great comfort—in fact are almost necessary if your headgear has no visor, merely as a protection from the excessive glare. Snowblinding is painful and often serious, and entirely unnecessary.
—**Frank H. Cheley, 1933**

WINTER BEDDING

Most winter campers camp at a permanent cabin, perhaps in the summer log camp itself; and in such cases, beds and bedding, in fact all the whole matter of general equipment, is cared for. Probably, for the average person, a good, log cabin with fireplace or stove should be considered essential to a winter camp, at least until he learns thoroughly how to camp in winter. However, it is entirely possible to make yourself comfortable in the winter woods with a tent or lean-to as shelter, or even with nothing but a shelter tent, for a brief period of days. Winter pack trips are not for novices, at least in a country of much snow and zero weather. It is fairly fine art at that, to handle yourself and a simple personal kit satisfactorily in snow-filled woods, without attempting to carry shelter of any kind save a good blanket.
—**Frank H. Cheley, 1933**

WINTER SLEEPING

Pipes, talk, and dish-cleaning occupy the remaining hours, and then, about nine o'clock, the beds are rolled out on the floor space. Mine is a caribou skin fur bag, warranted warm in a snow bank; my neighbor swears by a mess of blankets; the cow baron retires into a huge wool and canvas cowboy's bed-roll; and the Indian rolls himself in a couple of Navajo blankets and is content. I prefer the farthest corner of the tent, next the rear wall, and often have I raised the sod cloth a mite, to a hole that I know of through the snow bank, down which a column of cold forest air will come flowing into my nostrils.

The art of going to bed in a winter camp is one devised after some little personal study. While many sleep in their clothes, I have found that it is warmer to sleep in pajamas, with one's clothes pulled into the bag and wrapped loosely around. In a sleeping bag the problem of what to do with the unoccupied cold air spaces in the bag has puzzled many an outdoorsman. It goes without saying that your bag should fit you snugly, with just room to turn around in it without binding; too large a bag is always cold to sleep in, no matter how warm its texture. The blanket man does not have this trouble, his blankets fit him snugly and can be tucked in tight around the feet; but if he is a restless sleeper he soon unrolls them. I have found that one's extra clothes fill all waste space nicely inside the bag, and, if you find yourself getting cold, simply retrieve a few of them and pull them over the cold spot. If worn on you they will surely be cold, as they restrict blood circulation and fit so closely that there is no opportunity for heat-conserving dead air spaces.

One's head and feet need particular protection in sleeping when the snow is flying outside the tent. Without a night toque your head will soon be uncomfortably cold and keep you awake, crying out for protection, and no brimmed hat will be anything but an uncomfortable nuisance, always coming off and waking the sleeper with a cold head. Night socks are also essential; your feet are farthest from the source of heat, the lungs and heart, and the blood does not flow through them in such large currents. Wherefore, an extra pair of night socks with a pair of wool night slippers will be needed to keep them warm and comfortable, for, if they are cold, you cannot get to sleep. Finally comes the question of breathing. If you breathe the icy air of midnight directly through your nostrils it will surely cool you down, for no lungs can stand the constant influx of below-freezing air without distress. To put one's head entirely within the bag is what is generally done by Alaska mail team men in the snowy mountains, and trappers, but it is a suffocating business. I usually compromise by arranging my coat over my head, with a channel or hole leading out to the outside air. This channel tempers the incoming air by the warmth that your body is continually giving to the garment, and by morning it will become a veritable ice cave, crusted with white frost from your breath. But meanwhile you will have had a reasonable amount of fresh air to breathe all night, without getting chilled.

You and your sleeping bag thus become a sort of heat unit, independent of the tent heat which soon fades, your body giving out heat and the bag conserving it. When a condition of equilibrium is established you dose off to sleep, and there is energy enough left to restore tissues and rebuild the body for the next day. With inadequate clothing, no energy is left to replenish the body, and you arise worn and tired, all your vitality having gone into heat-making.
—Warren H. Miller, 1918

SNOWSHOEING

If snowshoeing is to consume even a reasonable portion of your time, you should see to it that you are fairly adept at that art before venturing on a long winter camp, for as a writer in *Outing* has so well said, "To enjoy such a winter outing you must know how to walk correctly on snowshoes. Your heels must come up first, because the tails of the shoes won't let you lift your toes first, and you will then lift the toes of the shoes high enough to clear the snow as instinctively as you would step over a log. It is well to remember, however, that if a fall is to come, it is better to let go and fall easily into the soft snow without straining. This is likely to happen over a soft spot, where a slim bush underneath has prevented packing, or around the bases of young evergreens, whose snow-buried branches give way beneath the shoes. Get up slowly and circumspectly, like some wise old skidding horse who knows better than to thrash around in such yielding medium. It's fun to watch the other fellow when he does all this, more so when he isn't wise, and throws snow around him like a harpooned whale."
—Frank H. Cheley, 1933

Take the Kodak along. Look up the birds that are wintering with you. Hunt up a half-frozen waterfall and listen to its half-drowned music. Put a feast of bread crumbs and a few bits of meat suet in your pocket and spread them on some accessible snow-white tablecloth for the birds. How they will thank you! Play the strenuous winter games such as fox and geese, dog and deer, and hare and hounds. Learn to become expert in the use of your ax. Cut and get in logs for improvements on the cabin, or for the building of indoor furniture. Perhaps you can fish through the ice, or even try your hand at trapping. Stay out-of-doors just as much as possible in order that you may keep a keen appetite, and sleep well, and enjoy the lazy fire after the sun has settled out of sight. Take in a couple of your best book friends for reading by the fire. It is an especially good time to delve into a book of fine poetry or a biography. Take time to sit and think and be friendly.
—Frank H. Cheley, 1933

FOOD THAT KEEPS ONE WARM

In point of fact your body is the real heat center—a sort of stove. It gives out quantities of heat, and if this is conserved by proper clothing and bedding you are comfortable, no matter what the weather may be doing. This is the whole secret of the matter, and, once mastered, winter camping proves the most enjoyable of all outdoor recreations, for those pests of all summer outings, the insects, are refreshingly conspicuous by their absence.
—Warren H. Miller, 1918

The winter trail of the trapper is often the only track on a freshly fallen snow.

Food in general for winter camps should be selected for its heat-giving qualities as well as its filling quantities. Incidentally, it will take a third to a half more grub for a given party than in summer. Winter campers will likely plan on at least a certain amount of simple hunting, so that meat will supply a good bulk of the ration. Avoid canned stuff that will burst when frozen, and be sure to include the necessaries for plenty of hot soup, stews, and drinks. There will be, of course, staples for hot cereal, bread, corn bread, pancakes and the like, as well as for rice, raisins, a general assortment of dried fruit, and sufficient bacon for drippings, seasoning, and emergency. Beans of all kinds are excellent winter rations, and should be given a large place in the commissary. Canned jam would seem to be a luxury, but in winter camps becomes a necessity, because of the sugar with its heat-producing qualities. Do not stint your menu. "Dress warmly, sleep dryly, and eat plenty," is an old woodsman's recipe for a successful winter camp, declaring that under such circumstances the cold stimulates the entire being, often even developing an undreamed of amount of vitality and vigor.

Under conditions one quickly adjusts himself to prolonged and even intense cold.
—Frank H. Cheley, 1933

If it is necessary to pack your equipment and food to your camp over the snow . . . construct a simple toboggan, and by means of a long rope or cross poles, let the party pull it in themselves. This is far better than attempting to carry it in by personal pack. Better, of course, is to plan enough in advance, so as to get at least the main part of your equipment in . . . before snow-fall, thus necessitating

WINTER CAMPSITES

It may be necessary to camp out one night en route. . . . If you should encounter much snow, choose a level, clear spot in a thick clump of trees, in close proximity to dry firewood trees. Dig out the snow, if deep, using your snowshoe as a snow shovel. Pitch camp facing at right angles to the wind. If it is stormy, bank your shelter with old logs, brush, or some of all these. If faced directly away from the wind, the eddy formed by the tent will suck the smoke back into the camp.
—Frank H. Cheley, 1933

In winter camping you may select a camp site irrespective of water supply, as plenty of good water may be made easily by melting ice or snow. The main things to look out for are shelter, good wood, and material for a good bed. . . .

If there is too much snow, so that getting down to the ground can only be accomplished by an excessive amount of hard labor, build a platform of small green logs for your fire and stamp down a place for your bed with your snowshoes, placing an extra large covering of boughs on top of the snow. Pitch the tent so as to catch all the fire heat possible, and save the largest of your wood for the night fire, building a green log reflector for it if possible. Heat your canteens and use them as hot-water bottles if you strike an excessively cold night.
—Frank H. Cheley, 1933

the carrying of only your personal effects, with perhaps your gun, pocket ax, and snowshoes as extras.
—Frank H. Cheley, 1933

We woke up to see the world buried in deep snowy white, the spruces laden thick with their white burden, and the big flakes coming on down swift and fast. The big "rag house," our 10 x 15 ft. wall tent, was buried heavily with snow, and my Forester tent almost out of sight, with high banks of whiteness driven up on its sides. We spent that day in making everything strong and secure, for it is the weight of snow that drags up tent pegs, and buckles in the eaves and ridge. Four whole trees were used up on the wall tent, each of them a four-inch dead lodgepole pine, one forming the ridge, two the eave poles and the last the post for the latter. The ground was not yet so deeply frozen but that a few cuts of the axe would get through the frost, letting these posts be driven in deep into the duff. One end of the ridge pole was lashed to a tree that in a measure sheltered the tent from snow fall, and the outer end was supported by stout shears cut from the tops of the four trees, which tops also furnished the supply of tent pegs. The eaves were guyed out and lashed to the side poles, making the roof strong and flat. For two weeks the rag house sheltered us, while for the same time the snow came down endlessly, with but two sunshiny days of intermission, and by that time the snow was three feet deep. The forester tent we let bury herself, simply clearing out a hollow in front large enough to hold the backlog fire. The snow soon formed a sort of self-supporting arch over the small roof of this tent, and this arch was lined inside with a skin of ice so that in time practically no weight of snow came on the canvas roof. With the big tent the roof problem was simple, one just slapped the snow off it from inside as it accumulated, a vigorous blow on the canvas from inside the tent sending the snow flying. If it had turned bitter cold we should have laid poles up from the side pole to the ridge and shingled them with balsam browse, but this is hardly worth the time necessary to do it if the temperatures are around twenty above zero.
—Warren H. Miller, 1918

WINTER SCENES

In the rag house a certain regime of order and neatness was instituted and lived up to. For four men to live in a space ten feet by fifteen and still have room for a tent stove, requires that during the day the bedding shall be neatly rolled and stowed in the back of the tent, leaving all the floor space for cooking and eating operations, also drying wet clothes at night. "A man'll as soon wade through hell on wax legs as go through packing snow without getting wet" is an old mountain saying, and I have never yet come across any fabric that will stand the constant pounding of caked snow against one's legs, nor any boot, however well greased, that will not finally become porous to snow and soak one through to the skin before nightfall during the day's tramp. The inevitable is usually warded off by boot grease until about four o'clock in the afternoon, when the wetness makes itself felt, and by night-fall, on returning to the tent, the first thing done is a change to dry clothes out of the kit bag, and an immediate drying of the freezing, soaking socks, drawers and trousers, worn during the day, needed again on the morrow. To this end not only is a clothes line run along the ridge under the pole, but a close-up drying rack is arranged around three sides of the stove, under the immediate eye of the cook, who transfers nearly-dry garments to the clothes line as fast as the fire has done the major part of the drying. As an auxiliary to this, a sock-drying fire is generally maintained outside the tent, in a cleared space in the snow, generally the same space reserved to the chopping block during the day. Drying socks is a fine art, and the punishment for carelessness or slovenliness is the loss of the sock, an irreparable loss when your nearest trading store is fifty miles away, over the Continental Divide and not to be reached until the trip's end! Some one must be on guard, all the time, when an open fire and a circle of socks are in proximity, and that some one must have his wits about him and be continually on the feel so that no sock be scorched.
—**Warren H. Miller, 1918**

Meanwhile the supper is being prepared on the stove. A huge six-quart mulligan of elk steaks, grouse breasts, onions, potatoes, macaroni, rice and tomatoes is bubbling back on the stove; a batch of corn bread is rising in the oven; a pot of tea simmering; a mess of prunes, apricots, peaches and apples is stewing, and soon these delicacies are served on a tarp, spread out on the tent door, and each man's place set with plate, cup and eating utensils; sugar, evaporated cream and butter gracing the center of the table. The above is a meal for four hungry hunters!
—**Warren H. Miller, 1918**

Eastern sports ready for a day on the winter trail.

TIPS FOR WINTER LIVING

For the last seven years I have camped out more or less every winter, and the following ideas seem to come in the category of things proven true and reliable:

- A closed tent and a tent stove are far preferable to an open tent and a backlog fire, for the latter uses too much wood to be worth the effort and its smoky and acrid atmosphere is always drifting into the tent, making it an eye-watering sort of living.

- The cold has nothing to do with living in the winter woods; you are the stove; see to it that you have warm clothing and warm bedding. And this does not mean heavy clothing or heavy bedding. In the daytime you labor so hard that even a Mackinaw is a burden; a good stag shirt is the best wear until nightfall when a sweater coat and perhaps a light pocket-sized rubber raincoat will be needed to counteract the cold and wind.

- A fur bag weighing ten pounds; a red Hudson's Bay blanket—four point, some twenty-eight feet long—folded four times and enclosed in a gabardine or shelter cloth covering; or a quilt bag of wool batts and sateen facing, plus a single 6 x 7-foot all-wool blanket inside; these three are, any of them, ample winter bedding, weighing ten pounds—take your choice!

- For winter clothes, as practical clothing for daily use, I have come to prefer long wool trousers to breeches; drab wool shirt with a stag shirt over it; and two pairs of socks under cruisers, moccasins, or rubber overs with leather tops. Add a Mackinaw in the East, or a wool sweater coat with a rubber coat over it in the West, or a khaki coat, fleece-lined with high collar, and you have protection handy when you get exposed to the cutting wind or the chill of night. You need one change of flannel underwear, two pairs of socks (besides the ones you're wearing), and a pair of night socks, night felt slippers, a set of pajamas, and a night toque. For a hat the broad-rimmed Stetson seems best, as snow is continually falling off saplings and bushes when you are poking through the woods, and a snow shower is a constant occurrence. A bandanna to tie around the whole works like a sunbonnet, when the cold is intense enough to attack your ears in the woods, is not to be sneezed at—you may have to put on the night toque too! But, as a rule, on the march or on the hunting trail, you warm up so much that it pays to endure the cold at first, in preference to lugging around a Mackinaw or other superfluous garment through all the day's hunt.

- As for accessories, in the matter of axes the two-pound Hudson's Bay, supplemented by a light one-man timber saw, will do very well for ordinary camping and a full axe if you have horse or toboggan transportation.

- For snowshoes, you will need bear-paws, 27 x 14 inches for eastern wet-packing snow; Adirondacks 12 x 50 inches for lightly drifted deep snow; and, for the intense cold, powdery dry snow of the Rockies, a still longer shoe, 60 x 13 inches, is generally used, often made three-bar. Most people do not seem to realize what the hole in a snowshoe is for, and so tie the thong so loose that their toe is continually getting over on the front bar and locking the shoe fast to the sole of the foot. The motion of snowshoeing is simply lifting the forward end, and to do this, your toe must go down into the hole, as your foot remains parallel to the ground when you lift it. So, in tying the thong, first put enough turns around the thong where it goes over your toe to insure that it will not permit the toe to slide forward, while not at the same time binding the toe too fast. The thongs then cross your foot and go back around your ankle, where they are finally tied in a bow knot in front of the ankle. To prevent shoveling up too much snow and thus carrying a heavy load, see that the toes turn well up.

- If you are going in powdery snow or bearpaws, it is well to make yourself as light as possible by transferring most of your belongings to the toboggan. This is a light sled of alternate oak and ash slats, usually 24 inches wide by 7 feet long, that will haul easily with 100 pounds of load wherever there is a trail. It is not a success in thick timber heavily grown up with underbrush and goes hard in powdery snow. But most woods going is along trails that get somewhere or, in winter, on level stretches of hard snow-covered lake or river ice, so that, next to horses, a toboggan is the best transportation. In loading it, the stove and camp kettle usually go in front, up under the curve, and then comes the duffel, well protected by waterproof tarps from getting wet by the snow that continually crowds aboard the toboggan.

- As to shelter I would place the large wall tent first for a party of hunters as producing the most warmth and comfort on the least expenditure of time and energy. It can be put up on a nomadic camp as quickly as any other of the same size, as you will note from my description of our Montana trip. For a party of two, the snow tent is a good selection, or, for three the Esquimaux tent. Particularly on a back-pack hike on snowshoes this is a fine tent because it provides a living room as well as a sleeping room. For in snowy weather, you are indoors a great deal more than in summer and want more room to live, move, and have your being in comfort.

—Warren Miller, 1915

Early rangers on winter patrol at Yellowstone.

CAMPING WESTERN STYLE

Sooner or later the Eastern sportsman takes the bit in his teeth and goes on a big-game trip in the Rockies. . . . [I]t's a new and entirely different country, alone worth the visit to camp in it; a country of big mountains and big distances, where, to get into the heart of the game districts, one must travel from 50 to a 100 miles in from the nearest railroad. The Eastern hunter finds it different from what he has been accustomed to; not that the wilderness is essentially different but that the means of transportation and the corresponding equipment are different, necessitating different clothing, more adequately suited to the needs of the country.
—Warren Miller, *Camp Craft*, 1915

Camping in the western style is another art born of the workplace. At the turn of the century, the methods and practices of the cowboy were still a required skill. No place is the stark reality of one way of life being given over to another so clear as on the western frontier. How odd to think that the Gibson Girl was popular the same year that Sitting Bull died, that Wyatt Earp lived for nearly fifteen years after the automobile was a household item, or that the same year Orville and Wilbur Wright flew at Kitty Hawk, Tom Horn was hung in Laramie for shooting suspected cattle rustlers.

Western style is the ultimate time-warp technology. Tack, clothing, and accessories remain virtually unchanged from 100 years ago. The style of the western camp, save a few concessions to convenience and good manners, are just as they would have been found back then. Place a photo from 1900 next to a photo of a camp from 1999, and the similarities speak volumes about western commitment to tradition . . . commitment that verges on muleheadedness at times, but founded in love and respect for a vibrant living heritage.

If you speak of how different things were 100 years ago compared to now in the East, things began to change a long time ago. Speak of changes in the West, and in most cases they are just now taking place. The first dude ranches came on the scene about 1902 and are still very popular today. The city-slickers movement, fueled by a contemporary clamoring for contact with things coming from tradition—things that have context— is the western style recaptured for all to enjoy.

THE HORSE

About the pleasantest way to travel and see the country leisurely and intimately is on horseback, or, as may be preferred, on foot, with an animal to carry one's pack.

The animal may be a horse, a mule, or a burro, depending upon the trail to be traveled, and other circumstances. If the trail is not too rugged, and is well watered, with plenty of good forage by the way, the horse is more tractable, and is a much better traveling companion than either the mule or the burro.
—Dillon Wallace, 1933

For main travel, instead of the canoe we have the horse . . . a willy-witted beast, whose principal motive in life is Fear, this emotion governing everything he thinks and does. He has no confidence in strangers, goes wild at the mere sight of your camera flashing in the sunlight over his head, shies all over the lot when you draw your rifle—let alone attempt to fire it (which action would probably land you over the moon)—and the scent of a grizzly track two days old crossing your trail will send him into fits. So much for your saddle-horse; your pack-horse is another born lunatic, perverse and pig-headed, full of original meanness, understanding no language outside of vigorous expletive, and you must know how to pack him, drive him, hobble him, catch him every morning, and extricate him from a thousand difficulties and misdemeanors into which he is always thrusting his foolish head.
—Warren Miller, *Camp Craft*, 1915

"THE RESULT OF NOT GETTING THE HITCH ON SNUG"

The horse rubs under a limb or against a big rock; the loosened rope scrapes off the top of the pack; something flops or rattles or falls—immediately causes him to arch his back, lower his head and begin to buck.

It is marvelous to what height the bowed back will send small articles catapult-wise into the air. First go the tarpauline and blankets; then the duffel bags; then one by one the contents of the alforjas; finally, after they have been sufficiently lightened, the alforjas as themselves in an abandoned parabola of debauched delight. In the meantime that horse, and all the others, has been running frantically all over the rough mountains, through the rocks, ravines, brush and forest trees. You have ridden recklessly trying to round them up, sweating, swearing, praying to the Red Gods that none of those indispensable animals is going to get lame in this insane hippodrome. Finally between you, you have succeeded in collecting and tying to trees all the culprits. Then you have to trail inch by inch along the track of the cyclone, picking up from where they have fallen, rolled, or been trampled, the contents of that pack flown to the smallest. It will take you the rest of the day; and then you'll miss some. Oh, it pays to get your hitch on snug!
—*Camp and Trail*, 1920

Here are several things to keep in mind, the principal of which is never to let your horse get out of hand. They are foolish enough when you are on them and, if starting in to gallop, may get excited and turn the affair into a genuine bolt; so it is well to check up before he gets out of hand. But, dismounted, your horse becomes as cunning as Satan himself. He will nibble quietly enough so long as you have his reins or do not attempt to regain them; but, once he has them, he knows enough not to let you get hold of them again. The beginner in such cases is apt to rush at the horse and try to catch him by his sprinting speed. As well try to catch the wind! Work up to him casually and regain the reins if you can, but it is much better on a stalk with a comparatively strange horse to tie him up somewhere. And, in doing this, be sure that it is in no place where he can hang himself or get tangled up in the reins while you are off on the stalk.
— Warren Miller, *Camp Craft*, 1915

BURROS AND MULES

For heavy loads in a rough country, the mule is the best of all. The burro, however, is cheap, eats little, and is not particular about his food, and can travel longer without water than either the horse or the mule. He can carry nearly as heavy a load as a horse, but not nearly so much as a mule. He is a stubborn little beast, though. When he has done what he considers an adequate day's work he stops. There is no use in urging or arguing with him. He has had enough for one day, and he knows it, and that is the end of it. But if one is hiking, the burro's day is usually quite long enough.
—Dillon Wallace, 1933

THE PACK HORSE

If one is going on a real camping excursion where one will need pack horses, one should, by all means, familiarize oneself with the proper method of packing a pack horse. This can be done in one's own cellar, attic or woodshed and without hiring a horse or keeping one for the purpose. The horse will be expensive enough when one needs it on the trail.

The drill in packing a horse should be taught in all scout camps, and all girl camps and all Y. M. C. A. camps, and all training camps; in fact, everywhere where anybody goes outdoors at all, or where anybody pretends to go outdoors; and after the tenderfeet have learned how to pack then it is the proper time to learn what to pack; consequently we put packing before outfitting, not the cart, but the pack before the horse, so to speak.
—**Daniel Carter Beard, 1920**

When packing a horse, except with such hitches as the "one man hitch," it requires two men or boys to "throw" the hitch. The first one is known as the head packer, and the other as the second packer. Remember that the left-hand side of the horse is the nigh side. The head packer stands on the nigh side of the horse.
—**Daniel Carter Beard, 1920**

Learn to pack at home and you will not lose your packs on the trail. In packing a live horse you will learn by practice not to pull in such a way as to cause the horse to step on your feet; you will also learn that a live horse will not stand as still as a wooden horse, but when you have learned to pack a wooden horse quickly and well, it will only take you a short time to become expert with a live horse.
—**Daniel Carter Beard, 1920**

A pack horse can carry two hundred pounds not more. Of course more can be piled on him, and he will stand up under it, but on a long trip he will deteriorate. Greater weights are carried only in text books, in camp-fire lies, and where a regular pack route permits of grain feeding. A good animal, with care, will take two hundred successfully enough, but I personally always pack much lighter. Feed costs nothing, so it is every bit as cheap to take three horses as two. The only expense is the slight bother of packing an extra animal. In return you can travel farther and more steadily, the chances of sore backs are minimized, your animals keep fat and strong, and in case one meets with an accident, you can still save all your effects on the other.
—*Camp and Trail*, **1920**

Anyone who travels with pack horses should know how to arrange the lead rope in a manner so that it may be quickly and easily loosened, and at the same time be out of the way, so that the horse will not get his foot over it when climbing or descending steep places, which often happens when the lead rope is fastened to the pack in the usual manner. If you will take the rope and wind it loosely around the horse's neck, behind his left ear and in front of his right ear, then tuck the end under the strands, the thing may be undone in an instant, and in the meantime the rope is out of the way where it will not bother either the man or the horse.
—**Daniel Carter Beard, 1920**

THE RIDER

It is the pounding of a rigid rider that makes a horse mad—that and his total lack of confidence in you as his rider and his alleged master.
—Warren Miller, 1915

In riding through timber your horse is always either sending you too near a tree or else he goes between two of them so that one of them is sure to take off your knee. Remember that a push with your hand on the tree will always shove the horse far enough over to one side to let your leg pass, and if done quickly enough you can even work him through two trees without either barking your leg.
—*Camp Craft*, Warren Miller, 1915

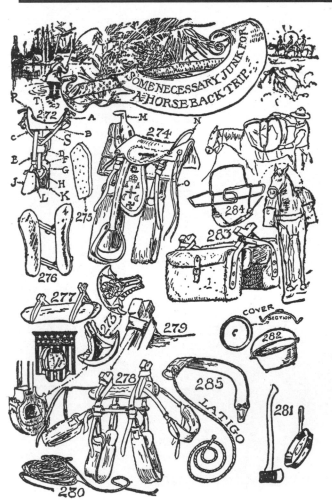

THE TACK

One must use Western ways; remember the horses were educated in the West if you were not.... [D]on't try a straight bit on a Western horse; he may spit it out and laugh at you; use the modern Western bits, saddles, and cinch and you will not go far wrong.
—**Daniel Carter Beard, 1920**

You will need a pack sawbuck.... [O]ver this saddle you can swing your two saddle bags, called alforjas, ... the cowboy favorite cooking utensil, the old Dutch oven, ... an axe and a frying pan.... Of course, one could write a whole book on horseback work, saddles and pack saddles.
—**Daniel Carter Beard, 1920**

LOADING A HORSE

Sling your rifle in its scabbard on the near side by the thongs. . . . Under your pommel is the place for your camera case. . . . In the cantle-thongs goes your slicker, with anything you want to carry rolled up inside of it. This may include a mackinaw and package of grub or fishing-tackle, but not much more, for you are limited as to the height of that package on behind for the excellent reason that one cannot throw one's leg over it in mounting if much more than about 6 inches in height. Finally, before mounting, see that you have no weighty and bulky articles about you in pockets or slung about your shoulders, for they will be sure to bounce out or loose or else dig a hole through your clothes. Also be sure that what you do need is not forgotten—pipe, matches, tobacco, watch, compass, binoculars, knife, revolver, and cartridges. All these will be wanted at one time or another, also any maps used on the route; and the place for them is stowed about you, not in the pockets of your clothing in the slicker roll, nor yet in the pack under the tarp on the pack-horse's back. For no one is going to stop the caravan to let you dig up these essentials once on the march. Chances at small game of all kinds are frequent along these mountain trails, and a good, accurate revolver and proficiency in its use are mighty valuable assets.
—Warren Miller, 1915

HITCHING THE HORSE

On some trail where there are no trees, sticks, or even stones; but if he is a good woodcrafter and plainsman, with his hunting knife he will proceed to dig as narrow and deep a hole possible in the earth, then he will tie a knot in the end of the picket rope and drop the knot to the bottom of the hole (the picket rope in reality should be one-half inch rope, fifty feet long); the only way to get that knot out of the hole is to stand directly over the opening and pull the knot up perpendicularly. It will never occur to the horse to shorten the line by taking hold of it with his teeth, so that it may stand over the hole and pull up the knot, consequently the animal will be as securely hitched as if tied to a post.
—Daniel Carter Beard, 1920

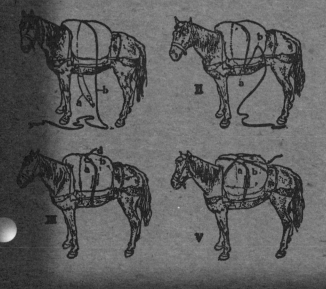

[W]e lashed on the bed rolls behind, with thongs running down to the top buckles of the girth bands and hung the haversacks in pairs over the front of the pommel, tying them back to the same buckles of the girth straps. My original scheme of tying these to the top of the stirrup fasteners did not work at all, as it did not produce enough downward pull on the cantle roll so that it would not stay put. We wore nothing hung or draped about us, for the obvious reason that such articles will forever be bouncing about and will hamper one's freedom of movement when riding.
—Warren Miller, 1918

SADDLE DIAGRAMS

[R]emember for the pack horse the necessary outfit is a horse blanket, the cincha and lash rope, the sling rope, the lead rope, the manta, which is a cover for the pack, sometimes called the tarp—short for tarpaulin, and the blind, but as a rule a handkerchief is used for a blinder. The aparejo is a sort of a leather mattress which goes over the horse's back and on which the pack rests, but you will find [out] all about that when you hit the trail with a pack train. The alforjas is a Spanish name for the saddle-bags used on a pack horse. When the reader knows how to pack his horse, knows all the Spanish names for the pack saddle and all that sort of thing, there may come a time when he will have a horse which needs to be hitched at night.
—Daniel Carter Beard, 1920

The packing that we shall consider here will be with the cross-tree type. The pack saddle should fit the animal, and it should be equipped with breeching and breast strap, or if it has no breast strap it should have a double cinch. This is to prevent the saddle and load from shifting and galling the animal.

The most convenient method of packing is with kyaks. These are usually from twenty to twenty-four inches long, depending upon the size of the animal, twenty inches deep, and ten inches wide. They are better if made of cowhide, but will do well enough if made of heavy canvas, with edges and corners reinforced with leather. Each kyak should be fitted with two heavy leather straps, with an adjustable loop at the top of each strap to drop over the protruding ends of the cross-tree forward and rear, to support it in position on the saddle. These straps should be attached to the kyak with leather "keepers," riveted or sewn into place, so that the straps will not work off the ends of the kyak, but may be removed from it if desired by pulling them through the keepers. There are, of course, to be two kyaks for each animal, one for each side.

At least three thicknesses of heavy woolen blanket should be used as padding under the pack saddle. This should fall low enough over the sides of the animal to prevent chafing by the kyaks.
—Dillon Wallace, 1933

To lash the load into place a half-inch lash or lair rope not less than thirty-three feet, but preferably forty feet, in length is necessary. We must also have a good broad cinch

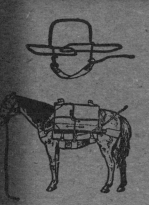

with a ring on one end and a cinch hook on the other end. This is attached to the rope by passing an end of the rope through the ring and knotting it firmly.
—Dillon Wallace, 1933

The pack outfit consists of the pack saddle, with the apparatus to keep it firm; its padding; the kyacks, or alforjas—sacks to sling on either side; and the lash rope and cinch with which to throw hitches.

The almost invariable type of pack saddle is the sawbuck. If it is bought with especial reference to the animal it is to be used on, it is undoubtedly the best. But nothing will more quickly gouge a hole in a horse's back than a saddle too narrow or too wide for his anatomy. A saddle of this sort bolted together can be taken apart for easier transportation by baggage or express.
—*Camp and Trail*, 1920

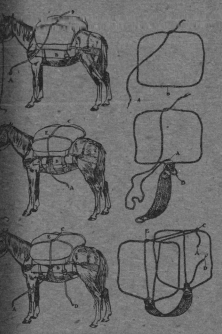

To the average wilderness traveler the possession of a pack saddle and canvas kyacks simplifies the problem considerably. If you were to engage in packing as a business, wherein probably you would be called on to handle packages of all shapes and sizes, however, you would be compelled to discard your kyacks in favor of a sling made of rope. And again it might very well happen that some time or another you might be called on to transport your plunder without appliances on an animal caught up from the pasture. For this reason you must further know how to hitch a pack securely to a naked horse.
—*Camp and Trail*, 1920

Hobbles—For the front legs may be purchased at any outfitter's, or home-made from unravelled rope. Make a loop from a strand from a large rope and then fasten it round one leg, as in diagram; after that twist the rope to make the connections between the two loops, tie another knot to prevent the rope from untwisting, then tie the two ends around the leg of the horse; the unravelled rope is soft and will not chafe the horse's leg.
—Daniel Carter Beard, 1920

Hobbles are made of two patterns. Both consist of heavy leather straps to buckle around either front leg and connected by two links and a swivel. In one the strap passes first through the ring to which the links are attached, and then to the buckle. The other buckles first, and then the end is carried through the ring. You will find the first mentioned a decided nuisance, especially on a wet or frosty morning, for the leather tends to atrophy in a certain position from which numbed fingers have more than a little difficulty in dislodging it. The latter, however, are comparatively easy to undo.

Hobbles should be lined. I have experimented with various materials, including the much lauded sheepskin with the wool on. The latter when wet chafes as much as raw leather, and when frozen is about as valuable as a wood rasp. The best lining is a piece of soft wash leather at least two inches wider than the hobble straps. With most horses it is sufficient to strap a pair of these around the forelegs and above the fetlocks. A gentle animal can be trusted with them fastened below. But many horses by dint of practice or plain native cussedness can hop along with hobbles nearly as fast as they could foot-free, and a lot too fast for you to catch them single handed. Such an animal is an unmitigated bother. Of course if there is good staking you can picket him out; but quite likely he is unused to the picket rope, or the feed is scant.
—*Camp and Trail*, 1920

So you have your horses ready for their burdens. Picket ropes should be of half-inch rope and about 50 feet long. The bell for the bell horse should be a loud one, with distinctive note not easily blended with natural sounds, and attached to a broad strap with safety buckle.
—*Camp and Trail*, 1920

RESOURCES

TENTS AND ACCESSORIES

EMPIRE CANVAS WORKS
Duane and Margot Lottig
11083 South Ellen Smith Road
Solon Springs, WI 54873
(715) 378-4216

FOUR DOG STOVES
John Kavalas
25909 Variolite Street NW
St. Francis, MN 55070
(612) 444-9587

HORIZONS UNLIMITED
Rick Driediger
P.O. Box 1110
La Ronge, Saskatchewan
S0J 1L0 CANADA
(306) 635-4420

OUTFITTERS PACK STATION
Richard Phillips
2070 West Broadway
Idaho Falls, ID 83402
(1-800) 657-2644

RILEY STOVE CO.
P.O. Box 817
Townsend, MT 59644
(1-800) 258-3611

TENTSMITHS
Peter Marques
P.O. Box 1748
Conway, NH 03818
(603) 447-2344

CLOTHING

C. C. FILSON COMPANY
P.O. Box 34020
Seattle, WA 98124
(206) 624-4437

BASKETS, KNIVES, CANOES, AND OTHER ITEMS

ASHAWAGH BASKET COMPANY
Peter Rickard, Inc.
R.D. #1, Box 292
Cobleskill, NY 12043
(1-800) 282-5663

BRADDOCK'S TRADE MERCANTILE
Paul Jones
9306 Roxanna Drive
Austin, TX 78748
(512) 292-4311

CLARK & SONS MERCANTLE. INC.
P.O. Box 28168
Lakewood, CO 80228
(303) 914-0028

CRAZY CROW TRADING POST
P.O. Box 847
Pottsboro, TX 75076-0847
(1-800) 786-6210

DULUTH PACK COMPANY
365 Canal Park Drive
Duluth, MN 55802
(1-800) 849-4489

GRANSFORS BRUKS
Snow and Nealley
P.O. Box 867
Bangor, ME 04402-0876
(1-800) 933-6642

CLINT ISHMAN
Knives, Axes, and Tools
Kestrel Tools
Rt. 1, Box 1762
Lopez, WA 98261
(360) 468-2103

LEHMAN'S NON-ELECTRIC
P.O. Box 41
Kidron, OH 44636-0041
(330) 857-5757

PAN WORLD TRADERS
P.O. Box 697
Santa Cruz, CA 95061
(831) 479-4803

SMOKEY MOUNTAIN KNIFE WORKS
P.O. Box 4430
Seveierville, TN 37864
(1-800) 251-9306

THREE RIVERS ARCHERY SUPPLY
P.O. Box 517
Ashley, IN 46705
(219) 587-9501

WOLF RIVER HANDICRAFTS
Lee and Duane Hanson
P.O. Box 205
Jackman, ME 04945
no phone # desired

PHOTOGRAPHIC AND LINE ART CREDITS

A special thanks to Adirondack State Park, Yellowstone National Park, C. C. Filson Company, Duluth Tent and Awning, Nabisco, and all others who generously contributed photographs to Camping in the Old Style.

Adirondack State Park: front cover and pages I, viii, xiv, 1, 2, 3, 7, 8, 14, 15, 16, 17, 18, 19, 20, 21, 22, 25, 26, 27, 28, 31, 33, 34, 37, 39, 46, 47, 78, 87, 89, 111, 119, 126, 134, 149, 150, 158, 164, 165, 166, 169, 171, 172, 174, 178, 190, 191, 197, 202, 213, and 214.

Beard, Daniel Carter: pages 42, 55, 60, 70, 71, 72, 75, 83, 95, 107, 108, 118, 132, 133, 135, 138, 139, 140, 146, 170, 182, 183, and 220.

Chelley, Frank: pages 49, 50, 51, 52, 54, 59, 106, and 152.

Duluth Tent and Awning: pages 49, 50, 51, 66, 89, 106, 112, 114, 193, and 194.

C. C, Filson Company: pages 30, 41, 43, and 44.

Miller, Warren: back cover and pages iii, vi, xiii, 24, 29, 32, 53, 57, 61, 63, 77, 79, 80, 87, 89, 90, 92, 93, 94, 95, 96, 97, 98, 99, 102, 103, 117, 118, 122, 142, 145, 146, 147, 156, 159, 162, 173, 177, 195, 199, 200, 201, 202, 203, 204, 205, 207, 208, 209, 210, 211, 212, 213, 218, and 219.

The Mountain Heritage Center, Cullowhee, North Carolina: pages x, 40, 149, and 175.

Nabisco: pages 62 and 69.

Seton, Ernest Thompson: page 48.

Wescott, David: back cover and pages 10, 11, 24, 35, 38, 48, 58, 61, 64, 66, 67, 68, 76, 81, 101, 102, 110, 114, 117, 127, 144, 163, 164, 167, 168, 179, 180, 184, 185, 186, 187, 188, and 196.

White, Stewart Edward: pages 216, 221, 222, 223, and 224.

Wilder, James Austin: front cover, back cover, and pages 59, 65, 91, 92, 109

Ye Sylvan Archer: page 100

Yellowstone National Park: pages 5, 6, 7, 9, 23, 115, 161, 212, 215, 220, and 225.

Yosemite National Park: 15, 82, 112, 113, 116, 192